GO!
Premium Media Site

Improve your grade with hands-on tools and resources!

- Master *Key Terms* to expand your vocabulary.
- Assess your knowledge with fun *Crossword Puzzles* and *Flipboards*, which let you flip through the definitions of the key terms and match them with the correct term.
- Prepare for exams by taking practice quizzes in the *Online Chapter Review*.
- Download *Student Data Files* for the application projects in each chapter.
- Answer matching and multiple choice questions to test what you learned in each chapter.

And for even more tools, you can access the following Premium Resources using your Access Code. Register now to get the most out of *GO!*.

- *Student Training Videos* for each Objective have been created by the author - a real instructor teaching the same types of courses that you take.*
- *GO! to Work* videos are short interviews with workers showing how they use Office in their job.*
- *GO! for Job Success* videos related to the projects in the chapter cover such important topics as Dressing for Success, Time Management, and Making Ethical Choices.*

*Access code required for these premium resources

Your Access Code is:

Note: If there is no silver foil covering the access code, it may already have been redeemed, and therefore may no longer be valid. In that case, you can purchase online access using a major credit card or PayPal account. To do so, go to **www.pearsonhighered.com/go**, select your book cover, click on "Buy Access" and follow the on-screen instructions.

To Register:

- To start you will need a valid email address and this access code.
- Go to **www.pearsonhighered.com/go** and scroll to find your text book.
- Once you've selected your text, on the Home Page for the book, click the link to access the Student Premium Content.
- Click the Register button and follow the on-screen instructions.
- After you register, you can sign in any time via the log-in area on the same screen.

System Requirements

Windows 7 Ultimate Edition; IE 8
Windows Vista Ultimate Edition SP1; IE 8
Windows XP Professional SP3; IE 7
Windows XP Professional SP3; Firefox 3.6.4
Mac OS 10.5.7; Firefox 3.6.4
Mac OS 10.6; Safari 5

Technical Support

http://247pearsoned.custhelp.com

Photo credits: Goodluz/wrangler/Elena Elisseeva/Shutterstock

Word 2013

Brief

GO!
with Microsoft®
Word 2013
Brief

Shelley Gaskin and Alicia Vargas

PEARSON

Boston Columbus Indianapolis New York San Francisco Upper Saddle River
Amsterdam Cape Town Dubai London Madrid Milan Munich Paris Montréal Toronto
Delhi Mexico City São Paulo Sydney Hong Kong Seoul Singapore Taipei Tokyo

Editor in Chief: Michael Payne
Executive Acquisitions Editor: Jenifer Niles
Editorial Project Manager: Carly Prakapas
Product Development Manager: Laura Burgess
Development Editor: Ginny Munroe
Editorial Assistant: Andra Skaalrud
Director of Marketing: Maggie Leen
Marketing Manager: Brad Forrester
Marketing Coordinator: Susan Osterlitz
Marketing Assistant: Darshika Vyas
Managing Editor: Camille Trentacoste
Senior Production Project Manager: Rhonda Aversa

Operations Specialist: Maura Zaldivar-Garcia
Senior Art Director: Jonathan Boylan
Cover Photo: © photobar/Fotolia
Associate Director of Design: Blair Brown
Director of Media Development: Taylor Ragan
Media Project Manager, Production: Renata Butera
Full-Service Project Management: PreMediaGlobal
Composition: PreMediaGlobal
Printer/Binder: Webcrafters, Inc.
Cover Printer: Lehigh-Phoenix Color/Hagerstown
Text Font: MinionPro

Credits and acknowledgments borrowed from other sources and reproduced, with permission, in this textbook appear on the appropriate page within text. Microsoft and/or its respective suppliers make no representations about the suitability of the information contained in the documents and related graphics published as part of the services for any purpose. All such documents and related graphics are provided "as is" without warranty of any kind.

Microsoft and/or its respective suppliers hereby disclaim all warranties and conditions with regard to this information, including all warranties and conditions of merchantability, whether express, implied or statutory, fitness for a particular purpose, title and non-infringement. In no event shall Microsoft and/or its respective suppliers be liable for any special, indirect or consequential damages or any damages whatsoever resulting from loss of use, data or profits, whether in an action of contract, negligence or other tortious action, arising out of or in connection with the use or performance of information available from the services.

The documents and related graphics contained herein could include technical inaccuracies or typographical errors. Changes are periodically added to the information herein. Microsoft and/or its respective suppliers may make improvements and/or changes in the product(s) and/or the program(s) described herein at any time.

Microsoft® and Windows® are registered trademarks of the Microsoft Corporation in the U.S.A. and other countries. This book is not sponsored or endorsed by or affiliated with the Microsoft Corporation.

Many of the designations by manufacturers and sellers to distinguish their products are claimed as trademarks. Where those designations appear in this book, and the publisher was aware of a trademark claim, the designations have been printed in initial caps or all caps.

Library of Congress data on file

10 9 8 7 6 5 4 3 2 1

ISBN 10: 0-13-334933-0
ISBN 13: 978-0-13-334933-7

Brief Contents

Table of Contents

Word Introduction to Microsoft Word 2013   49

Chapter 1   Creating Documents with Microsoft Word 2013..........51

Chapter 2   Using Tables and Templates to Create Resumes and Cover Letters......................... 109

Chapter 3   Creating Research Papers, Newsletters, and Merged Mailing Labels 167

About the Authors

Shelley Gaskin, Series Editor, is a professor in the Business and Computer Technology Division at Pasadena City College in Pasadena, California. She holds a bachelor's degree in Business Administration from Robert Morris College (Pennsylvania), a master's degree in Business from Northern Illinois University, and a doctorate in Adult and Community Education from Ball State University (Indiana). Before joining Pasadena City College, she spent 12 years in the computer industry, where she was a systems analyst, sales representative, and director of Customer Education with Unisys Corporation. She also worked for Ernst & Young on the development of large systems applications for their clients. She has written and developed training materials for custom systems applications in both the public and private sector, and has also written and edited numerous computer application textbooks.

This book is dedicated to my students, who inspire me every day.

Alicia Vargas is a faculty member in Business Information Technology at Pasadena City College. She holds a master's and a bachelor's degree in business education from California State University, Los Angeles, and has authored several textbooks and training manuals on Microsoft Word, Microsoft Excel, and Microsoft PowerPoint.

This book is dedicated with all my love to my husband Vic, who makes everything possible; and to my children Victor, Phil, and Emmy, who are an unending source of inspiration and who make everything worthwhile.

GO! with Word 2013

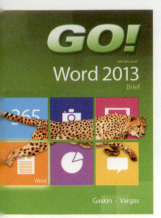

GO! with Word 2013 is the right solution for you and your students in today's fast-moving, mobile environment. The GO! Series content focuses on the real-world job skills students need to succeed in the workforce. They learn Office by working step-by-step through practical job-related projects that put the core functionality of Office in context. And as has always been true of the GO! Series, students learn the important concepts when they need them, and they never get lost in instruction, because the GO! Series uses Microsoft procedural syntax. Students learn how and learn why—at the teachable moment.

After completing the instructional projects, students are ready to apply the skills in a wide variety of progressively challenging projects that require them to solve problems, think critically, and create projects on their own. And, for those who want to go beyond the classroom and become certified, GO! provides clear MOS preparation guidelines so students know what is needed to ace the Core exam!

What's New

New Design reflects the look of Windows 8 and Office 2013 and enhances readability.

Enhanced Chapter Opener now includes a deeper introduction to the A and B instructional projects and more highly defined chapter Objectives and Learning Outcomes.

New Application Introductions provide a brief overview of the application and put the chapters in context for students.

Coverage of New Features of Office 2013 ensures that students are learning the skills they need to work in today's job market.

New Application Capstone Projects ensure that students are ready to move on to the next set of chapters. Each Application Capstone Project can be found on the Instructor Resource Center and is also a Grader project in MyITLab.

More Grader Projects based on the E, F, and G mastering-level projects, both homework and assessment versions! These projects are written by our GO! authors, who are all instructors in colleges like yours!

New Training and Assessment Simulations are now written by the authors to match the book one-to-one!

New MOS Map on the Instructor Resource Site and in the Annotated Instructor's Edition indicates clearly where each required MOS Objective is covered.

Three Types of Videos help students understand and succeed in the real world:

- *Student Training Videos* are broken down by Objective and created by the author—a real instructor teaching the same types of courses that you do. Real personal instruction.
- *GO! to Work* videos are short interviews with workers showing how they use Office in their jobs.
- *GO! for Job Success* videos relate to the projects in the chapter and cover important career topics such as *Dressing for Success*, *Time Management*, and *Making Ethical Choices*.

New GO! Learn It Online section at the end of the chapter indicates where various student learning activities can be found, including multiple choice and matching activities.

New Styles for In-Text Boxed Content: Another Way, Notes, More Knowledge, Alerts, and **new** *By Touch* **instructions** are included in line with the instruction and not in the margins so that the student is more likely to read this information.

Clearly Indicated Build from Scratch Projects: GO! has always had many projects that begin "from scratch," and now we have an icon to really call them out!

New Visual Summary focuses on the four key concepts to remember from each chapter.

New Review and Assessment Guide summarizes the end-of-chapter assessments for a quick overview of the different types and levels of assignments and assessments for each chapter.

New Skills and Procedures Summary Chart (online at the Instructor Resource Center) summarizes all of the shortcuts and commands covered in the chapter.

New End-of-Chapter Key Term Glossary with Definitions for each chapter, plus a comprehensive end-of-book glossary.

New Flipboards and Crossword Puzzles enable students to review the concepts and key terms learned in each chapter by completing online challenges.

Teach the Course You Want in Less Time

A Microsoft® Office textbook designed for student success!

- **Project-Based** – Students learn by creating projects that they will use in the real world.

- **Microsoft Procedural Syntax** – Steps are written to put students in the right place at the right time.

- **Teachable Moment** – Expository text is woven into the steps—at the moment students need to know it—not chunked together in a block of text that will go unread.

- **Sequential Pagination** – Students have actual page numbers instead of confusing letters and abbreviations.

New Feature

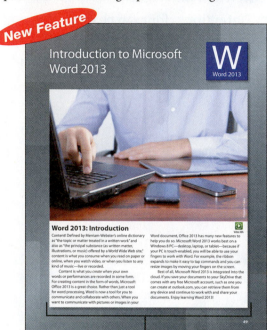

Student Outcomes and Learning Objectives – Objectives are clustered around projects that result in student outcomes.

New Design – Provides a more visually appealing and concise display of important content.

New Application Introductions – Provide an overview of the application to prepare students for the upcoming chapters.

Simulation Training and Assessment – Gives your students the most realistic Office 2013 experience with open, realistic, high-fidelity simulations.

Project Activities – A project summary stated clearly and quickly.

Scenario – Each chapter opens with a job-related scenario that sets the stage for the projects the student will create.

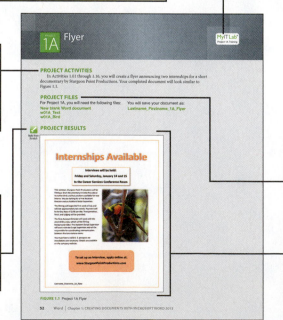

New Build from Scratch Icons – Enable you to easily see all the projects that the student builds from scratch.

Project Files – Clearly show students which files are needed for the project and the names they will use to save their documents.

Project Results – Show students what successful completion looks like.

In-Text Features
Another Way, Notes, *More* Knowledge, Alerts, and By Touch Instructions

Microsoft Procedural Syntax – Steps are written to put the student at the right place at the right time.

Color Coding – Each chapter has two instructional projects, which is less overwhelming for students than one large chapter project. The two projects are differentiated by different colored numbering and headings.

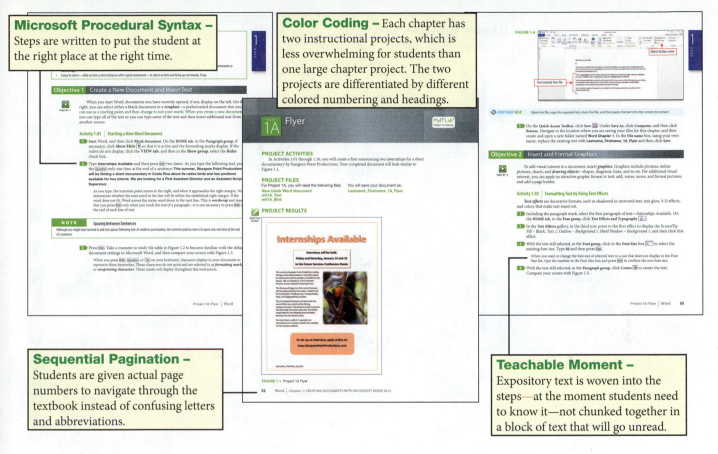

FIGURE 1.1 Project 1A Flyer

Sequential Pagination – Students are given actual page numbers to navigate through the textbook instead of confusing letters and abbreviations.

Teachable Moment – Expository text is woven into the steps—at the moment students need to know it—not chunked together in a block of text that will go unread.

End-of-Chapter
Content-Based Assessments – Assessments with defined solutions.

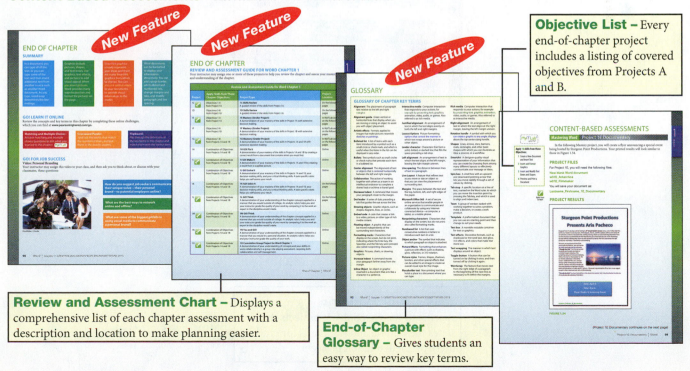

Objective List – Every end-of-chapter project includes a listing of covered objectives from Projects A and B.

Review and Assessment Chart – Displays a comprehensive list of each chapter assessment with a description and location to make planning easier.

End-of-Chapter Glossary – Gives students an easy way to review key terms.

End-of-Chapter

Content-Based Assessments – Assessments with defined solutions. (continued)

Grader Projects – Each chapter has six MyITLab Grader projects—three homework and three assessment—clearly indicated by the MyITLab logo.

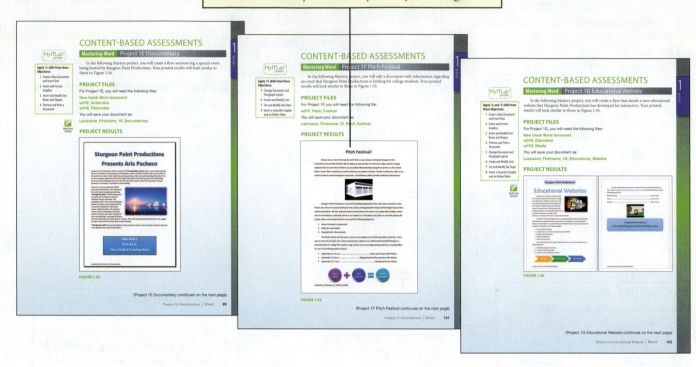

Task-Specific Rubric – A matrix specific to the GO! Solve It projects that states the criteria and standards for grading these defined-solution projects.

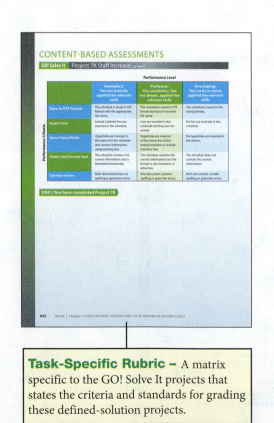

End-of-Chapter

Outcomes-Based Assessments – Assessments with open-ended solutions.

Sample Solution – Outcomes-based assessments include a sample solution so the instructor can compare student work with an example of expert work.

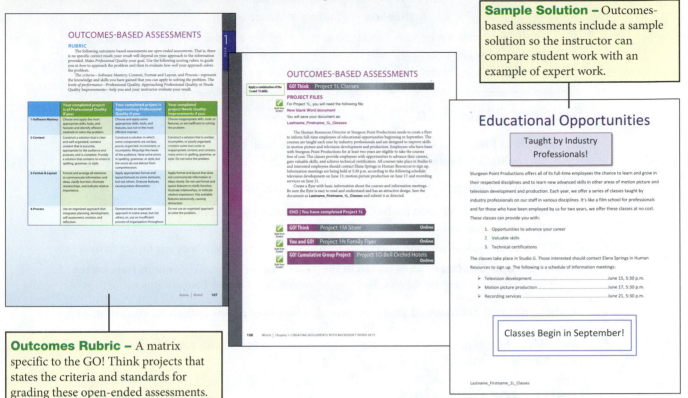

Outcomes Rubric – A matrix specific to the GO! Think projects that states the criteria and standards for grading these open-ended assessments.

GO! with Microsoft Office 365 – A collaboration project for each chapter teaches students how to use the cloud-based tools of Office 365 to communicate and collaborate from any device, anywhere.

Office Web Apps – For each instructional project, students can create the same or similar result in the corresponding Office Web Apps - 24 projects in all!

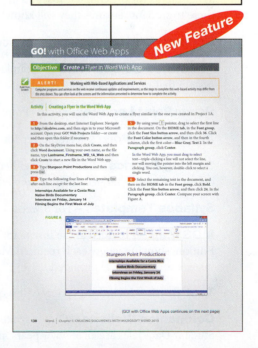

Student Materials

Student Data Files – All student data files are available to all on the companion website: www.pearsonhighered.com/go.

3 Types of Videos help students understand and succeed in the real world:

- **Student Training Videos** are by Objective and created by the author—a real instructor teaching the same types of courses that you teach.
- *GO! to Work* videos are short interviews with workers showing how they use Office in their job.
- *GO! for Job Success* videos related to the projects in the chapter cover important career topics such as *Dressing for Success*, *Time Management*, and *Making Ethical Choices*.

Flipboards and crossword puzzles provide a variety of review options for content in each chapter.

Available on the companion website using the access code included with your book.
pearsonhighered.com/go.

All Instructor and Student materials available at pearsonhighered.com/go

Instructor Materials

Annotated Instructor Edition – An instructor tool includes a full copy of the student textbook and a guide to implementing your course in three different ways, depending on the emphasis you want to place on digital engagement. Also included are teaching tips, discussion topics, and other useful pieces for teaching each chapter.

Student Assignment Tracker (previously called Assignment Sheets) – Lists all the assignments for the chapter. Just add the course information, due dates, and points. Providing these to students ensures they will know what is due and when.

Scripted Lectures – A script to guide your classroom lecture of each instructional project.

Annotated Solution Files – Coupled with the scorecards, these create a grading and scoring system that makes grading easy and efficient.

PowerPoint Lectures – PowerPoint presentations for each chapter.

Audio PowerPoints – Audio versions of the PowerPoint presentations for each chapter.

Scoring Rubrics – Can be used either by students to check their work or by you as a quick check-off for the items that need to be corrected.

Syllabus Templates – For 8-week, 12-week, and 16-week courses.

MOS Map – Provided at the Instructor Resource Center site and in the Annotated Instructor's Edition, showing where each required MOS Objective is covered either in the book or via additional instructional material provided.

Test Bank – Includes a variety of test questions for each chapter.

Companion Website – Online content such as the Online Chapter Review, Glossary, and Student Data Files are all at www.pearsonhighered.com/go.

Reviewers

GO! Focus Group Participants

Kenneth Mayer	Heald College
Carolyn Borne	Louisiana State University
Toribio Matamoros	Miami Dade College
Lynn Keane	University of South Carolina
Terri Hayes	Broward College
Michelle Carter	Paradise Valley Community College

GO! Reviewers

Abul Sheikh	Abraham Baldwin Agricultural College
John Percy	Atlantic Cape Community College
Janette Hicks	Binghamton University
Shannon Ogden	Black River Technical College
Karen May	Blinn College
Susan Fry	Boise State University
Chigurupati Rani	Borough of Manhattan Community College / CUNY
Ellen Glazer	Broward College
Kate LeGrand	Broward College
Mike Puopolo	Bunker Hill Community College
Nicole Lytle-Kosola	California State University, San Bernardino
Nisheeth Agrawal	Calhoun Community College
Pedro Diaz-Gomez	Cameron
Linda Friedel	Central Arizona College
Gregg Smith	Central Community College
Norm Cregger	Central Michigan University
Lisa LaCaria	Central Piedmont Community College
Steve Siedschlag	Chaffey College
Terri Helfand	Chaffey College
Susan Mills	Chambersburg
Mandy Reininger	Chemeketa Community College
Connie Crossley	Cincinnati State Technical and Community College
Marjorie Deutsch	City University of New York - Queensborough Community College
Mary Ann Zlotow	College of DuPage
Christine Bohnsak	College of Lake County
Gertrude Brier	College of Staten Island
Sharon Brown	College of The Albemarle
Terry Rigsby	Columbia College
Vicki Brooks	Columbia College
Donald Hames	Delgado Community College
Kristen King	Eastern Kentucky University
Kathie Richer	Edmonds Community College
Gary Smith	Elmhurst College
Wendi Kappersw	Embry-Riddle Aeronautical University
Nancy Woolridge	Fullerton College
Abigail Miller	Gateway Community & Technical College
Deep Ramanayake	Gateway Community & Technical College
Gwen White	Gateway Community & Technical College
Debbie Glinert	Gloria K School
Dana Smith	Golf Academy of America
Mary Locke	Greenville Technical College
Diane Marie Roselli	Harrisburg Area Community College
Linda Arnold	Harrisburg Area Community College - Lebanon
Daniel Schoedel	Harrisburg Area Community College - York Campus
Ken Mayer	Heald College
Xiaodong Qiao	Heald College
Donna Lamprecht	Hopkinsville Community College
Kristen Lancaster	Hopkinsville Community College
Johnny Hurley	Iowa Lakes Community College
Linda Halverson	Iowa Lakes Community College
Sarah Kilgo	Isothermal Community College
Chris DeGeare	Jefferson College
David McNair	Jefferson College
Diane Santurri	Johnson & Wales University
Roland Sparks	Johnson & Wales University
Ram Raghuraman	Joliet Junior College
Eduardo Suniga	Lansing Community College
Kenneth A. Hyatt	Lone Star College - Kingwood
Glenn Gray	Lone Star College - North Harris
Gene Carbonaro	Long Beach City College
Betty Pearman	Los Medanos College
Diane Kosharek	Madison College
Peter Meggison	Massasoit Community College
George Gabb	Miami Dade College
Lennie Alice Cooper	Miami Dade College
Richard Mabjish	Miami Dade College
Victor Giol	Miami Dade College
John Meir	Midlands Technical College
Greg Pauley	Moberly Area Community College
Catherine Glod	Mohawk Valley Community College
Robert Huyck	Mohawk Valley Community College
Kevin Engellant	Montana Western
Philip Lee	Nashville State Community College
Ruth Neal	Navarro College
Sharron Jordan	Navarro College
Richard Dale	New Mexico State University
Lori Townsend	Niagara County Community College
Judson Curry	North Park University
Mary Zegarski	Northampton Community College
Neal Stenlund	Northern Virginia Community College
Michael Goeken	Northwest Vista College
Mary Beth Tarver	Northwestern State University
Amy Rutledge	Oakland University
Marcia Braddock	Okefenokee Technical College
Richard Stocke	Oklahoma State University - OKC
Jane Stam	Onondaga Community College
Mike Michaelson	Palomar College
Kungwen (Dave) Chu	Purdue University Calumet
Wendy Ford	City University of New York - Queensborough Community College
Lewis Hall	Riverside City College
Karen Acree	San Juan College
Tim Ellis	Schoolcraft College
Dan Combellick	Scottsdale Community College
Pat Serrano	Scottsdale Community College
Rose Hendrickson	Sheridan College
Kit Carson	South Georgia College
Rebecca Futch	South Georgia State College
Brad Hagy	Southern Illinois University Carbondale
Mimi Spain	Southern Maine Community College
David Parker	Southern Oregon University
Madeline Baugher	Southwestern Oklahoma State University
Brian Holbert	St. Johns River State College
Bunny Howard	St. Johns River State College
Stephanie Cook	State College of Florida
Sharon Wavle	Tompkins Cortland Community College
George Fiori	Tri-County Technical College
Steve St. John	Tulsa Community College
Karen Thessing	University of Central Arkansas
Richard McMahon	University of Houston-Downtown
Shohreh Hashemi	University of Houston-Downtown
Donna Petty	Wallace Community College
Julia Bell	Walters State Community College
Ruby Kowaney	West Los Angeles College
Casey Thompson	Wiregrass Georgia Technical College
DeAnnia Clements	Wiregrass Georgia Technical College

Introduction to Microsoft Office 2013 Features

PROJECT 1A

OUTCOMES
Create, save, and print a Microsoft Office 2013 document.

OBJECTIVES

1. Use File Explorer to Download, Extract, and Locate Files and Folders
2. Use Start Search to Locate and Start a Microsoft Office 2013 Desktop App
3. Enter, Edit, and Check the Spelling of Text in an Office 2013 Program
4. Perform Commands from a Dialog Box
5. Create a Folder and Name and Save a File
6. Insert a Footer, Add Document Properties, Print a File, and Close a Desktop App

PROJECT 1B

OUTCOMES
Use the ribbon and dialog boxes to perform commands in Microsoft Office 2013.

OBJECTIVES

7. Open an Existing File and Save It with a New Name
8. Sign In to Office and Explore Options for a Microsoft Office Desktop App
9. Perform Commands from the Ribbon and Quick Access Toolbar
10. Apply Formatting in Office Programs
11. Compress Files and Use the Microsoft Office 2013 Help System
12. Install Apps for Office and Create a Microsoft Account

etse1112/Fotolia

In This Chapter

In this chapter, you will use File Explorer to navigate the Windows folder structure, create a folder, and save files in Microsoft Office 2013 programs. You will also practice using features in Microsoft Office 2013 that work similarly across Word, Excel, Access, and PowerPoint. These features include managing files, performing commands, adding document properties, signing in to Office, applying formatting, and using Help. You will also practice compressing files and installing Apps for Office from the Office Store. In this chapter, you will also learn how to set up a free Microsoft account so that you can use SkyDrive.

The projects in this chapter relate to **Skyline Metro Grill**, which is a chain of 25 casual, full-service restaurants based in Boston. The Skyline Metro Grill owners are planning an aggressive expansion program. To expand by 15 additional restaurants in Chicago, San Francisco, and Los Angeles by 2018, the company must attract new investors, develop new menus, develop new marketing strategies, and recruit new employees, all while adhering to the company's quality guidelines and maintaining its reputation for excellent service. To succeed, the company plans to build on its past success and maintain its quality elements.

PROJECT 1A

Note Form

MyITLab®
Project 1A Training

PROJECT ACTIVITIES

In Activities 1.01 through 1.09, you will create a note form using Microsoft Word, save it in a folder that you create by using File Explorer, and then print the note form or submit it electronically as directed by your instructor. Your completed note form will look similar to Figure 1.1.

PROJECT FILES

For Project 1A, you will need the following file:
New blank Word document

You will save your file as:
Lastname_Firstname_1A_Note_Form

PROJECT RESULTS

Build from Scratch

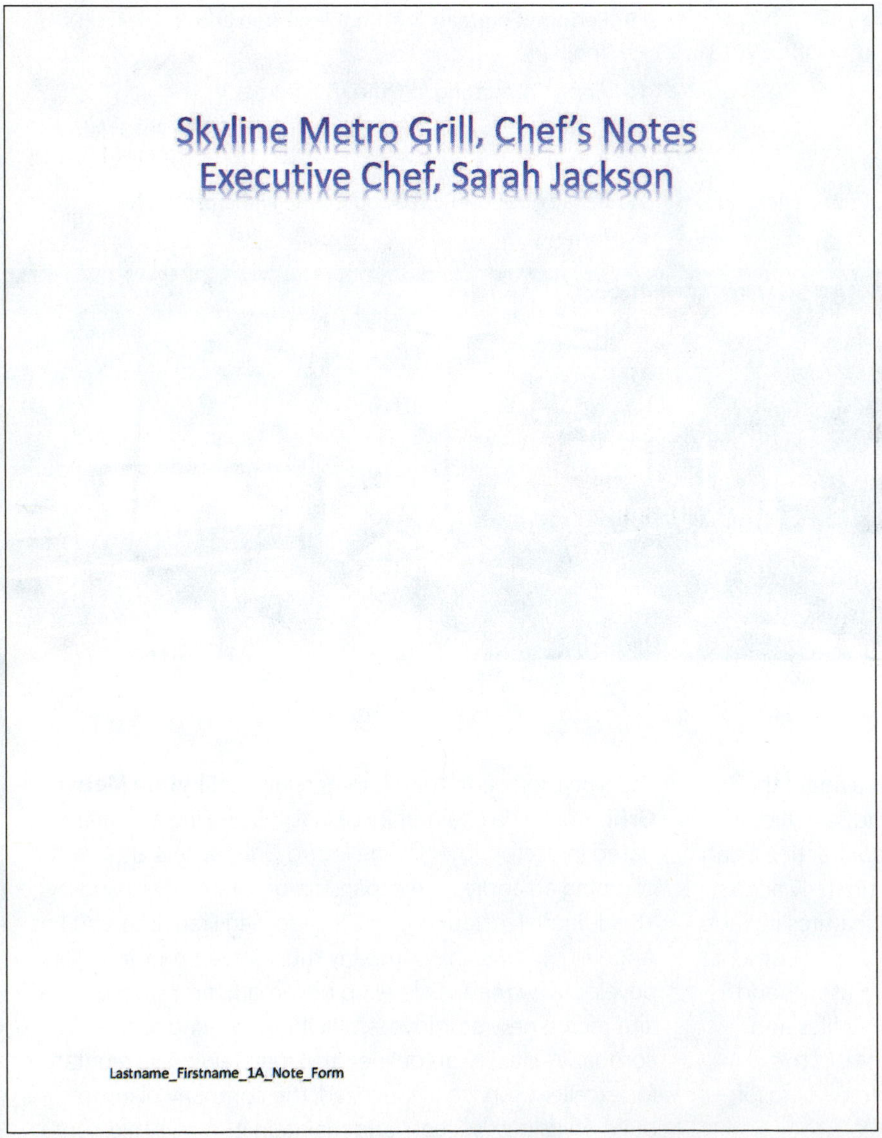

Skyline Metro Grill, Chef's Notes
Executive Chef, Sarah Jackson

Lastname_Firstname_1A_Note_Form

FIGURE 1.1 Project 1A Note Form

Objective 1   Use File Explorer to Download, Extract, and Locate Files and Folders

Video OF1-1

A *file* is a collection of information stored on a computer under a single name, for example, a Word document or a PowerPoint presentation. A file is stored in a *folder*—a container in which you store files—or a *subfolder*, which is a folder within a folder. The Windows operating system stores and organizes your files and folders, which is a primary task of an operating system.

You *navigate*—explore within the organizing structure of Windows—to create, save, and find your files and folders by using the *File Explorer* program. File Explorer displays the files and folders on your computer and is at work anytime you are viewing the contents of files and folders in a *window*. A window is a rectangular area on a computer screen in which programs and content appear; a window can be moved, resized, minimized, or closed.

Activity 1.01   Using File Explorer to Download, Extract, and Locate Files and Folders

ALERT! You Will Need a USB Flash Drive

You will need a USB flash drive for this activity to download the Student Data Files for this chapter. If your instructor is providing the files to you, for example by placing the files at your learning management system, be sure you have downloaded them to a location where you can access the files and then skip to Activity 1.02.

NOTE Creating a Microsoft Account

Use a free Microsoft account to sign in to Windows 8 and Office 2013 so that you can work on different PCs and use your SkyDrive. You need not use the Microsoft account as your primary email address unless you want to do so. To create a Microsoft account, go to **www.outlook.com**.

1 ▶ Sign in to Windows 8 with your Microsoft account—or the account provided by your instructor—to display the Windows 8 **Start screen**, and then click the **Desktop** tile. Insert a **USB flash drive** in your computer; **Close** ☒ any messages or windows that display.

The *desktop* is the screen in Windows that simulates your work area. A *USB flash drive* is a small data storage device that plugs into a computer USB port.

2 ▶ On the taskbar, click **Internet Explorer** 🅔. Click in the **address bar** to select the existing text, type **www.pearsonhighered.com/go** and press ⏎. Locate and click the name of this textbook, and then click the **STUDENT DATA FILES tab**.

The *taskbar* is the area along the lower edge of the desktop that displays buttons representing programs—also referred to as desktop apps. In the desktop version of Internet Explorer 10, the *address bar* is the area at the top of the Internet Explorer window that displays, and where you can type, a *URL—Uniform Resource Locator*—which is an address that uniquely identifies a location on the Internet.

3 On the list of files, move your mouse pointer over—*point* to—**Office Features Chapter 1** and then *click*—press the left button on your mouse pointing device one time.

4 In the **Windows Internet Explorer** dialog box, click **Save As**.

A *dialog box* is a small window that contains options for completing a task.

5 In the **Save As** dialog box, on the left, locate the **navigation pane**, and point to the vertical **scroll bar**.

The Save As dialog box is an example of a *common dialog box*; that is, this dialog box looks the same in Excel and in PowerPoint and in most other Windows-based desktop applications—also referred to as programs.

Use the *navigation pane* on the left side of the Save As dialog box to navigate to, open, and display favorites, libraries, folders, saved searches, and an expandable list of drives. A *pane* is a separate area of a window.

A *scroll bar* displays when a window, or a pane within a window, has information that is not in view. You can click the up or down scroll arrows—or the left and right scroll arrows in a horizontal scroll bar—to scroll the contents up and down or left and right in small increments.

You can also drag the *scroll box*—the box within the scroll bar—to scroll the window or pane in either direction.

This is a *compressed folder*—also called a *zipped folder*—which is a folder containing one or more files that have been reduced in size. A compressed folder takes up less storage space and can be transferred to other computers faster.

NOTE | **Comparing Your Screen with the Figures in This Textbook**

Your screen will match the figures shown in this textbook if you set your screen resolution to 1280 × 768. At other resolutions, your screen will closely resemble, but not match, the figures shown. To view your screen's resolution, on the desktop, right-click in a blank area, and then click Screen resolution.

---

6 In the **navigation pane**, if necessary, on the scroll bar click ☑ to scroll down. If necessary, to the left of **Computer**, click ▷ to expand the list. Then click the name of your **USB flash drive**.

7 With *Office_Features* displayed in the **File name** box, in the lower right corner click **Save**.

At the bottom of your screen, the *Notification bar* displays information about pending downloads, security issues, add-ons, and other issues related to the operation of your computer.

8 In the **Notification bar**, when the download is complete, click **Open folder** to display the folder window for your **USB flash drive**.

A *folder window* displays the contents of the current location—folder, library, or drive—and contains helpful parts so that you can navigate within the file organizing structure of Windows.

9 With the compressed **Office_Features** folder selected, on the ribbon, click the **Extract tab** to display the **Compressed Folder Tools**, and then click **Extract all**.

The *ribbon* is a user interface in both Office 2013 and Windows 8 that groups the commands for performing related tasks on tabs across the upper portion of a window.

In the dialog box, you can *extract*—decompress or pull out—files from a compressed folder.

You can navigate to some other location by clicking the Browse button and navigating within your storage locations.

10 In the **Extract Compressed (Zipped) Folders** dialog box, click to the right of the selected text, and then press (Backspace) until only the drive letter of your USB and the colon following it display—for example G:—and then click **Extract**. Notice that a progress bar indicates the progress of the extract process, and that when the extract is complete, the **Office_Features** folder displays on the file list of your **USB flash drive**.

In a dialog box or taskbar button, a **progress bar** indicates visually the progress of a task such as a download or file transfer.

The **address bar** in File Explorer displays your current location in the folder structure as a series of links separated by arrows, which is referred to as the **path**—a sequence of folders that leads to a specific file or folder.

By pressing (Backspace) in the Extract dialog box, you avoid creating an unneeded folder level.

11 Because you no longer need the compressed (zipped) version of the folder, be sure it is selected, click the **Home tab**, and then click **Delete**. In the upper right corner of the **USB drive** folder window, click **Close** ☒. **Close** ☒ the **Internet Explorer** window and in the Internet Explorer message, click **Close all tabs**.

Your desktop redisplays.

Objective 2   Use Start Search to Locate and Start a Microsoft Office 2013 Desktop App

Video OF1-2

The term **desktop app** commonly refers to a computer program that is installed on your computer and requires a computer operating system such as Microsoft Windows or Apple OS to run. The programs in Microsoft Office 2013 are considered to be desktop apps. Apps that run from the *device software* on a smartphone or a tablet computer—for example, iOS, Android, or Windows Phone—or apps that run from *browser software* such as Internet Explorer, Safari, Firefox, or Chrome on a desktop PC or laptop PC are referred to simply as **apps**.

Activity 1.02   Using Start Search to Locate and Start a Microsoft Office 2013 Desktop App

The easiest and fastest way to search for an app is to use the **Start search** feature—simply display the Windows 8 Start screen and start typing. By default, Windows 8 searches for apps; you can change it to search for files or settings.

1 With your desktop displayed, press ⊞ to display the Windows 8 **Start screen**, and then type **word 2013** With *word 2013* bordered in white in the search results, press (Enter) to return to the desktop and open Word. If you want to do so, in the upper right corner, sign in with your Microsoft account, and then compare your screen with Figure 1.2.

Documents that you have recently opened, if any, display on the left. On the right, you can select either a blank document or a **template**—a preformatted document that you can use as a starting point and then change to suit your needs.

 BY TOUCH   Swipe from the right edge of the screen to display the charms, and then tap Search. Tap in the Apps box, and then use the onscreen keyboard that displays to type *word 2013*. Tap the selected Word 2013 app name to open Word.

FIGURE 1.2

Recently opened documents, if any, display here

Start a blank document here

User signed in; this is optional

Templates to start different types of documents

2 ▶ Click **Blank document**. Compare your screen with Figure 1.3, and then take a moment to study the description of these screen elements in the table in Figure 1.4.

N O T E	**Displaying the Full Ribbon**

If your full ribbon does not display, click any tab, and then at the right end of the ribbon, click ⊞ to pin the ribbon to keep it open while you work.

FIGURE 1.3

Quick Access Toolbar

Ribbon tabs

Help and window control buttons

Application icon

Title bar

Ribbon

FILE tab

Group names

Signed-in user

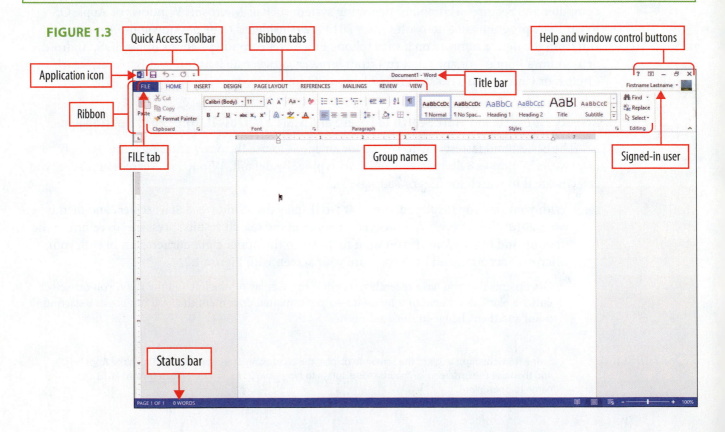

Status bar

FIGURE 1.4

MICROSOFT OFFICE SCREEN ELEMENTS	
SCREEN ELEMENT	**DESCRIPTION**
FILE tab	Displays Microsoft Office Backstage view, which is a centralized space for all of your file management tasks such as opening, saving, printing, publishing, or sharing a file—all the things you can do *with* a file.
Group names	Indicate the names of the groups of related commands on the displayed tab.
Help and window control buttons	Display Word Help and Full Screen Mode and enable you to Minimize, Restore Down, or Close the window.
Application icon	When clicked, displays a menu of window control commands including Restore, Minimize, and Close.
Quick Access Toolbar	Displays buttons to perform frequently used commands and use resources with a single click. The default commands include Save, Undo, and Redo. You can add and delete buttons to customize the Quick Access Toolbar for your convenience.
Ribbon	Displays a group of task-oriented tabs that contain the commands, styles, and resources you need to work in an Office 2013 desktop app. The look of your ribbon depends on your screen resolution. A high resolution will display more individual items and button names on the ribbon.
Ribbon tabs	Display the names of the task-oriented tabs relevant to the open program.
Status bar	Displays file information on the left; on the right displays buttons for Read Mode, Print Layout, and Web Layout views; on the far right displays Zoom controls.
Title bar	Displays the name of the file and the name of the program. The Help and window control buttons are grouped on the right side of the title bar.
Signed-in user	Name of the Windows 8 signed-in user.

Objective 3 Enter, Edit, and Check the Spelling of Text in an Office 2013 Program

Video OF1-3

All of the programs in Office 2013 require some typed text. Your keyboard is still the primary method of entering information into your computer. Techniques to enter text and to *edit*—make changes to—text are similar among all of the Office 2013 programs.

Activity 1.03 | Entering and Editing Text in an Office 2013 Program

1 On the ribbon, on the HOME tab, in the Paragraph group, if necessary, click Show/Hide ¶ so that it is active—shaded. If necessary, on the VIEW tab, in the Show group, select the Ruler check box so that rulers display below the ribbon and on the left side of your window.

The *insertion point*—a blinking vertical line that indicates where text or graphics will be inserted—displays. In Office 2013 programs, the mouse *pointer*—any symbol that displays on your screen in response to moving your mouse device—displays in different shapes depending on the task you are performing and the area of the screen to which you are pointing.

When you press Enter, Spacebar, or Tab on your keyboard, characters display to represent these keystrokes. These screen characters do not print and are referred to as *formatting marks* or *nonprinting characters*.

2 ▸ Type **Skyline Grille Info** and notice how the insertion point moves to the right as you type. Point slightly to the right of the letter *e* in *Grille* and click to place the insertion point there. Compare your screen with Figure 1.5.

A *paragraph symbol* (¶) indicates the end of a paragraph and displays each time you press Enter. This is a type of formatting mark and does not print.

FIGURE 1.5

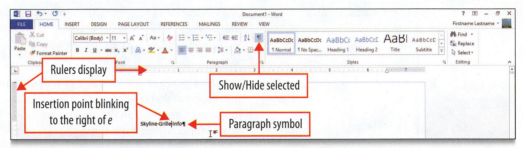

3 ▸ On your keyboard, locate and then press the Backspace key to delete the letter *e*.

Pressing Backspace removes a character to the left of the insertion point.

4 ▸ Press → one time to place the insertion point to the left of the *I* in *Info*. Type **Chef's** and then press Spacebar one time.

By *default*, when you type text in an Office program, existing text moves to the right to make space for new typing. Default refers to the current selection or setting that is automatically used by a program unless you specify otherwise.

5 ▸ Press Del four times to delete *Info* and then type **Notes**

Pressing Del removes a character to the right of the insertion point.

6 ▸ With your insertion point blinking after the word *Notes*, on your keyboard, hold down the Ctrl key. While holding down Ctrl, press ← three times to move the insertion point to the beginning of the word *Grill*.

This is a *keyboard shortcut*—a key or combination of keys that performs a task that would otherwise require a mouse. This keyboard shortcut moves the insertion point to the beginning of the previous word.

A keyboard shortcut is commonly indicated as Ctrl + ← (or some other combination of keys) to indicate that you hold down the first key while pressing the second key. A keyboard shortcut can also include three keys, in which case you hold down the first two and then press the third. For example, Ctrl + Shift + ← selects one word to the left.

7 ▸ With the insertion point blinking at the beginning of the word *Grill*, type **Metro** and press Spacebar.

8 ▸ Press Ctrl + End to place the insertion point after the letter *s* in *Notes*, and then press Enter one time. With the insertion point blinking, type the following and include the spelling error:
Exective Chef, Madison Dunham

9 With your mouse, point slightly to the left of the *M* in *Madison*, hold down the left mouse button, and then *drag*—hold down the left mouse button while moving your mouse—to the right to select the text *Madison Dunham* but not the paragraph mark following it, and then release the mouse button. Compare your screen with Figure 1.6.

> The *mini toolbar* displays commands that are commonly used with the selected object, which places common commands close to your pointer. When you move the pointer away from the mini toolbar, it fades from view.

> *Selecting* refers to highlighting, by dragging or clicking with your mouse, areas of text or data or graphics so that the selection can be edited, formatted, copied, or moved. The action of dragging includes releasing the left mouse button at the end of the area you want to select.

> The Office programs recognize a selected area as one unit to which you can make changes. Selecting text may require some practice. If you are not satisfied with your result, click anywhere outside of the selection, and then begin again.

 BY TOUCH Tap once on *Madison* to display the gripper—small circle that acts as a handle—directly below the word. This establishes the start gripper. If necessary, with your finger, drag the gripper to the beginning of the word. Then drag the gripper to the end of Dunham to select the text and display the end gripper.

FIGURE 1.6

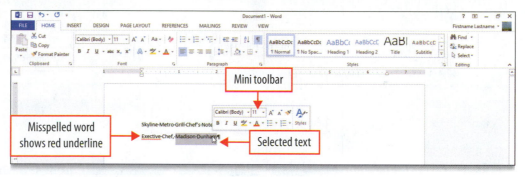

Mini toolbar

Misspelled word shows red underline

Selected text

10 With the text *Madison Dunham* selected, type **Sarah Jackson**

> In any Windows-based program, such as the Microsoft Office 2013 programs, selected text is deleted and then replaced when you begin to type new text. You will save time by developing good techniques for selecting and then editing or replacing selected text, which is easier than pressing the ⌷Del⌷ key numerous times to delete text.

Activity 1.04 | Checking Spelling

Office 2013 has a dictionary of words against which all entered text is checked. In Word and PowerPoint, words that are not in the dictionary display a wavy red line, indicating a possible misspelled word or a proper name or an unusual word—none of which are in the Office 2013 dictionary.

In Excel and Access, you can initiate a check of the spelling, but red underlines do not display.

1 Notice that the misspelled word *Exective* displays with a wavy red underline.

2 Point to *Exective* and then *right-click*—click your right mouse button one time.

> A *shortcut menu* displays, which displays commands and options relevant to the selected text or object. These are *context-sensitive commands* because they relate to the item you right-clicked. These types of menus are also referred to as *context menus*. Here, the shortcut menu displays commands related to the misspelled word.

 BY TOUCH Tap and hold a moment to select the misspelled word, then release your finger to display the shortcut menu.

3 Press `Esc` to cancel the shortcut menu, and then in the lower left corner of your screen, on the **status bar**, click the **Proofing** icon, which displays an *X* because some errors are detected. Compare your screen with Figure 1.7.

The Spelling pane displays on the right. Here you have many more options for checking spelling than you have on the shortcut menu. The suggested correct word, *Executive*, is highlighted.

You can click the speaker icon to hear the pronunciation of the selected word. You can also see some synonyms for *Executive*. Finally, if you have not already installed a dictionary, you can click *Get a Dictionary*—if you are signed in to Office with a Microsoft account—to find and install one from the online Office store; or if you have a dictionary app installed, it will display here and you can search it for more information.

In the Spelling pane, you can ignore the word one time or in all occurrences, change the word to the suggested word, select a different suggestion, or add a word to the dictionary against which Word checks.

FIGURE 1.7

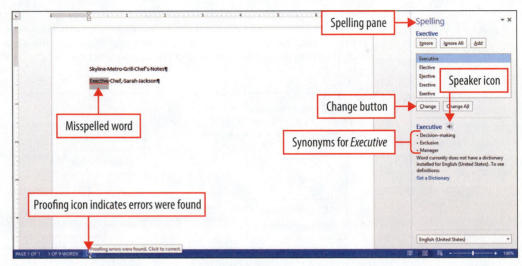

 **ANOTHER WAY** Press `F7` to display the Spelling pane; or, on the Review tab, in the Proofing group, click Spelling & Grammar.

4 In the **Spelling** pane, click **Change** to change the spelling to *Executive*. In the message box that displays, click **OK**.

Objective 4 Perform Commands from a Dialog Box

Video OF1-4

In a dialog box, you make decisions about an individual object or topic. In some dialog boxes, you can make multiple decisions in one place.

Activity 1.05 | Performing Commands from a Dialog Box

1 On the ribbon, click the **DESIGN tab**, and then in the **Page Background group**, click **Page Color**.

2 At the bottom of the menu, notice the command **Fill Effects** followed by an **ellipsis** (…). Compare your screen with Figure 1.8.

An *ellipsis* is a set of three dots indicating incompleteness. An ellipsis following a command name indicates that a dialog box will display when you click the command.

FIGURE 1.8

3 ▶ Click **Fill Effects** to display the **Fill Effects** dialog box. Compare your screen with Figure 1.9.

Fill is the inside color of a page or object. The Gradient tab is active. In a *gradient fill*, one color fades into another. Here, the dialog box displays a set of tabs across the top from which you can display different sets of options. Some dialog boxes display the option group names on the left.

FIGURE 1.9

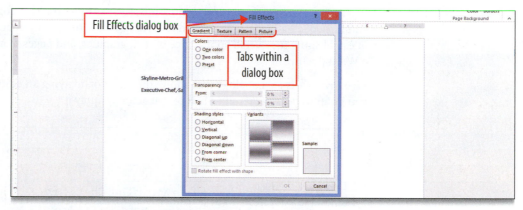

4 ▶ Under **Colors**, click the **One color** option button.

The dialog box displays settings related to the One color option. An *option button* is a round button that enables you to make one choice among two or more options.

5 ▶ Click the **Color 1 arrow**—the arrow under the text *Color 1*—and then in the third column, point to the second color to display the ScreenTip *Gray-25%, Background 2, Darker 10%*.

A *ScreenTip* displays useful information about mouse actions, such as pointing to screen elements or dragging.

6 ▶ Click **Gray-25%, Background 2, Darker 10%**, and then notice that the fill color displays in the **Color 1** box. In the **Dark Light** bar, click the **Light arrow** as many times as necessary until the scroll box is all the way to right. Under **Shading styles**, click the **Diagonal down** option button. Under **Variants**, click the upper right variant. Compare your screen with Figure 1.10.

FIGURE 1.10

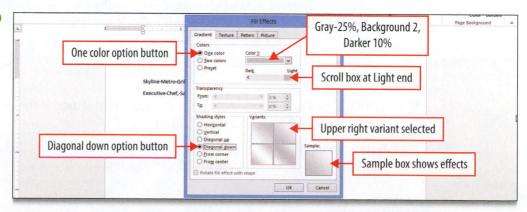

7 ▶ At the bottom of the dialog box, click **OK**, and notice the subtle page color.

In Word, the gray shading page color will not print—even on a color printer—unless you set specific options to do so. However a subtle background page color is effective if people will be reading the document on a screen. Microsoft's research indicates that two-thirds of people who open Word documents never edit them; they only read them.

Activity 1.06 | Using Undo

1 ▶ Point to the *S* in *Skyline*, and then drag down and to the right to select both paragraphs of text and include the paragraph marks. On the mini toolbar, click **Styles,** and then *point to* but do not click **Title**. Compare your screen with Figure 1.11.

A **style** is a group of **formatting** commands, such as font, font size, font color, paragraph alignment, and line spacing that can be applied to a paragraph with one command. Formatting is the process of establishing the overall appearance of text, graphics, and pages in an Office file—for example, in a Word document.

Live Preview is a technology that shows the result of applying an editing or formatting change as you point to possible results—before you actually apply it.

FIGURE 1.11

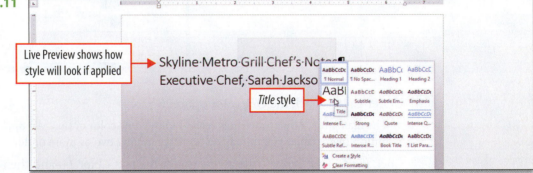

2 ▶ In the **Styles** gallery, click **Title**.

A **gallery** is an Office feature that displays a list of potential results.

3 ▶ On the ribbon, on the **HOME tab**, in the **Paragraph group**, click **Center** ☰ to center the two paragraphs.

Alignment refers to the placement of paragraph text relative to the left and right margins. **Center alignment** refers to text that is centered horizontally between the left and right margins. You can also align text at the left margin, which is the default alignment for text in Word, or at the right.

ANOTHER WAY   Press Ctrl + E to use the Center command.

4 ▶ With the two paragraphs still selected, on the **HOME tab**, in the **Font Group**, click **Text Effects and Typography** A▾ to display a gallery.

5 ▶ In the second row, click the first effect—**Gradient Fill – Gray**. Click anywhere to *deselect*—cancel the selection—the text and notice the text effect.

6 Because this effect might be difficult to read, in the upper left corner of your screen, on the **Quick Access Toolbar**, click **Undo** .

The **Undo** command reverses your last action.

🔄 **ANOTHER WAY**   Press Ctrl + Z as the keyboard shortcut for the Undo command.

7 Display the **Text Effects and Typography** gallery again, and then in the second row, click the second effect—**Gradient Fill – Blue, Accent 1, Reflection**. Click anywhere to deselect the text and notice the text effect. Compare your screen with Figure 1.12.

As you progress in your study of Microsoft Office, you will practice using many dialog boxes and applying interesting effects such as this to your Word documents, Excel worksheets, Access database objects, and PowerPoint slides.

FIGURE 1.12

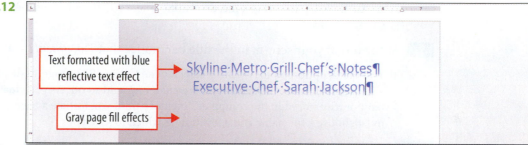

Text formatted with blue reflective text effect →

Skyline·Metro·Grill·Chef's·Notes¶
Executive·Chef,·Sarah·Jackson¶

Gray page fill effects →

Objective 5   Create a Folder and Name and Save a File

Video OF1-5

A *location* is any disk drive, folder, or other place in which you can store files and folders. Where you store your files depends on how and where you use your data. For example, for your college classes, you might decide to store on a removable USB flash drive so that you can carry your files to different locations and access your files on different computers.

If you do most of your work on a single computer, for example your home desktop system or your laptop computer that you take with you to school or work, then you can store your files in one of the Libraries—Documents, Music, Pictures, or Videos—that the Windows 8 operating system creates on your hard drive.

The best place to store files if you want them to be available anytime, anywhere, from almost any device is on your *SkyDrive*, which is Microsoft's free *cloud storage* for anyone with a free Microsoft account. Cloud storage refers to online storage of data so that you can access your data from different places and devices. *Cloud computing* refers to applications and services that are accessed over the Internet, rather than to applications that are installed on your local computer.

Because many people now have multiple computing devices—desktop, laptop, tablet, smartphone—it is common to store data *in the cloud* so that it is always available. *Synchronization*, also called *syncing*—pronounced SINK-ing—is the process of updating computer files that are in two or more locations according to specific rules. So if you create and save a Word document on your SkyDrive using your laptop, you can open and edit that document on your tablet. And then when you close the document again, the file is properly updated to reflect your changes.

You need not be connected to the Internet to access documents stored on SkyDrive because an up-to-date version of your content is synched to your local system and available on SkyDrive. You must, however, be connected to the Internet for the syncing to occur. Saving to SkyDrive will keep the local copy on your computer and the copy in the cloud synchronized for as long as you need it. If you open and edit on a different computer, log into the SkyDrive website, and then edit using Office 2013, Office 2010, or the **Office Web Apps**, you can save any changes back to SkyDrive. Office Web Apps are the free online companions to Microsoft Word, Excel, PowerPoint, Access, and OneNote. These changes will be synchronized back to any of your computers that run the SkyDrive for Windows application, which you get for free simply by logging in with your Microsoft account at skydrive.com.

The Windows operating system helps you to create and maintain a logical folder structure, so always take the time to name your files and folders consistently.

Activity 1.07 | Creating a Folder and Naming and Saving a File

A Word document is an example of a file. In this activity, you will create a folder on your USB flash drive in which to store your files. If you prefer to store on your SkyDrive or in the Documents library on your hard drive, you can use similar steps.

1 If necessary, insert your **USB flash drive** into your computer.

> As the first step in saving a file, determine where you want to save the file, and if necessary, insert a storage device.

2 At the top of your screen, in the title bar, notice that *Document1 – Word* displays.

> The Blank option on the opening screen of an Office 2013 program displays a new unsaved file with a default name—*Document1, Presentation1*, and so on. As you create your file, your work is temporarily stored in the computer's memory until you initiate a Save command, at which time you must choose a file name and a location in which to save your file.

3 In the upper left corner of your screen, click the **FILE tab** to display **Backstage** view. Compare your screen with Figure 1.13.

> **Backstage view** is a centralized space that groups commands related to *file* management; that is why the tab is labeled *FILE*. File management commands include opening, saving, printing, publishing, or sharing a file. The **Backstage tabs**—*Info*, *New*, *Open*, *Save*, *Save As*, *Print*, *Share*, *Export*, and *Close*—display along the left side. The tabs group file-related tasks together.

> Here, the **Info tab** displays information—*info*—about the current file, and file management commands display under Info. For example, if you click the Protect Document button, a list of options that you can set for this file that relate to who can open or edit the document displays.

> On the right, you can also examine the **document properties**. Document properties, also known as **metadata**, are details about a file that describe or identify it, such as the title, author name, subject, and keywords that identify the document's topic or contents. To close Backstage view and return to the document, you can click ⬅ in the upper left corner or press Esc.

FIGURE 1.13

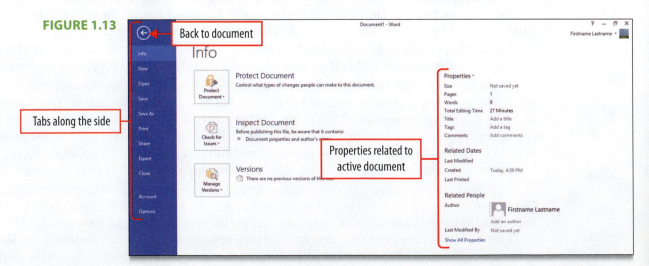

4 On the left, click **Save As**, and notice that the default location for storing Office files is your **SkyDrive**—if you are signed in. Compare your screen with Figure 1.14.

> When you are saving something for the first time, for example a new Word document, the Save and Save As commands are identical. That is, the Save As commands will display if you click Save or if you click Save As.

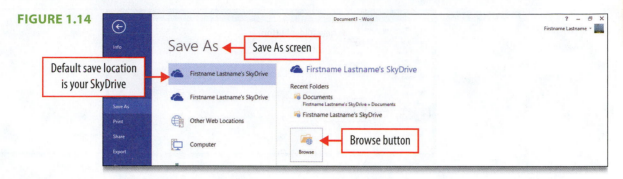

> **NOTE** **Saving after Your File Is Named**
>
> After you name and save a file, the Save command on the Quick Access Toolbar saves any changes you make to the file without displaying Backstage view. The Save As command enables you to name and save a *new* file based on the current one—in a location that you choose. After you name and save the new document, the original document closes, and the new document—based on the original one—displays.

5 To store your Word file on your **USB flash drive**—instead of your SkyDrive—click the **Browse** button to display the **Save As** dialog box. On the left, in the navigation pane, scroll down, and then under **Computer**, click the name of your **USB flash drive**. Compare your screen with Figure 1.15.

> In the Save As dialog box, you must indicate the name you want for the file and the location where you want to save the file. When working with your own data, it is good practice to pause at this point and determine the logical name and location for your file.

> In the Save As dialog box, a *toolbar* displays. This is a row, column, or block of buttons or icons, that usually displays across the top of a window and that contains commands for tasks you perform with a single click.

FIGURE 1.15

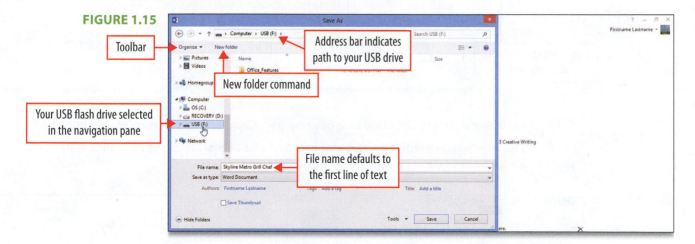

6 On the toolbar, click **New folder**.

In the file list, Word creates a new folder, and the text *New folder* is selected.

7 Type **Office Features Chapter 1** and press Enter. Compare your screen with Figure 1.16.

In Windows-based programs, the Enter key confirms an action.

8 In the **file list**, double-click the name of your new folder to open it and display its name in the **address bar**.

9 In the lower portion of the dialog box, click in the **File name** box to select the existing text. Notice that Office inserts the text at the beginning of the document as a suggested file name.

10 On your keyboard, locate the hyphen ⊟ key. Notice that the Shift of this key produces the underscore character. With the text still selected and using your own name, type **Lastname_Firstname_1A_Note_Form** and then compare your screen with Figure 1.17.

You can use spaces in file names, however, some people prefer not to use spaces. Some programs, especially when transferring files over the Internet, may insert the extra characters *%20* in place of a space. This can happen in *SharePoint*, so using underscores instead of spaces can be a good habit to adopt. SharePoint is Microsoft's collaboration software with which people in an organization can set up team sites to share information, manage documents, and publish reports for others to see. In general, however, unless you encounter a problem, it is OK to use spaces. In this textbook, underscores are used instead of spaces in file names.

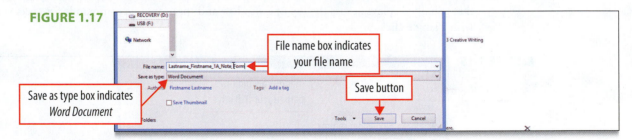

11 In the lower right corner, click **Save** or press Enter. Compare your screen with Figure 1.18.

The Word window redisplays and your new file name displays in the title bar, indicating that the file has been saved to a location that you have specified.

12 ▶ In the first paragraph, click to place the insertion point after the word *Grill* and type **,** (a comma). In the upper left corner of your screen, on the **Quick Access Toolbar**, click **Save** 🖫.

After a document is named and saved in a location, you can save any changes you have made since the last Save operation by using the Save command on the Quick Access Toolbar. When working on a document, it is good practice to save your changes from time to time.

Video OF1-6

For most of your files, especially in a workplace setting, it is useful to add identifying information to help in finding files later. You might also want to print your file on paper or create an electronic printout. The process of printing a file is similar in all of the Office applications.

Activity 1.08 | Inserting a Footer, Inserting Document Info, and Adding Document Properties

> **N O T E** | **Are You Printing or Submitting Your Files Electronically?**
> In this activity, you can either produce a paper printout or create an electronic file to submit to your instructor if required.

1 ▶ On the ribbon, click the **INSERT tab**, and then in the **Header & Footer group**, click **Footer**.

2 ▶ At the bottom of the list, click **Edit Footer**. On the ribbon, notice that the **HEADER & FOOTER TOOLS** display.

The *Header & Footer Tools Design* tab displays on the ribbon. The ribbon adapts to your work and will display additional tabs like this one—referred to as ***contextual tabs***—when you need them.

A ***footer*** is a reserved area for text or graphics that displays at the bottom of each page in a document. Likewise, a ***header*** is a reserved area for text or graphics that displays at the top of each page in a document. When the footer (or header) area is active, the document area is dimmed, indicating it is unavailable.

3 ▶ On the ribbon, under **HEADER & FOOTER TOOLS**, on the **DESIGN tab**, in the **Insert group**, click **Document Info**, and then click **File Name** to insert the name of your file in the footer, which is a common business practice. Compare your screen with Figure 1.19.

Ribbon commands that display ▼ will, when clicked, display a list of options for the command.

FIGURE 1.19

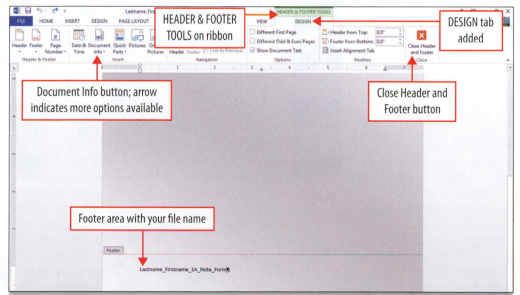

4 At the right end of the ribbon, click **Close Header and Footer**.

>  **ANOTHER WAY**   Double-click anywhere in the dimmed document to close the footer.

5 Click the **FILE tab** to display **Backstage** view. On the right, at the bottom of the **Properties** list, click **Show All Properties**.

>  **ANOTHER WAY**   Click the arrow to the right of Properties, and then click Show Document Panel to show and edit properties at the top of your document window.

6 On the list of **Properties**, click to the right of **Tags** to display an empty box, and then type **chef, notes, form**

> *Tags*, also referred to as *keywords*, are custom file properties in the form of words that you associate with a document to give an indication of the document's content. Adding tags to your documents makes it easier to search for and locate files in File Explorer and in systems such as Microsoft SharePoint document libraries.

>  **BY TOUCH**   Tap to the right of Tags to display the Tags box and the onscreen keyboard.

7 Click to the right of **Subject** to display an empty box, and then type your course name and section #; for example *CIS 10, #5543*.

8 Under **Related People**, be sure that your name displays as the author. If necessary, right-click the author name, click Edit Property, type your name, click outside of the Edit person dialog box, and then click OK. Compare your screen with Figure 1.20.

FIGURE 1.20

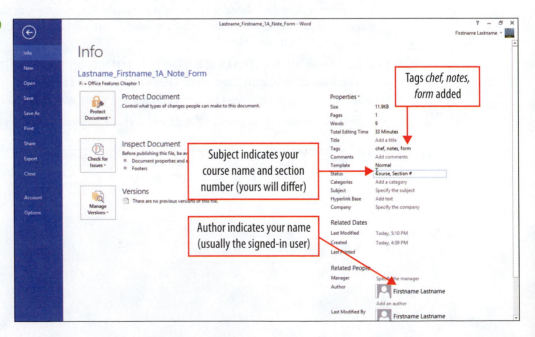

Activity 1.09 | Printing a File and Closing a Desktop App

1 On the left, click **Print**, and then compare your screen with Figure 1.21.

Here you can select any printer connected to your system and adjust the settings related to how you want to print. On the right, the ***Print Preview*** displays, which is a view of a document as it will appear on paper when you print it.

At the bottom of the Print Preview area, in the center, the number of pages and page navigation arrows with which you can move among the pages in Print Preview display. On the right, the Zoom slider enables you to shrink or enlarge the Print Preview. ***Zoom*** is the action of increasing or decreasing the viewing area of the screen.

ANOTHER WAY   From the document screen, press Ctrl + P or Ctrl + F2 to display Print in Backstage view.

FIGURE 1.21

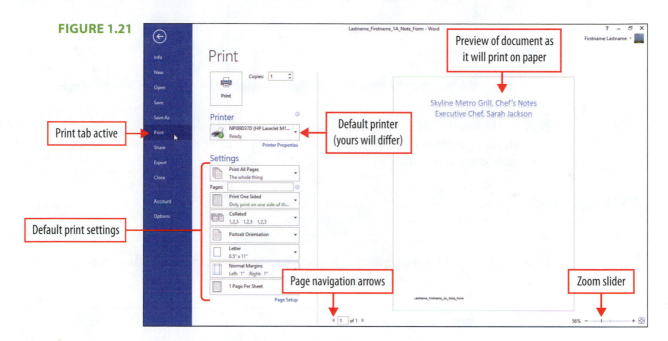

2 To submit your file electronically, skip this step and continue to Step 3. To print your document on paper using the default printer on your system, in the upper left portion of the screen, click the **Print** button.

The document will print on your default printer; if you do not have a color printer, the blue text will print in shades of gray. The gray page color you applied to the document does not display in Print Preview nor does it print unless you specifically adjust some of Word's options. Backstage view closes and your file redisplays in the Word window.

3 To create an electronic file, on the left click **Export**. On the right, click the **Create PDF/XPS** button to display the **Publish as PDF or XPS** dialog box.

PDF stands for ***Portable Document Format***, which is a technology that creates an image that preserves the look of your file. This is a popular format for sending documents electronically, because the document will display on most computers.

XPS stands for ***XML Paper Specification***—a Microsoft file format that also creates an image of your document and that opens in the XPS viewer.

4 On the left in the **navigation pane**, if necessary expand ▷ Computer, and then navigate to your **Office Features Chapter 1** folder on your **USB flash drive**. Compare your screen with Figure 1.22.

FIGURE 1.22

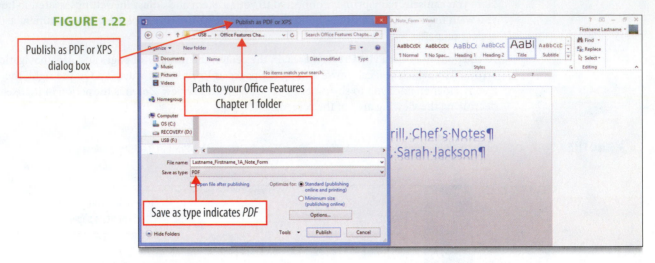

Publish as PDF or XPS dialog box

Path to your Office Features Chapter 1 folder

Save as type indicates *PDF*

5 In the lower right corner of the dialog box, click **Publish**; if your Adobe Acrobat or Adobe Reader program displays your PDF, in the upper right corner, click Close ✖. Notice that your document redisplays in Word.

ANOTHER WAY   In Backstage view, click Save As, navigate to the location of your Chapter folder, click the Save as type arrow, on the list click PDF, and then click Save.

6 Click the **FILE tab** to redisplay **Backstage** view. On the left, click **Close**, if necessary click Save, and then compare your screen with Figure 1.23.

FIGURE 1.23

Close button

Word window with all documents closed

7 In the upper right corner of the Word window, click **Close** ✖ . If directed by your instructor to do so, submit your paper or electronic file.

END | You have completed Project 1A

PROJECT ACTIVITIES

In Activities 1.10 through 1.21, you will open, edit, and then compress a Word file. You will also use the Office Help system and install an app for Office. Your completed document will look similar to Figure 1.24.

PROJECT FILES

For Project 1B, you will need the following file:

of01B_Rehearsal_Dinner

You will save your file as:

Lastname_Firstname_1B_Rehearsal_Dinner

PROJECT RESULTS

Skyline Metro Grill

TO: Sarah Jackson, Executive Chef

FROM: Laura Mabry Hernandez, General Manager

DATE: February 17, 2016

SUBJECT: Wedding Rehearsal Dinners

In the spring and summer months, wedding rehearsal dinners provide a new marketing opportunity for Skyline Metro Grill at all of our locations. A rehearsal dinner is an informal meal following a wedding rehearsal at which the bride and groom typically thank those who have helped them make their wedding a special event.

Our smaller private dining rooms with sweeping city views are an ideal location for a rehearsal dinner. At each of our locations, I have directed the Sales and Marketing Coordinator to partner with local wedding planners to promote Skyline Metro Grill as a relaxed yet sophisticated venue for rehearsal dinners. The typical rehearsal dinner includes the wedding party, the immediate family of the bride and groom, and out-of-town guests.

Please develop six menus—in varying price ranges—to present to local wedding planners so that they can easily promote Skyline Metro Grill to couples who are planning a rehearsal dinner. In addition to a traditional dinner, we should also include options for a buffet-style dinner and a family-style dinner.

This marketing effort will require extensive communication with our Sales and Marketing Coordinators and with local wedding planners. Let's meet to discuss the details and the marketing challenges, and to create a promotional piece that begins something like this:

Skyline Metro Grill for Your Rehearsal Dinner

Lastname_Firstname_1B_Rehearsal_Dinner

FIGURE 1.24 Project 1B Memo

Video OF1-7

In any Office program, you can display the *Open dialog box*, from which you can navigate to and then open an existing file that was created in that same program.

The Open dialog box, along with the Save and Save As dialog boxes, is a common dialog box. These dialog boxes, which are provided by the Windows programming interface, display in all Office programs in the same manner. So the Open, Save, and Save As dialog boxes will all look and perform the same regardless of the Office program in which you are working.

Activity 1.10 | Opening an Existing File and Saving It with a New Name

In this activity, you will display the Open dialog box, open an existing Word document, and then save it in your storage location with a new name.

1 Sign in to your computer, and then on the Windows 8 Start screen, type **word 2013** Press Enter to open Word on your desktop. If you want to do so, on the taskbar, right-click the **Word icon**, and then click **Pin this program to taskbar** to keep the Word program available from your desktop.

2 On Word's opening screen, on the left, click **Open Other Documents**. Under **Open**, click **Computer**, and then on the right click **Browse**.

3 In the **Open** dialog box, on the left in the **navigation pane**, scroll down, if necessary expand ▷ Computer, and then click the name of your **USB flash drive**. In the **file list**, double-click the **Office_Features** folder that you downloaded.

4 Double-click **of01B_Rehearsal_Dinner**. If **PROTECTED VIEW** displays at the top of your screen, in the center click **Enable Editing**.

In Office 2013, a file will open in *Protected View* if the file appears to be from a potentially risky location, such as the Internet. Protected View is a security feature in Office 2013 that protects your computer from malicious files by opening them in a restricted environment until you enable them. *Trusted Documents* is another security feature that remembers which files you have already enabled.

You might encounter these security features if you open a file from an email or download files from the Internet; for example, from your college's learning management system or from the Pearson website. So long as you trust the source of the file, click Enable Editing or Enable Content—depending on the type of file you receive—and then go ahead and work with the file.

5 With the document displayed in the Word window, be sure that **Show/Hide** is active; if necessary, on the HOME tab, in the Paragraph group, click Show/Hide to activate it. Compare your screen with Figure 1.25.

FIGURE 1.25

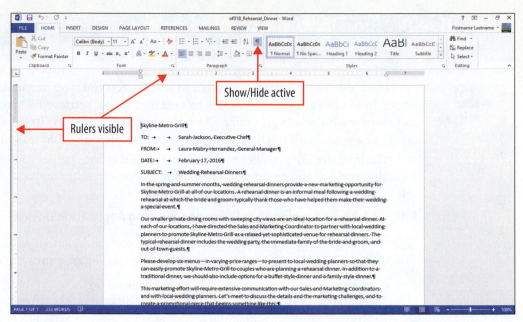

Show/Hide active

Rulers visible

Skyline-Metro-Grill¶

TO: →   →   Sarah-Jackson,-Executive-Chef¶

FROM:→   →   Laura-Mabry-Hernandez,-General-Manager¶

DATE:→   →   February-17,-2016¶

SUBJECT: →   →   Wedding-Rehearsal-Dinners¶

In-the-spring-and-summer-months,-wedding-rehearsal-dinners-provide-a-new-marketing-opportunity-for-Skyline-Metro-Grill-at-all-of-our-locations.-A-rehearsal-dinner-is-an-informal-meal-following-a-wedding-rehearsal-at-which-the-bride-and-groom-typically-thank-those-who-have-helped-them-make-their-wedding-a-special-event.¶

Our-smaller,-private-dining-rooms-with-sweeping-city-views-are-an-ideal-location-for-a-rehearsal-dinner.-At-each-of-our-locations,-I-have-directed-the-Sales-and-Marketing-Coordinator-to-partner-with-local-wedding-planners-to-promote-Skyline-Metro-Grill-as-a-relaxed-yet-sophisticated-venue-for-rehearsal-dinners.-The-typical-rehearsal-dinner-includes-the-wedding-party,-the-immediate-family-of-the-bride-and-groom,-and-out-of-town-guests.¶

Please-develop-six-menus—in-varying-price-ranges—to-present-to-local-wedding-planners-so-that-they-can-easily-promote-Skyline-Metro-Grill-to-couples-who-are-planning-a-rehearsal-dinner.-In-addition-to-a-traditional-dinner,-we-should-also-include-options-for-a-buffet-style-dinner-and-a-family-style-dinner.¶

This-marketing-effort-will-require-extensive-communication-with-our-Sales-and-Marketing-Coordinators-and-with-local-wedding-planners.-Let's-meet-to-discuss-the-details-and-the-marketing-challenges,-and-to-create-a-promotional-piece-that-begins-something-like-this:¶

6 ▸ Click the **FILE tab** to display **Backstage** view, and then on the left, click **Save As**. On the right, click the folder under **Current Folder** to open the **Save As** dialog box. Notice that the current folder is the **Office_Features** folder you downloaded.

🔄 **ANOTHER WAY**   Press F12 to display the Save As dialog box.

7 ▸ In the upper left corner of the **Save As** dialog box, click the **Up** button ↑ to move up one level in the File Explorer hierarchy. In the **file list**, double-click your **Office Features Chapter 1** folder to open it.

8 ▸ Click in the **File name** box to select the existing text, and then, using your own name, type **Lastname_Firstname_1B_Rehearsal_Dinner** Compare your screen with Figure 1.26.

FIGURE 1.26

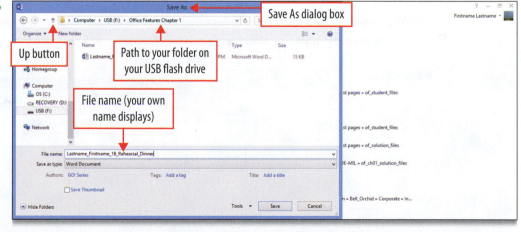

Save As dialog box

Up button

Path to your folder on your USB flash drive

File name (your own name displays)

File name: Lastname_Firstname_1B_Rehearsal_Dinner

Save as type: Word Document

9 ▸ Click **Save** or press Enter; notice that your new file name displays in the title bar.

The original document closes, and your new document, based on the original, displays with the name in the title bar.

More Knowledge   **Read-Only**

Some files might display **Read-Only** in the title bar, which is a property assigned to a file that prevents the file from being modified or deleted; it indicates that you cannot save any changes to the displayed document unless you first save it with a new name.

Video OF1-8

If you sign in to Windows 8 with a Microsoft account, you may notice that you are also signed in to Office. This enables you to save files to and retrieve files from your SkyDrive and to ***collaborate*** with others on Office files when you want to do so. To collaborate means to work with others as a team in an intellectual endeavor to complete a shared task or to achieve a shared goal.

Within each Office application, an ***Options dialog box*** enables you to select program settings and other options and preferences. For example, you can set preferences for viewing and editing files.

Activity 1.11 | Signing In to Office and Viewing Application Options

1 ▶ In the upper right corner of your screen, if you are signed in with a Microsoft account, click the arrow to the right of your name, and then compare your screen with Figure 1.27.

Here you can change your photo, go to About me to edit your profile, examine your Account settings, or switch accounts to sign in with a different Microsoft account.

FIGURE 1.27

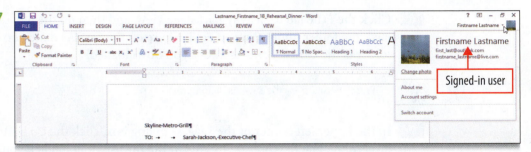

2 ▶ Click the **FILE tab** to display **Backstage** view. On the left, click the last tab—**Options**.

3 ▶ In the **Word Options** dialog box, on the left, click **Display**, and then on the right, locate the information under **Always show these formatting marks on the screen**.

4 ▶ Under **Always show these formatting marks on the screen**, be sure the last check box, **Show all formatting marks**, is selected—select it if necessary. Compare your screen with Figure 1.28.

FIGURE 1.28

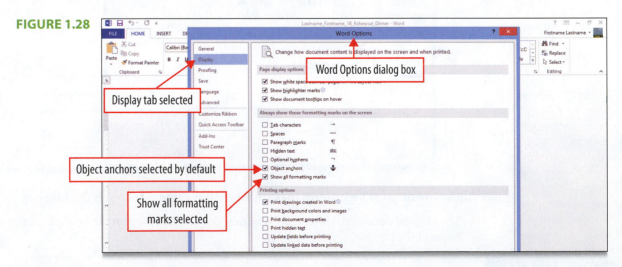

5 ▶ In the lower right corner of the dialog box, click **OK**.

Video OF1-9

The ribbon that displays across the top of the program window groups commands in a manner that you would most logically use them. The ribbon in each Office program is slightly different, but all contain the same three elements: *tabs*, *groups*, and *commands*.

Tabs display across the top of the ribbon, and each tab relates to a type of activity; for example, laying out a page. Groups are sets of related commands for specific tasks. Commands—instructions to computer programs—are arranged in groups and might display as a button, a menu, or a box in which you type information.

You can also minimize the ribbon so only the tab names display, which is useful when working on a smaller screen such as a tablet computer where you want to maximize your screen viewing area.

Activity 1.12 | Performing Commands from and Customizing the Ribbon and the Quick Access Toolbar

1 ▶ Take a moment to examine the document on your screen. If necessary, on the ribbon, click the VIEW tab, and then in the Show group, click to place a check mark in the Ruler check box. Compare your screen with Figure 1.29.

This document is a memo from the General Manager to the Executive Chef regarding a new restaurant promotion for wedding rehearsal dinners.

When working in Word, display the rulers so that you can see how margin settings affect your document and how text and objects align. Additionally, if you set a tab stop or an indent, its location is visible on the ruler.

FIGURE 1.29

Ruler checkbox selected

VIEW tab active

Show group

Rulers display

2 ▶ In the upper left corner of your screen, above the ribbon, locate the **Quick Access Toolbar**.

Recall that the Quick Access Toolbar contains commands that you use frequently. By default, only the commands Save, Undo, and Redo display, but you can add and delete commands to suit your needs. Possibly the computer at which you are working already has additional commands added to the Quick Access Toolbar.

3 ▶ At the end of the **Quick Access Toolbar**, click the **Customize Quick Access Toolbar** button ⬇ , and then compare your screen with Figure 1.30.

A list of commands that Office users commonly add to their Quick Access Toolbar displays, including New, Open, Email, Quick Print, and Print Preview and Print. Commands already on the Quick Access Toolbar display a check mark. Commands that you add to the Quick Access Toolbar are always just one click away.

Here you can also display the More Commands dialog box, from which you can select any command from any tab on the ribbon to add to the Quick Access Toolbar.

 BY TOUCH   Tap once on Quick Access Toolbar commands.

FIGURE 1.30

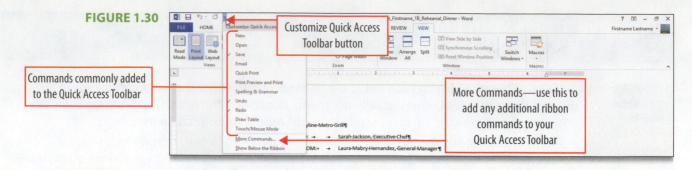

Customize Quick Access Toolbar button

Commands commonly added to the Quick Access Toolbar

More Commands—use this to add any additional ribbon commands to your Quick Access Toolbar

4 On the list, click **Print Preview and Print**, and then notice that the icon is added to the **Quick Access Toolbar**. Compare your screen with Figure 1.31.

The icon that represents the Print Preview command displays on the Quick Access Toolbar. Because this is a command that you will use frequently while building Office documents, you might decide to have this command remain on your Quick Access Toolbar.

ANOTHER WAY Right-click any command on the ribbon, and then on the shortcut menu, click Add to Quick Access Toolbar.

FIGURE 1.31

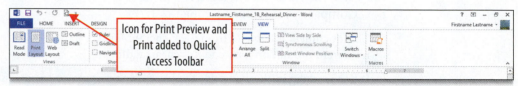

Icon for Print Preview and Print added to Quick Access Toolbar

5 In the first line of the document, if necessary, click to the left of the *S* in *Skyline* to position the insertion point there, and then press Enter one time to insert a blank paragraph. Press ↑ one time to position the insertion point in the new blank paragraph. Compare your screen with Figure 1.32.

FIGURE 1.32

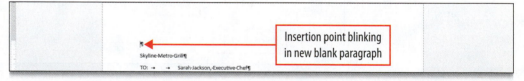

Insertion point blinking in new blank paragraph

6 On the ribbon, click the **INSERT tab**. In the **Illustrations group**, *point* to the **Online Pictures** button to display its ScreenTip.

Many buttons on the ribbon have this type of *enhanced ScreenTip*, which displays useful descriptive information about the command.

7 Click **Online Pictures**, and then compare your screen with Figure 1.33.

In the Insert Pictures dialog box you can search for online pictures using Microsoft's Clip Art collection. *Clip art* refers to royalty-free photos and illustrations you can download from Microsoft's Office.com site.

Here you can also search for images using the Bing search engine, and if you are signed in with your Microsoft account, you can also find images on your SkyDrive or on your computer by clicking Browse. At the bottom, you can click the Flickr logo and download pictures from your Flickr account if you have one.

FIGURE 1.33

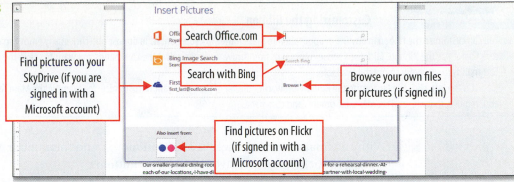

8 ▸ Click **Office.com Clip Art** and in the box that displays to the right, type **salad in a bowl** and press Enter. As shown in Figure 1.34, point to the illustration of the salad bowl to display its keywords.

You can use various keywords to find clip art that is appropriate for your documents.

FIGURE 1.34

9 ▸ Click the illustration of the salad to select it, and then in the lower right corner, click **Insert**. In the upper right corner of the picture, point to the **Layout Options** button ▣ to display its ScreenTip, and then compare your screen with Figure 1.35. If you cannot find the image, select a similar image, and then drag one of the corner sizing handles to match the approximate size shown in the figure.

Inserted pictures anchor—attach to—the paragraph at the insertion point location—as indicated by the anchor symbol. *Layout Options* enable you to choose how the *object*—in this instance an inserted picture—interacts with the surrounding text. An object is a picture or other graphic such as a chart or table that you can select and then move and resize.

When a picture is selected, the PICTURE TOOLS become available on the ribbon. Additionally, *sizing handles*—small squares that indicate an object is selected—surround the selected picture.

FIGURE 1.35

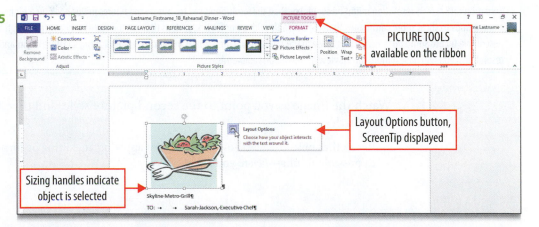

10 With the image selected, click **Layout Options** , and then under **With Text Wrapping**, in the second row, click the first layout—**Top and Bottom**.

11 Point to the image to display the pointer, hold down the left mouse button to display a green line at the left margin, and then drag the image to the right and slightly upward until a green line displays in the center of the image and at the top of the image, as shown in Figure 1.36, and then release the left mouse button. If you are not satisfied with your result, on the Quick Access Toolbar, click Undo and begin again.

> *Alignment Guides* are green lines that display to help you align objects with margins or at the center of a page.

FIGURE 1.36

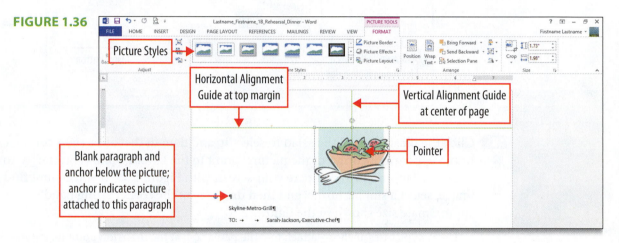

12 On the ribbon, in the **Picture Styles group**, point to the first style to display the ScreenTip *Simple Frame, White*, and notice that the image displays with a white frame.

NOTE   **The Size of Groups on the Ribbon Varies with Screen Resolution**

Your monitor's screen resolution might be set higher than the resolution used to capture the figures in this book. At a higher resolution, the ribbon expands some groups to show more commands than are available with a single click, such as those in the Picture Styles group. Or, the group expands to add descriptive text to some buttons, such as those in the Adjust group. Regardless of your screen resolution, all Office commands are available to you. In higher resolutions, you will have a more robust view of the ribbon commands.

13 Watch the image as you point to the second picture style, and then to the third, and then to the fourth.

> Recall that Live Preview shows the result of applying an editing or formatting change as you point to possible results—*before* you actually apply it.

14 In the **Picture Styles group**, click the second style—**Beveled Matte, White**—and then click anywhere outside of the image to deselect it. Notice that the *PICTURE TOOLS* no longer display on the ribbon. Compare your screen with Figure 1.37.

Contextual tabs on the ribbon display only when you need them.

FIGURE 1.37

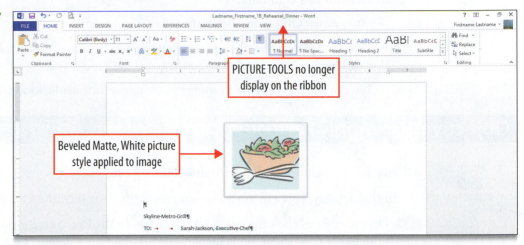

15 On the **Quick Access Toolbar**, click **Save** 🖫 to save the changes you have made.

Activity 1.13 | Minimizing and Using the Keyboard to Control the Ribbon

Instead of a mouse, some individuals prefer to navigate the ribbon by using keys on the keyboard.

1 On your keyboard, press [Alt], and then on the ribbon, notice that small labels display. Press [N] to activate the commands on the **INSERT tab**, and then compare your screen with Figure 1.38.

Each label represents a *KeyTip*—an indication of the key that you can press to activate the command. For example, on the INSERT tab, you can press [F] to open the Online Pictures dialog box.

FIGURE 1.38

2 Press [Esc] to redisplay the KeyTips for the tabs. Then, press [Alt] or [Esc] again to turn off keyboard control of the ribbon.

3 Point to any tab on the ribbon and right-click to display a shortcut menu.

Here you can choose to display the Quick Access Toolbar below the ribbon or collapse the ribbon to maximize screen space. You can also customize the ribbon by adding, removing, renaming, or reordering tabs, groups, and commands, although this is not recommended until you become an expert Office user.

4 ▸ Click **Collapse the Ribbon**. Notice that only the ribbon tabs display. Click the **HOME tab** to display the commands. Click anywhere in the document, and notice that the ribbon goes back to the collapsed display.

5 ▸ Right-click any ribbon tab, and then click **Collapse the Ribbon** again to remove the check mark from this command.

Many expert Office users prefer the full ribbon display.

6 ▸ Point to any tab on the ribbon, and then on your mouse device, roll the mouse wheel. Notice that different tabs become active as you roll the mouse wheel.

You can make a tab active by using this technique instead of clicking the tab.

Objective 10   Apply Formatting in Office Programs

Video OF1-10

Activity 1.14 | Changing Page Orientation and Zoom Level

In this activity, you will practice common formatting techniques used in Office applications.

1 ▸ On the ribbon, click the **PAGE LAYOUT tab**. In the **Page Setup group**, click **Orientation**, and notice that two orientations display—*Portrait* and *Landscape*. Click **Landscape**.

In **portrait orientation**, the paper is taller than it is wide. In **landscape orientation**, the paper is wider than it is tall.

2 ▸ In the lower right corner of the screen, locate the **Zoom slider**.

Recall that to zoom means to increase or decrease the viewing area. You can zoom in to look closely at a section of a document, and then zoom out to see an entire page on the screen. You can also zoom to view multiple pages on the screen.

3 ▸ Drag the **Zoom slider** to the left until you have zoomed to approximately *60%*. Compare your screen with Figure 1.39.

FIGURE 1.39

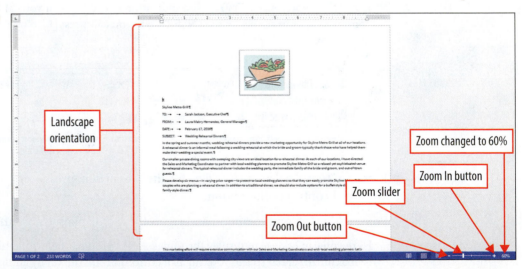

> 🔄 **BY TOUCH**   Drag the Zoom slider with your finger.

4 ▸ Use the technique you just practiced to change the **Orientation** back to **Portrait**.

The default orientation in Word is Portrait, which is commonly used for business documents such as letters and memos.

5 In the lower right corner, click the **Zoom In** button ➕ as many times as necessary to return to the **100%** zoom setting.

> Use the zoom feature to adjust the view of your document for editing and for your viewing comfort.

 **ANOTHER WAY**   You can also control Zoom from the ribbon. On the VIEW tab, in the Zoom group, you can control the Zoom level and also zoom to view multiple pages.

6 On the **Quick Access Toolbar**, click **Save** 🖫.

Activity 1.15 | Formatting Text by Using Fonts, Alignment, Font Colors, and Font Styles

1 If necessary, on the right side of your screen, drag the vertical scroll box to the top of the scroll bar. To the left of *Skyline Metro Grill*, point in the margin area to display the 🔄 pointer and click one time to select the entire paragraph. Compare your screen with Figure 1.40.

> Use this technique to select complete paragraphs from the margin area—drag downward to select multiple-line paragraphs—which is faster and more efficient than dragging through text.

FIGURE 1.40

2 On the ribbon, click the **HOME tab**, and then in the **Paragraph group**, click **Center** ☰ to center the paragraph.

3 On the **HOME tab**, in the **Font group**, click the **Font button arrow** [Calibri (Body) ▾]. On the alphabetical list of font names, scroll down and then locate and *point to* **Cambria**.

> A *font* is a set of characters with the same design and shape. The default font in a Word document is Calibri, which is a *sans serif* font—a font design with no lines or extensions on the ends of characters.

> The Cambria font is a *serif font*—a font design that includes small line extensions on the ends of the letters to guide the eye in reading from left to right.

> The list of fonts displays as a gallery showing potential results. For example, in the Font gallery, you can point to see the actual design and format of each font as it would look if applied to text.

4 Point to several other fonts and observe the effect on the selected text. Then, scroll back to the top of the **Font** gallery. Under **Theme Fonts**, click **Calibri Light**.

> A *theme* is a predesigned combination of colors, fonts, line, and fill effects that look good together and is applied to an entire document by a single selection. A theme combines two sets of fonts—one for text and one for headings. In the default Office theme, Calibri Light is the suggested font for headings.

5 With the paragraph *Skyline Metro Grill* still selected, on the **HOME tab**, in the **Font group**, click the **Font Size button arrow** [11 ▾], point to **36**, and then notice how Live Preview displays the text in the font size to which you are pointing. Compare your screen with Figure 1.41.

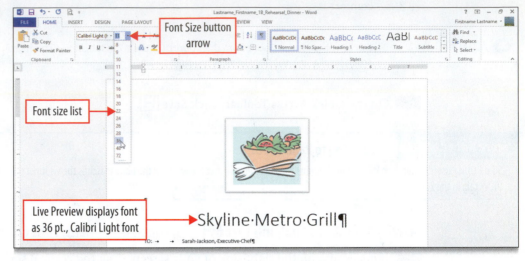

Font Size button arrow

Font size list

Live Preview displays font as 36 pt., Calibri Light font

Skyline·Metro·Grill¶

6 On the list of font sizes, click **20**.

Fonts are measured in *points*, with one point equal to 1/72 of an inch. A higher point size indicates a larger font size. Headings and titles are often formatted by using a larger font size. The word *point* is abbreviated as *pt*.

7 With *Skyline Metro Grill* still selected, on the **HOME tab**, in the **Font group**, click the **Font Color button arrow** [A ▾]. Under **Theme Colors**, in the last column, click the last color—**Green, Accent 6, Darker 50%**. Click anywhere to deselect the text.

8 To the left of *TO:*, point in the left margin area to display the [⤢] pointer, hold down the left mouse button, and then drag down to select the four memo headings. Compare your screen with Figure 1.42.

Use this technique to select complete paragraphs from the margin area—drag downward to select multiple paragraphs—which is faster and more efficient than dragging through text.

↻ **BY TOUCH**   Tap once on TO: to display the gripper, then with your finger, drag to the right and down to select the four paragraphs.

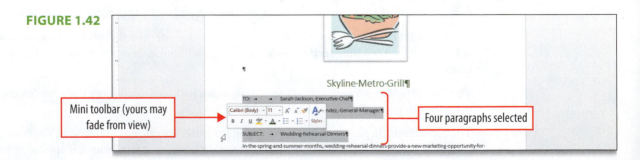

Mini toolbar (yours may fade from view)

Four paragraphs selected

9 With the four paragraphs selected, on the mini toolbar, click the **Font Color** button ▣ ▾, and notice that the text color of the four paragraphs changes.

The font color button retains its most recently used color—Green, Accent 6, Darker 50%. As you progress in your study of Microsoft Office, you will use other buttons that behave in this manner; that is, they retain their most recently used format. This is commonly referred to as **MRU**—most recently used.

Recall that the mini toolbar places commands that are commonly used for the selected text or object close by so that you reduce the distance that you must move your mouse to access a command. If you are using a touchscreen device, most commands that you need are close and easy to touch.

10 On the right, drag the vertical scroll box down slightly to position more of the text on the screen. Click anywhere in the paragraph that begins *In the spring*, and then *triple-click*—click the left mouse button three times—to select the entire paragraph. If the entire paragraph is not selected, click in the paragraph and begin again.

11 With the entire paragraph selected, on the mini toolbar, click the **Font Color button arrow** ▣ ▾, and then under **Theme Colors**, in the sixth column, click the last color— **Orange, Accent 2, Darker 50%**.

12 In the memo headings, select the guide word *TO:* and then on the mini toolbar, click **Bold** B and **Italic** I.

Font styles include bold, italic, and underline. Font styles emphasize text and are a visual cue to draw the reader's eye to important text.

13 On the mini toolbar, click **Italic** I again to turn off the Italic formatting.

A *toggle button* is a button that can be turned on by clicking it once, and then turned off by clicking it again.

Activity 1.16 | Using Format Painter

Use the Format Painter to copy the formatting of specific text or of a paragraph and then apply it in other locations in your document.

1 With *TO:* still selected, on the mini toolbar, click **Format Painter** ◆. Then, move your mouse under the word *Sarah*, and notice the ▣I mouse pointer. Compare your screen with Figure 1.43.

The pointer takes the shape of a paintbrush, and contains the formatting information from the paragraph where the insertion point is positioned. Information about the Format Painter and how to turn it off displays in the status bar.

FIGURE 1.43

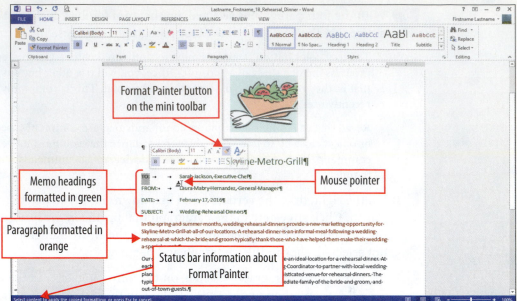

2 With the ▲I pointer, drag to select the guide word *FROM:* and notice that Bold formatting is applied. Then, point to the selected text *FROM:* and on the mini toolbar, *double-click* **Format Painter** 🖌.

3 Select the guide word *DATE:* to copy the Bold formatting, and notice that the pointer retains the ▲I shape.

> When you *double-click* the Format Painter button, the Format Painter feature remains active until you either click the Format Painter button again, or press Esc to cancel it—as indicated on the status bar.

4 With Format Painter still active, select the guide word *SUBJECT:*, and then on the ribbon, on the **HOME tab**, in the **Clipboard group**, notice that **Format Painter** 🖌 is selected, indicating that it is active. Compare your screen with Figure 1.44.

FIGURE 1.44

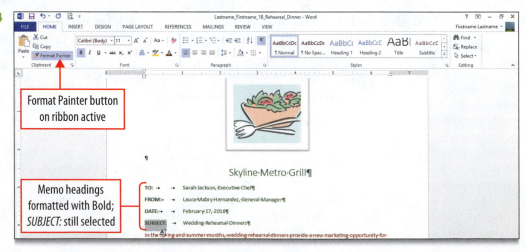

5 On the ribbon, click **Format Painter** 🖌 to turn the command off.

 **ANOTHER WAY**   Press Esc to turn off Format Painter.

6 In the paragraph that begins *In the spring*, triple-click again to select the entire paragraph. On the mini toolbar, click **Bold** [B] and **Italic** [I]. Click anywhere to deselect.

7 On the **Quick Access Toolbar**, click **Save** [💾] to save the changes you have made to your document.

Activity 1.17 | Using Keyboard Shortcuts and Using the Clipboard to Copy, Cut, and Paste

The *Clipboard* is a temporary storage area that holds text or graphics that you select and then cut or copy. When you *copy* text or graphics, a copy is placed on the Clipboard and the original text or graphic remains in place. When you *cut* text or graphics, a copy is placed on the Clipboard, and the original text or graphic is removed—cut—from the document.

After copying or cutting, the contents of the Clipboard are available for you to *paste*—insert—in a new location in the current document, or into another Office file.

1 Hold down [Ctrl] and press [Home] to move to the beginning of your document, and then take a moment to study the table in Figure 1.45, which describes similar keyboard shortcuts with which you can navigate quickly in a document.

FIGURE 1.45

KEYBOARD SHORTCUTS TO NAVIGATE IN A DOCUMENT	
TO MOVE	**PRESS**
To the beginning of a document	[Ctrl] + [Home]
To the end of a document	[Ctrl] + [End]
To the beginning of a line	[Home]
To the end of a line	[End]
To the beginning of the previous word	[Ctrl] + [←]
To the beginning of the next word	[Ctrl] + [→]
To the beginning of the current word (if insertion point is in the middle of a word)	[Ctrl] + [←]
To the beginning of the previous paragraph	[Ctrl] + [↑]
To the beginning of the next paragraph	[Ctrl] + [↓]
To the beginning of the current paragraph (if insertion point is in the middle of a paragraph)	[Ctrl] + [↑]
Up one screen	[PgUp]
Down one screen	[PgDn]

2 To the left of *Skyline Metro Grill*, point in the left margin area to display the [⇗] pointer, and then click one time to select the entire paragraph. On the **HOME tab**, in the **Clipboard group**, click **Copy** [📋].

Because anything that you select and then copy—or cut—is placed on the Clipboard, the Copy command and the Cut command display in the Clipboard group of commands on the ribbon. There is no visible indication that your copied selection has been placed on the Clipboard.

🔄 **ANOTHER WAY**   Right-click the selection, and then click Copy on the shortcut menu; or, use the keyboard shortcut [Ctrl] + [C].

3 On the **HOME tab**, in the **Clipboard group**, to the right of the group name *Clipboard*, click the **Dialog Box Launcher** button, and then compare your screen with Figure 1.46.

The Clipboard pane displays with your copied text. In any ribbon group, the *Dialog Box Launcher* displays either a dialog box or a pane related to the group of commands. It is not necessary to display the Clipboard in this manner, although sometimes it is useful to do so.

FIGURE 1.46

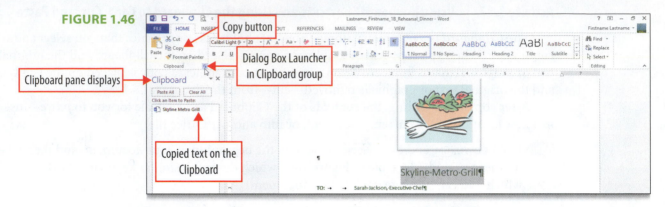

4 In the upper right corner of the **Clipboard** pane, click **Close**.

5 Press Ctrl + End to move to the end of your document. Press Enter one time to create a new blank paragraph. On the **HOME tab**, in the **Clipboard group**, point to **Paste**, and then click the *upper* portion of this split button.

The Paste command pastes the most recently copied item on the Clipboard at the insertion point location. If you click the lower portion of the Paste button, a gallery of Paste Options displays. A *split button* is divided into two parts; clicking the main part of the button performs a command, and clicking the arrow displays a list or gallery with choices.

ANOTHER WAY   Right-click, on the shortcut menu under Paste Options, click the desired option button; or, press Ctrl + V.

6 Below the pasted text, click **Paste Options** as shown in Figure 1.47.

Here you can view and apply various formatting options for pasting your copied or cut text. Typically you will click Paste on the ribbon and paste the item in its original format. If you want some other format for the pasted item, you can choose another format from the *Paste Options gallery*.

The Paste Options gallery provides a Live Preview of the various options for changing the format of the pasted item with a single click. The Paste Options gallery is available in three places: on the ribbon by clicking the lower portion of the Paste button—the Paste button arrow; from the Paste Options button that displays below the pasted item following the paste operation; or on the shortcut menu if you right-click the pasted item.

FIGURE 1.47

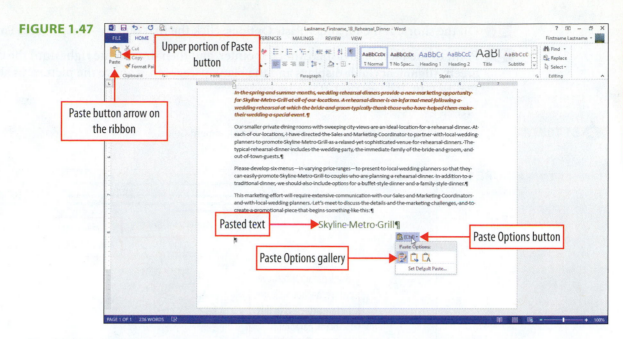

Upper portion of Paste button

Paste button arrow on the ribbon

Pasted text

Paste Options button

Paste Options gallery

7 In the **Paste Options** gallery, *point* to each option to see the Live Preview of the format that would be applied if you clicked the button.

The contents of the Paste Options gallery are contextual; that is, they change based on what you copied and where you are pasting.

8 Press [Esc] to close the gallery; the button will remain displayed until you take some other screen action.

9 Press [Ctrl] + [Home] to move to the top of the document, and then click the **salad image** one time to select it. While pointing to the selected image, right-click, and then on the shortcut menu, click **Cut**.

Recall that the Cut command cuts—removes—the selection from the document and places it on the Clipboard.

ANOTHER WAY   On the HOME tab, in the Clipboard group, click the Cut button; or, use the keyboard shortcut [Ctrl] + [X].

10 Press [Del] one time to remove the blank paragraph from the top of the document, and then press [Ctrl] + [End] to move to the end of the document.

11 With the insertion point blinking in the blank paragraph at the end of the document, right-click, and notice that the **Paste Options** gallery displays on the shortcut menu. Compare your screen with Figure 1.48.

FIGURE 1.48

Paste Options on the shortcut menu

12 On the shortcut menu, under **Paste Options**, click the first button—**Keep Source Formatting**.

13 Point to the picture to display the pointer, and then drag to the right until the center green **Alignment Guide** displays and the blank paragraph is above the picture, as shown in Figure 1.49. Release the left mouse button.

FIGURE 1.49

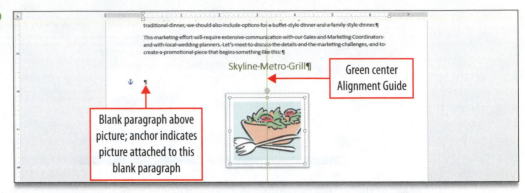

14 Above the picture, click to position the insertion point at the end of the word *Grill*, press [Spacebar] one time, type **for Your Rehearsal Dinner** and then **Save** 🖫 your document. Compare your screen with Figure 1.50.

FIGURE 1.50

15 On the **INSERT tab**, in the **Header & Footer group**, click **Footer**. At the bottom of the list, click **Edit Footer**, and then with the **HEADER & FOOTER Design tab** active, in the **Insert group**, click **Document Info**. Click **File Name** to add the file name to the footer.

16 On the right end of the ribbon, click **Close Header and Footer**.

17 On the **Quick Access Toolbar**, point to the **Print Preview and Print icon** 🔍 you placed there, right-click, and then click **Remove from Quick Access Toolbar**.

If you are working on your own computer and you want to do so, you can leave the icon on the toolbar; in a lab setting, you should return the software to its original settings.

18 Click **Save** 🖫 and then click the **FILE tab** to display **Backstage** view. With the **Info tab** active, in the lower right corner click **Show All Properties**. As **Tags**, type **weddings, rehearsal dinners, marketing**

19 As the **Subject**, type your course name and number—for example *CIS 10, #5543*. Under **Related People**, be sure your name displays as the author (edit it if necessary), and then on the left, click **Print** to display the Print Preview. Compare your screen with Figure 1.51.

FIGURE 1.51

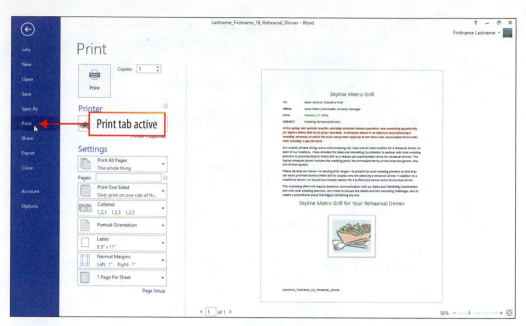

> Print tab active

20 ▶ On the left side of **Backstage** view, click **Save**. As directed by your instructor, print or submit your file electronically as described in Project 1A, and then in the upper right corner of the Word window, click **Close** ❌ .

21 ▶ If a message indicates *Would you like to keep the last item you copied?* click **No**.

This message displays if you have copied some type of image to the Clipboard. If you click Yes, the items on the Clipboard will remain for you to use in another program or document.

Objective 11 | Compress Files and Use the Microsoft Office 2013 Help System

Video OF1-11

A *compressed file* is a file that has been reduced in size. Compressed files take up less storage space and can be transferred to other computers faster than uncompressed files. You can also combine a group of files into one compressed folder, which makes it easier to share a group of files.

Within each Office program, the Help feature provides information about all of the program's features and displays step-by-step instructions for performing many tasks.

Activity 1.18 | Compressing Files

In this activity, you will combine the two files you created in this chapter into one compressed file.

1 ▶ On the Windows taskbar, click **File Explorer** 📁 . On the left, in the **navigation pane**, navigate to your **USB flash drive**, and then open your **Office Features Chapter 1** folder. Compare your screen with Figure 1.52.

FIGURE 1.52

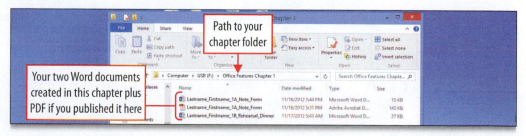

> Path to your chapter folder

> Your two Word documents created in this chapter plus PDF if you published it here

2 In the **file list**, click your **Lastname_Firstname_1A_Note_Form** Word file one time to select it. Then, hold down Ctrl, and click your **Lastname_Firstname_1B_Rehearsal_Dinner** file to select the files in the list.

In any Windows-based program, holding down Ctrl while selecting enables you to select multiple items.

3 On the **File Explorer** ribbon, click **Share**, and then in the **Send group**, click **Zip**. Compare your screen with Figure 1.53.

Windows creates a compressed folder containing a *copy* of each of the selected files. The folder name is selected—highlighted in blue—so that you can rename it.

 BY TOUCH   Tap the ribbon commands.

FIGURE 1.53

 ANOTHER WAY   Point to the selected files in the File List, right-click, point to Send to, and then click Compressed (zipped) folder.

4 Using your own name, type **Lastname_Firstname_Office_Features_Chapter_1** and press Enter.

The compressed folder is ready to attach to an email or share in some other format.

5 In the upper right corner of the folder window, click **Close** ⊠.

Activity 1.19 | Using the Microsoft Office 2013 Help System in Excel

In this activity, you will use the Microsoft Help feature to find information about formatting numbers in Excel.

1 Press ⊞ to display the Windows 8 **Start screen**, and then type **excel 2013** Press Enter to open the Excel desktop app.

2 On Excel's opening screen, click **Blank workbook**, and then in the upper right corner, click **Microsoft Excel Help** ❔.

 ANOTHER WAY   Press F1 to display Help in any Office program.

3 In the **Excel Help** window, click in the **Search online help** box, type **formatting numbers** and then press Enter.

4 On the list of results, click **Format numbers as currency**. Compare your screen with Figure 1.54.

FIGURE 1.54

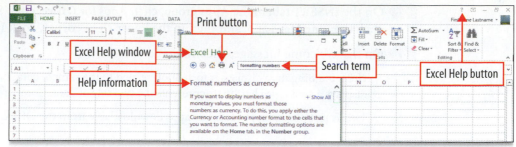

5 ▶ If you want to do so, at the top of the **Excel Help** window, click Print 🖨 to print a copy of this information for your reference.

6 ▶ In the upper right corner of the Help window, click **Close** ☒ .

7 ▶ Leave Excel open for the next activity.

Objective 12 Install Apps for Office and Create a Microsoft Account

> **A L E R T !**   **Working with Web-Based Applications and Services**
>
> Computer programs and services on the web receive continuous updates and improvements. Thus, the steps to complete the following web-based activities may differ from the ones shown. You can often look at the screens and the information presented to determine how to complete the activity.

Video OF1-12

Apps for Office 2013 and SharePoint 2013 are a collection of downloadable apps that enable you to create and view information within your familiar Office programs. Some of these apps are developed by Microsoft, but many more are developed by specialists in different fields. As new apps are developed, they will be available from the online Office Store.

An *app for Office* is a webpage that works within one of the Office applications, such as Excel, that you download from the Office Store. Office apps combine cloud services and web technologies within the user interface of Office and SharePoint. For example, in Excel, you can use an app to look up and gather search results for a new apartment by placing the information in an Excel worksheet, and then use maps to determine the distance of each apartment to work and to family members.

Activity 1.20 │ Installing Apps for Office

> **A L E R T !**   **You Must Be Signed In to Office with a Microsoft Account to Complete This Activity**
>
> To download an Office app, you must be signed in to Office with a free Microsoft account. If you do not have a Microsoft account, refer to the next activity to create one by using Microsoft's outlook.com email service, which includes free SkyDrive cloud storage.

1 ▶ On the Excel ribbon, click the **INSERT tab**. In the **Apps group**, click the **Apps for Office** arrow, and then click **See All**.

2 ▶ Click **FEATURED APPS**, and then on the right, click in the **Search for apps on the Office Store** box, type **Bing Maps** and press Enter.

3 ▶ Click the **Bing logo**, and then click the **Add** button, and then if necessary, click Continue.

4 ▶ **Close** ☒ Internet Explorer, and then **Close** ☒ the **Apps for Office** box.

5 On the **INSERT tab**, in the **Apps group**, click **Apps for Office**, click **See All**, click **MY APPS**, click the **Bing Maps** app, and then in the lower right corner, click **Insert**.

6 On the Welcome message, click **Insert Sample Data**.

Here, the Bing map displays information related to the sample data. Each state in the sample data displays a small pie chart that represents the two sets of data. Compare your screen with Figure 1.55.

This is just one example of many apps downloadable from the Office store.

FIGURE 1.55

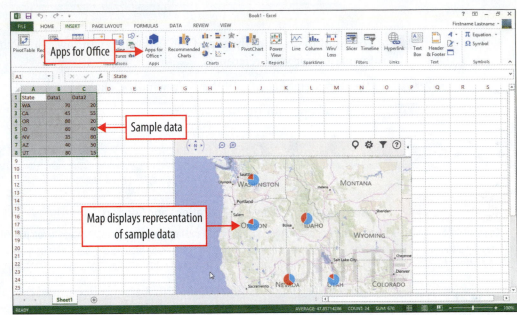

7 **Close** ☒ Excel without saving.

Activity 1.21 | Creating a Microsoft Account

> **ALERT!** **This Is an Optional Activity**
>
> You will find both Windows 8 and Office 2013 to be much more useful if you sign in with a Microsoft account. If you already have an email account from msn.com, hotmail.com, live.com, or outlook.com, then you already have a Microsoft account. If you do not, you can create a free Microsoft account by following the steps in this activity.

In Windows 8, you can create a Microsoft account, and then use that account to sign in to *any* Windows 8 PC. Signing in with a Microsoft account is recommended because you can:

- Download Windows 8 apps from the Windows Store.
- Get your online content—email, social network updates, updated news—automatically displayed in an app on the Windows 8 Start screen when you sign in.
- Synch settings online to make every Windows 8 computer you use look and feel the same.
- Sign in to Office so that you can store documents on your SkyDrive and download Office apps.

1 Open Internet Explorer 🌐, and then go to **www.outlook.com**

2 Locate and click **Sign up now** to display a screen similar to Figure 1.56. Complete the form to create your account.

FIGURE 1.56

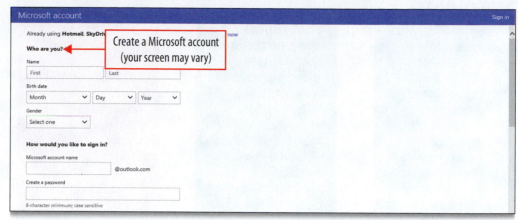

3 Close ✖ Internet Explorer.

END | You have completed Project 1B

END OF CHAPTER

SUMMARY

Many Office features and commands, such as the Open and Save As dialog boxes, performing commands from the ribbon and from dialog boxes, and using the Clipboard are the same in all Office desktop apps.

A desktop app is installed on your computer and requires a computer operating system such as Microsoft Windows or Apple OS to run. The programs in Microsoft Office 2013 are considered to be desktop apps.

Apps that run on a smartphone or tablet computer—for example, iOS, Android, or Windows Phone—or apps that run from browser software such as Internet Explorer or Chrome on a PC, are referred to as apps.

Within each Office app, you can install additional Apps for Office from the Office Store. You must have a Microsoft account, which includes free SkyDrive storage, to download Windows 8 or Office apps.

GO! LEARN IT ONLINE

Review the concepts and key terms in this chapter by completing these online challenges, which you can find at **www.pearsonhighered.com/go**.

Matching and Multiple Choice:
Answer matching and multiple choice questions to test what you learned in this chapter. MyITLab®

Crossword Puzzle:
Spell out the words that match the numbered clues, and put them in the puzzle squares.

Flipboard:
Flip through the definitions of the key terms in this chapter and match them with the correct term.

GLOSSARY

GLOSSARY OF CHAPTER KEY TERMS

Address bar (Internet Explorer) The area at the top of the Internet Explorer window that displays, and where you can type, a URL—Uniform Resource Locator—which is an address that uniquely identifies a location on the Internet.

Address bar (Windows) The bar at the top of a folder window with which you can navigate to a different folder or library, or go back to a previous one.

Alignment The placement of text or objects relative to the left and right margins.

Alignment guides Green lines that display when you move an object to assist in alignment.

App The term that commonly refers to computer programs that run from the device software on a smartphone or a tablet computer—for example, iOS, Android, or Windows Phone—or computer programs that run from the browser software on a desktop PC or laptop PC—for example Internet Explorer, Safari, Firefox, or Chrome.

App for Office A webpage that works within one of the Office applications, such as Excel, and that you download from the Office Store.

Apps for Office 2013 and SharePoint 2013 A collection of downloadable apps that enable you to create and view information within your familiar Office programs.

Backstage tabs The area along the left side of Backstage view with tabs to display screens with related groups of commands.

Backstage view A centralized space for file management tasks; for example, opening, saving, printing, publishing, or sharing a file. A navigation pane displays along the left side with tabs that group file-related tasks together.

Center alignment The alignment of text or objects that is centered horizontally between the left and right margins.

Click The action of pressing and releasing the left button on a mouse pointing device one time.

Clip art Downloadable predefined graphics available online from Office.com and other sites.

Clipboard A temporary storage area that holds text or graphics that you select and then cut or copy.

Cloud computing Refers to applications and services that are accessed over the Internet, rather than to applications that are installed on your local computer.

Cloud storage Online storage of data so that you can access your data from different places and devices.

Collaborate To work with others as a team in an intellectual endeavor to complete a shared task or to achieve a shared goal.

Commands An instruction to a computer program that causes an action to be carried out.

Common dialog boxes The set of dialog boxes that includes Open, Save, and Save As, which are provided by the Windows programming interface, and which display and operate in all of the Office programs in the same manner.

Compressed file A file that has been reduced in size and thus takes up less storage space and can be transferred to other computers quickly.

Compressed folder A folder that has been reduced in size and thus takes up less storage space and can be transferred to other computers quickly; also called a *zipped* folder.

Context menus Menus that display commands and options relevant to the selected text or object; also called *shortcut menus*.

Context-sensitive commands Commands that display on a shortcut menu that relate to the object or text that you right-clicked.

Contextual tabs Tabs that are added to the ribbon automatically when a specific object, such as a picture, is selected, and that contain commands relevant to the selected object.

Copy A command that duplicates a selection and places it on the Clipboard.

Cut A command that removes a selection and places it on the Clipboard.

Default The term that refers to the current selection or setting that is automatically used by a computer program unless you specify otherwise.

Deselect The action of canceling the selection of an object or block of text by clicking outside of the selection.

Desktop In Windows, the screen that simulates your work area.

Desktop app The term that commonly refers to a computer program that is installed on your computer and requires a computer operating system like Microsoft Windows or Apple OS to run.

Dialog box A small window that contains options for completing a task.

Dialog Box Launcher A small icon that displays to the right of some group names on the ribbon, and which opens a related dialog box or pane providing additional options and commands related to that group.

Document properties Details about a file that describe or identify it, including the title, author name, subject, and keywords that identify the document's topic or contents; also known as *metadata*.

Drag The action of holding down the left mouse button while moving your mouse.

Edit The process of making changes to text or graphics in an Office file.

Ellipsis A set of three dots indicating incompleteness; an ellipsis following a command name indicates that a dialog box will display if you click the command.

Enhanced ScreenTip A ScreenTip that displays more descriptive text than a normal ScreenTip.

Extract To decompress, or pull out, files from a compressed form.

File A collection of information stored on a computer under a single name, for example, a Word document or a PowerPoint presentation.

File Explorer The program that displays the files and folders on your computer, and which is at work anytime you are viewing the contents of files and folders in a window.

Fill The inside color of an object.

Folder A container in which you store files.

Folder window In Windows, a window that displays the contents of the current folder, library, or device, and contains helpful parts so that you can navigate the Windows file structure.

Font A set of characters with the same design and shape.

Font styles Formatting emphasis such as bold, italic, and underline.

Footer A reserved area for text or graphics that displays at the bottom of each page in a document.

Formatting The process of establishing the overall appearance of text, graphics, and pages in an Office file—for example, in a Word document.

Formatting marks Characters that display on the screen, but do not print, indicating where the Enter key, the Spacebar, and the Tab key were pressed; also called *nonprinting characters*.

Gallery An Office feature that displays a list of potential results instead of just the command name.

Gradient fill A fill effect in which one color fades into another.

Groups On the Office ribbon, the sets of related commands that you might need for a specific type of task.

Header A reserved area for text or graphics that displays at the top of each page in a document.

Info tab The tab in Backstage view that displays information about the current file.

Insertion point A blinking vertical line that indicates where text or graphics will be inserted.

Keyboard shortcut A combination of two or more keyboard keys, used to perform a task that would otherwise require a mouse.

KeyTip The letter that displays on a command in the ribbon and that indicates the key you can press to activate the command when keyboard control of the ribbon is activated.

Keywords Custom file properties in the form of words that you associate with a document to give an indication of the document's content; used to help find and organize files. Also called *tags*.

Landscape orientation A page orientation in which the paper is wider than it is tall.

Layout Options A button that displays when an object is selected and that has commands to choose how the object interacts with surrounding text.

Live Preview A technology that shows the result of applying an editing or formatting change as you point to possible results—*before* you actually apply it.

Location Any disk drive, folder, or other place in which you can store files and folders.

Metadata Details about a file that describe or identify it, including the title, author name, subject, and keywords that identify the document's topic or contents; also known as *document properties*.

Mini toolbar A small toolbar containing frequently used formatting commands that displays as a result of selecting text or objects.

MRU Acronym for *most recently used*, which refers to the state of some commands that retain the characteristic most recently applied; for example, the Font Color button retains the most recently used color until a new color is chosen.

Navigate The process of exploring within the organizing structure of Windows.

Navigation pane In a folder window, the area on the left in which you can navigate to, open, and display favorites, libraries, folders, saved searches, and an expandable list of drives.

Nonprinting characters Characters that display on the screen, but do not print, indicating where the Enter key, the Spacebar, and the Tab key were pressed; also called *formatting marks*.

Notification bar An area at the bottom of an Internet Explorer window that displays information about pending downloads, security issues, add-ons, and other issues related to the operation of your computer.

Object A text box, picture, table, or shape that you can select and then move and resize.

Office Web Apps The free online companions to Microsoft Word, Excel, PowerPoint, Access, and OneNote.

Open dialog box A dialog box from which you can navigate to, and then open on your screen, an existing file that was created in that same program.

Option button In a dialog box, a round button that enables you to make one choice among two or more options.

Options dialog box A dialog box within each Office application where you can select program settings and other options and preferences.

Pane A separate area of a window.

Paragraph symbol The symbol ¶ that represents the end of a paragraph.

Paste The action of placing text or objects that have been copied or cut from one location to another location.

Paste Options gallery A gallery of buttons that provides a Live Preview of all the Paste options available in the current context.

Path A sequence of folders that leads to a specific file or folder.

PDF The acronym for Portable Document Format, which is a file format that creates an image that preserves the look of your file; this is a popular format for sending documents electronically because the document will display on most computers.

Point The action of moving your mouse pointer over something on your screen.

Pointer Any symbol that displays on your screen in response to moving your mouse.

Points A measurement of the size of a font; there are 72 points in an inch.

Portable Document Format A file format that creates an image that preserves the look of your file, but that cannot be easily changed; a popular format for sending documents electronically, because the document will display on most computers.

Portrait orientation A page orientation in which the paper is taller than it is wide.

Print Preview A view of a document as it will appear when you print it.

Progress bar In a dialog box or taskbar button, a bar that indicates visually the progress of a task such as a download or file transfer.

Protected View A security feature in Office 2013 that protects your computer from malicious files by opening them in a restricted environment until you enable them; you might encounter this feature if you open a file from an email or download files from the Internet.

pt The abbreviation for *point*; for example, when referring to a font size.

Quick Access Toolbar In an Office program window, the small row of buttons in the upper left corner of the screen from which you can perform frequently used commands.

Read-Only A property assigned to a file that prevents the file from being modified or deleted; it indicates that you cannot save any changes to the displayed document unless you first save it with a new name.

Ribbon A user interface in both Office 2013 and File Explorer that groups the commands for performing related tasks on tabs across the upper portion of the program window.

Right-click The action of clicking the right mouse button one time.

Sans serif font A font design with no lines or extensions on the ends of characters.

ScreenTip A small box that that displays useful information when you perform various mouse actions such as pointing to screen elements or dragging.

Scroll bar A vertical or horizontal bar in a window or a pane to assist in bringing an area into view, and which contains a scroll box and scroll arrows.

Scroll box The box in the vertical and horizontal scroll bars that can be dragged to reposition the contents of a window or pane on the screen.

Selecting Highlighting, by dragging with your mouse, areas of text or data or graphics, so that the selection can be edited, formatted, copied, or moved.

Serif font A font design that includes small line extensions on the ends of the letters to guide the eye in reading from left to right.

SharePoint Collaboration software with which people in an organization can set up team sites to share information, manage documents, and publish reports for others to see.

Shortcut menu A menu that displays commands and options relevant to the selected text or object; also called a *context menu*.

Sizing handles Small squares that indicate a picture or object is selected.

SkyDrive Microsoft's free cloud storage for anyone with a free Microsoft account.

Split button A button divided into two parts and in which clicking the main part of the button performs a command and clicking the arrow opens a menu with choices.

Start search The search feature in Windows 8 in which, from the Start screen, you can begin to type and by default, Windows 8 searches for apps; you can adjust the search to search for files or settings.

Status bar The area along the lower edge of an Office program window that displays file information on the left and buttons to control how the window looks on the right.

Style A group of formatting commands, such as font, font size, font color, paragraph alignment, and line spacing that can be applied to a paragraph with one command.

Subfolder A folder within a folder.

Synchronization The process of updating computer files that are in two or more locations according to specific rules—also called *syncing*.

Syncing The process of updating computer files that are in two or more locations according to specific rules—also called *synchronization*.

Tabs (ribbon) On the Office ribbon, the name of each activity area.

Tags Custom file properties in the form of words that you associate with a document to give an indication of the document's content; used to help find and organize files. Also called *keywords*.

Taskbar The area along the lower edge of the desktop that displays buttons representing programs.

Template A preformatted document that you can use as a starting point and then change to suit your needs.

Theme A predesigned combination of colors, fonts, and effects that look good together and is applied to an entire document by a single selection.

Title bar The bar at the top edge of the program window that indicates the name of the current file and the program name.

Toggle button A button that can be turned on by clicking it once, and then turned off by clicking it again.

Toolbar In a folder window, a row of buttons with which you can perform common tasks, such as changing the view of your files and folders or burning files to a CD.

Triple-click The action of clicking the left mouse button three times in rapid succession.

Trusted Documents A security feature in Office that remembers which files you have already enabled; you might encounter this feature if you open a file from an email or download files from the Internet.

Uniform Resource Locator An address that uniquely identifies a location on the Internet.

URL The acronym for Uniform Resource Locator, which is an address that uniquely identifies a location on the Internet.

USB flash drive A small data storage device that plugs into a computer USB port.

Window A rectangular area on a computer screen in which programs and content appear, and which can be moved, resized, minimized, or closed.

XML Paper Specification A Microsoft file format that creates an image of your document and that opens in the XPS viewer.

XPS The acronym for XML Paper Specification—a Microsoft file format that creates an image of your document and that opens in the XPS viewer.

Zipped folder A folder that has been reduced in size and thus takes up less storage space and can be transferred to other computers quickly; also called a *compressed* folder.

Zoom The action of increasing or decreasing the size of the viewing area on the screen.

Introduction to Microsoft Word 2013

W Word 2013

Fotowerk / Fotolia

Video WA

Word 2013: Introduction

Content! Defined by Merriam-Webster's online dictionary as "the topic or matter treated in a written work" and also as "the principal substance (as written matter, illustrations, or music) offered by a World Wide Web site," content is what you consume when you read on paper or online, when you watch video, or when you listen to any kind of music—live or recorded.

Content is what you *create* when your own words or performances are recorded in some form. For creating content in the form of words, Microsoft Office 2013 is a great choice. Rather than just a tool for word processing, Word is now a tool for you to communicate and collaborate with others. When you want to communicate with pictures or images in your

Word document, Office 2013 has many new features to help you do so. Microsoft Word 2013 works best on a Windows 8 PC—desktop, laptop, or tablet—because if your PC is touch-enabled, you will be able to use your fingers to work with Word. For example, the ribbon expands to make it easy to tap commands and you can resize images by moving your fingers on the screen.

Best of all, Microsoft Word 2013 is integrated into the cloud. If you save your documents to your SkyDrive that comes with any free Microsoft account, such as one you can create at outlook.com, you can retrieve them from any device and continue to work with and share your documents. Enjoy learning Word 2013!

Creating Documents with Microsoft Word 2013

GO! to Work
Video W1

PROJECT 1A	OUTCOMES
	Create a flyer with a picture.

OBJECTIVES

1. Create a New Document and Insert Text
2. Insert and Format Graphics
3. Insert and Modify Text Boxes and Shapes
4. Preview and Print a Document

PROJECT 1B	OUTCOMES
	Format text, paragraphs, and documents.

OBJECTIVES

5. Change Document and Paragraph Layout
6. Create and Modify Lists
7. Set and Modify Tab Stops
8. Insert a SmartArt Graphic and an Online Video

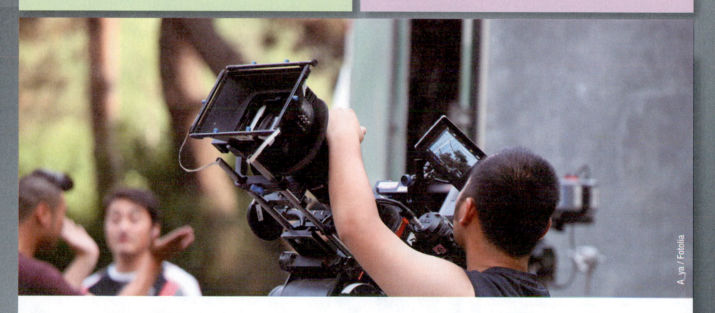

A_ya / Fotolia

In This Chapter

In this chapter, you will begin your study of Microsoft Word, which is one of the most popular computer programs and one that almost everyone has a reason to use. You will use many of the new tools in Word 2013 such as applying attractive styles to your documents. You can use Microsoft Word to perform basic word processing tasks such as writing a memo, a report, or a letter. You can also use Word to complete complex tasks, such as creating sophisticated tables, embedding graphics, writing blogs, and creating publications. Word is a program that you can learn gradually, and then add more advanced skills, one at a time.

The projects in this chapter relate to **Sturgeon Point Productions**, which is an independent film company based in Miami and with offices in Detroit and Milwaukee. The film professionals produce effective broadcast and branded content for many industries, and provide a wide array of film and video production services. Sturgeon Point Productions has won awards for broadcast advertising, business media, music videos, and social media. The mission of the company is to help clients tell their stories—whether the story is about a social issue, a new product, a geographical location, a new company, or a person.

MyITLab®
Project 1A Training

PROJECT ACTIVITIES

In Activities 1.01 through 1.16, you will create a flyer announcing two internships for a short documentary by Sturgeon Point Productions. Your completed document will look similar to Figure 1.1.

PROJECT FILES

For Project 1A, you will need the following files:

New blank Word document
w01A_Text
w01A_Bird

You will save your document as:

Lastname_Firstname_1A_Flyer

PROJECT RESULTS

Build from
Scratch

Internships Available

Interviews will be held:

Friday and Saturday, January 14 and 15

In the Career Services Conference Room

This summer, Sturgeon Point Productions will be filming a short documentary in Costa Rica about its native birds and has positions available for two interns. We are looking for a first Assistant Director and an Assistant Script Supervisor.

The filming will begin the first week of July and will last approximately two weeks. Payment will be by Day Rate of $100 per day. Transportation, food, and lodging will be provided.

The First Assistant Director will work with the second film crew, which will be filming background video. The Assistant Script Supervisor will work with the Script Supervisor and will be responsible for coordinating communication between the two camera crews.

You must have a valid U. S. passport; no inoculations are necessary. Details are available on the company website.

To set up an interview, apply online at:

www.SturgeonPointProductions.com

Lastname_Firstname_1A_Flyer

FIGURE 1.1 Project 1A Flyer

Objective 1   Create a New Document and Insert Text

Video W1-1

When you start Word, documents you have recently opened, if any, display on the left. On the right, you can select either a blank document or a *template*—a preformatted document that you can use as a starting point and then change to suit your needs. When you create a new document, you can type all of the text or you can type some of the text and then insert additional text from another source.

Activity 1.01 | Starting a New Word Document

1 **Start** Word, and then click **Blank document**. On the **HOME tab**, in the **Paragraph group**, if necessary, click **Show/Hide** ¶ so that it is active and the formatting marks display. If the rulers do not display, click the **VIEW tab**, and then in the **Show group**, select the **Ruler** check box.

2 Type **Internships Available** and then press Enter two times. As you type the following text, press the Spacebar only one time at the end of a sentence: **This summer, Sturgeon Point Productions will be filming a short documentary in Costa Rica about its native birds and has positions available for two interns. We are looking for a First Assistant Director and an Assistant Script Supervisor.**

As you type, the insertion point moves to the right, and when it approaches the right margin, Word determines whether the next word in the line will fit within the established right margin. If the word does not fit, Word moves the entire word down to the next line. This is *wordwrap* and means that you press Enter *only* when you reach the end of a paragraph—it is not necessary to press Enter at the end of each line of text.

NOTE   **Spacing between Sentences**

Although you might have learned to add two spaces following end-of-sentence punctuation, the common practice now is to space only one time at the end of a sentence.

3 Press Enter. Take a moment to study the table in Figure 1.2 to become familiar with the default document settings in Microsoft Word, and then compare your screen with Figure 1.3.

When you press Enter, Spacebar, or Tab on your keyboard, characters display in your document to represent these keystrokes. These characters do not print and are referred to as *formatting marks* or *nonprinting characters*. These marks will display throughout this instruction.

FIGURE 1.2

DEFAULT DOCUMENT SETTINGS IN A NEW WORD DOCUMENT	
SETTING	**DEFAULT FORMAT**
Font and font size	The default font is Calibri and the default font size is 11 points.
Margins	The default left, right, top, and bottom page margins are 1 inch.
Line spacing	The default line spacing is 1.08, which provides slightly more space between lines than single spacing does.
Paragraph spacing	The default spacing after a paragraph is 8 points, which is slightly less than the height of one blank line of text.
View	The default view is Print Layout view, which displays the page borders and displays the document as it will appear when printed.

FIGURE 1.3

More Knowledge   **Word's Default Settings Are Easier to Read Online**

Until just a few years ago, word processing programs used single spacing, an extra blank paragraph to separate paragraphs, and 12 pt Times New Roman as the default formats. Now, studies show that individuals find the Word default formats described in Figure 1.2 to be easier to read online, where many documents are now viewed and read.

Activity 1.02 | Inserting Text from Another Document

1 ▶ On the ribbon, click the **INSERT tab**. In the **Text group**, click the **Object button arrow**, and then click **Text from File**.

A L E R T !   **Does the Object Dialog Box Display?**

If the Object dialog box displays, you probably clicked the Object *button* instead of the Object *button arrow*. Close the Object dialog box, and then in the Text group, click the Object button arrow, as shown in Figure 1.4. Click *Text from File*, and then continue with Step 2.

2 ▶ In the **Insert File** dialog box, navigate to the student files that accompany this textbook, locate and select **w01A_Text**, and then click **Insert**. Compare your screen with Figure 1.4.

A *copy* of the text from the w01A_Text file displays at the insertion point location; the text is not removed from the original file.

FIGURE 1.4

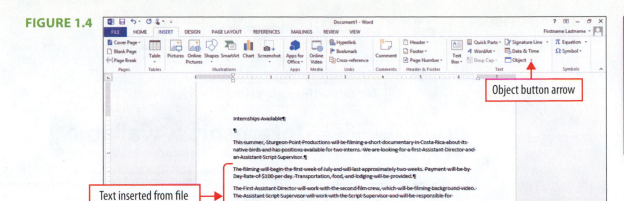

Object button arrow

Text inserted from file

🔄 **ANOTHER WAY**   Open the file, copy the required text, close the file, and then paste the text into the current document.

3 ▸ On the **Quick Access Toolbar**, click **Save** 🖫. Under **Save As**, click **Computer**, and then click **Browse**. Navigate to the location where you are saving your files for this chapter, and then create and open a new folder named **Word Chapter 1**. In the **File name** box, using your own name, replace the existing text with **Lastname_Firstname_1A_Flyer** and then click **Save**.

Objective 2   Insert and Format Graphics

Video W1-2

To add visual interest to a document, insert *graphics*. Graphics include pictures, online pictures, charts, and *drawing objects*—shapes, diagrams, lines, and so on. For additional visual interest, you can apply an attractive graphic format to text; add, resize, move, and format pictures; and add a page border.

Activity 1.03 | Formatting Text by Using Text Effects

Text effects are decorative formats, such as shadowed or mirrored text, text glow, 3-D effects, and colors that make text stand out.

1 ▸ Including the paragraph mark, select the first paragraph of text—*Internships Available*. On the **HOME tab**, in the **Font group**, click **Text Effects and Typography** 🅰⏷.

2 ▸ In the **Text Effects** gallery, in the third row, point to the first effect to display the ScreenTip *Fill – Black, Text 1, Outline – Background 1, Hard Shadow – Background 1*, and then click this effect.

3 ▸ With the text still selected, in the **Font group**, click in the **Font Size** box ⏹ to select the existing font size. Type **52** and then press Enter.

> When you want to change the font size of selected text to a size that does not display in the Font Size list, type the number in the Font Size box and press Enter to confirm the new font size.

4 ▸ With the text still selected, in the **Paragraph group**, click **Center** ⬌ to center the text. Compare your screen with Figure 1.5.

FIGURE 1.5

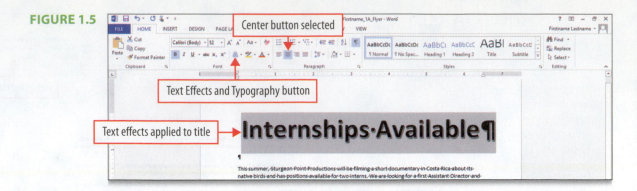

5 With the text still selected, in the **Font group**, click **Text Effects and Typography** ![A icon]. Point to **Shadow**, and then under **Outer**, in the second row, click the third style—**Offset Left**.

6 With the text still selected, in the **Font group**, click the **Font Color button arrow** ![A icon]. Under **Theme Colors**, in the sixth column, click the first color—**Orange, Accent 2**.

7 Click anywhere in the document to deselect the text, click **Save** ![save icon], and then compare your screen with Figure 1.6.

FIGURE 1.6

More Knowledge | **Clear Existing Formatting**

If you do not like your text effect, you can remove all formatting from any selected text. To do so, on the HOME tab, in the Font group, click Clear All Formatting ![icon].

Activity 1.04 | Inserting Pictures

1 In the paragraph that begins *This summer*, click to position the insertion point at the beginning of the paragraph.

2 On the **INSERT tab**, in the **Illustrations group**, click **Pictures**. In the **Insert Picture** dialog box, navigate to your student data files, locate and click **w01A_Bird**, and then click **Insert**.

Word inserts the picture as an ***inline object***; that is, the picture is positioned directly in the text at the insertion point, just like a character in a sentence. The Layout Options button displays to the right of the picture. You can change the ***Layout Options*** to control the manner in which text wraps around a picture or other object. Sizing handles surround the picture indicating it is selected.

3 Notice the square sizing handles around the border of the selected picture, as shown in Figure 1.7.

The corner sizing handles resize the graphic proportionally. The center sizing handles resize a graphic vertically or horizontally only; however, sizing with these will distort the graphic. A ***rotation handle***, with which you can rotate the graphic to any angle, displays above the top center sizing handle.

FIGURE 1.7

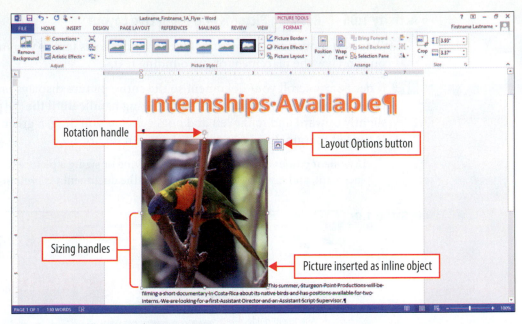

Activity 1.05 | Wrapping Text around a Picture Using Layout Options

Recall that Layout Options enable you to control **text wrapping**—the manner in which text displays around an object.

1 Be sure the picture is selected—you know it is selected if the sizing handles display.

2 To the right of the picture, click **Layout Options** to display a gallery of text wrapping arrangements. Point to each layout option icon to view its ScreenTip.

Each icon visually depicts how text will wrap around an object.

ANOTHER WAY   On the FORMAT tab, in the Arrange group, click Wrap Text.

3 From the gallery, under **With Text Wrapping**, click the first layout—**Square**. Compare your screen with Figure 1.8.

Select Square text wrapping when you want to wrap the text to the left or right of an image. To the left of the picture, an **object anchor** displays indicating that the selected object is anchored to the text at this location in the document.

FIGURE 1.8

4 **Close** the **Layout Options**, and then **Save** your document.

Activity 1.06 | Resizing Pictures and Using Live Layout

When you move or size a picture, **Live Layout** reflows text as you move or size an object so that you can view the placement of surrounding text.

1 If necessary, scroll your document so the entire picture displays on the screen. At the lower right corner of the picture, point to the sizing handle until the [↖] pointer displays. Drag slightly upward and to the left and notice that as you drag, a green alignment guide displays at the left margin. Compare your screen with Figure 1.9.

> *Alignment guides* display when you are moving or sizing a picture to help you with object placement, and Live Layout shows you how the document text will flow and display on the page.

FIGURE 1.9

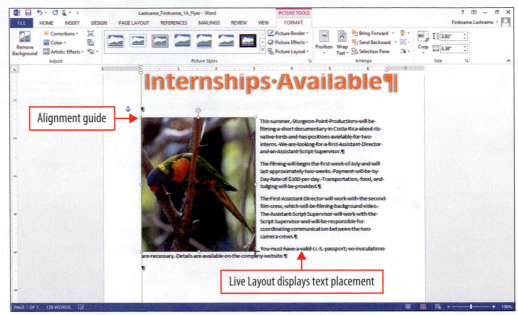

2 Continue to drag up and to the left until the bottom of the graphic is aligned at approximately **4 inches on the vertical ruler** and notice that the graphic is proportionally resized.

3 On the **Quick Access Toolbar**, click **Undo** [↺] to restore the picture to its original size.

ANOTHER WAY   On the FORMAT tab, in the Adjust group, click Reset Picture.

4 On the ribbon, under **PICTURE TOOLS**, on the **FORMAT tab**, in the **Size group**, click the **Shape Height spin box arrows** [↕ Height: 0.19" ▲▼] as necessary to change the height of the picture to **3.8"**. If necessary, scroll down to view the entire picture on your screen, and then compare your screen with Figure 1.10.

> A *spin box* is a small box with an upward- and downward-pointing arrow that lets you move rapidly through a set of values by clicking. When you use the Shape Height and Shape Width spin boxes to change the size of a graphic, the graphic will always resize proportionally; that is, the width adjusts as you change the height and vice versa.

FIGURE 1.10

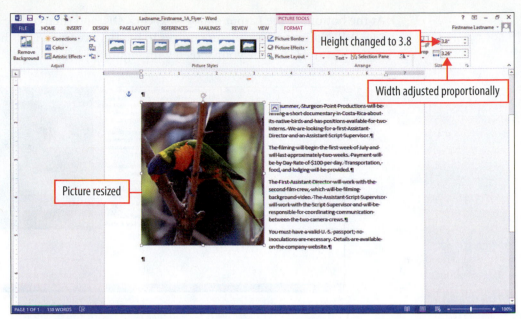

Height changed to 3.8

Width adjusted proportionally

Picture resized

5 Save 🖫 your document.

Activity 1.07 | Moving a Picture

There are two ways to move a picture in a document. You can point to the picture and then drag it to a new position. You can also change the picture settings in a dialog box, which gives you more precise control over the picture location.

1 Be sure the picture is selected. On the ribbon, click the **FORMAT tab**. In the **Arrange group**, click **Position**, and then click **More Layout Options**.

2 In the **Layout** dialog box, be sure the **Position tab** is selected. Under **Horizontal**, click the **Alignment** option button. To the right of **Alignment**, click the **arrow**, and then click **Right**. To the right of **relative to**, click the **arrow**, and then click **Margin**.

3 Under **Vertical**, click the **Alignment** option button. Change the **Alignment** options to **Top relative to Line**. Compare your screen with Figure 1.11.

With these alignment settings, the picture will move to the right margin of the page and the top edge will align with the top of the first line of the paragraph to which it is anchored.

FIGURE 1.11

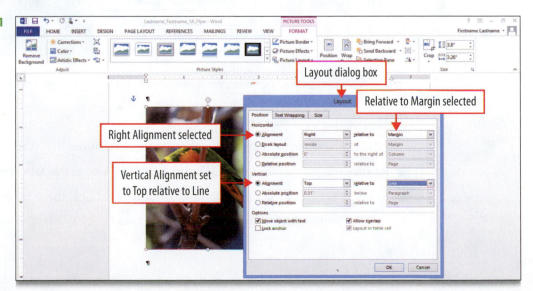

Layout dialog box

Relative to Margin selected

Right Alignment selected

Vertical Alignment set to Top relative to Line

4 At the bottom of the **Layout** dialog box, click **OK**, and then on the **Quick Access Toolbar**, click **Save** 💾. Notice that the picture moves to the right margin, and the text wraps on the left side of the picture. Compare your screen with Figure 1.12.

FIGURE 1.12

Activity 1.08 | Applying Picture Effects

Picture styles include shapes, shadows, frames, borders, and other special effects with which you can stylize an image. *Picture Effects* enhance a picture with effects such as shadow, glow, reflection, or 3-D rotation.

1 Be sure the picture is selected. On the **FORMAT tab**, in the **Picture Styles group**, click **Picture Effects**.

2 Point to **Soft Edges**, and then click **5 Point**.

The Soft Edges feature fades the edges of the picture. The number of points you choose determines how far the fade goes inward from the edges of the picture.

3 Compare your screen with Figure 1.13, and then **Save** 💾 your document.

FIGURE 1.13

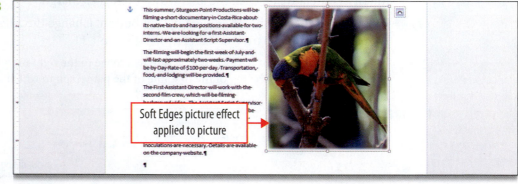

Activity 1.09 | Applying Artistic Effects

Artistic effects are formats that make pictures look more like sketches or paintings.

1 Be sure the picture is selected. On the **FORMAT tab**, in the **Adjust group**, click **Artistic Effects**.

2 In the first row of the gallery, point to, but do not click, the third effect—**Pencil Grayscale**.

Live Preview displays the picture with the *Pencil Grayscale* effect added.

3 In the second row of the gallery, click the third effect—**Paint Brush**. **Save** 💾 your document, and then notice that the picture looks more like a painting than a photograph. Compare your screen with Figure 1.14.

FIGURE 1.14

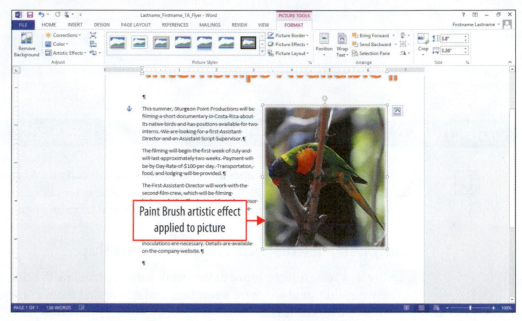

Paint Brush artistic effect applied to picture

Activity 1.10 | Adding a Page Border

Page borders frame a page and help to focus the information on the page.

1 Click anywhere outside the picture to deselect it. On the **DESIGN tab**, in the **Page Background group**, click **Page Borders**.

2 In the **Borders and Shading** dialog box, on the **Page Border tab**, under **Setting**, click **Box**. Under **Style**, scroll the list and click the seventh style—double lines.

3 Click the **Color arrow**, and then in the sixth column, click the first color—**Orange, Accent 2**.

4 Under **Apply to**, be sure **Whole document** is selected, and then compare your screen with Figure 1.15.

FIGURE 1.15

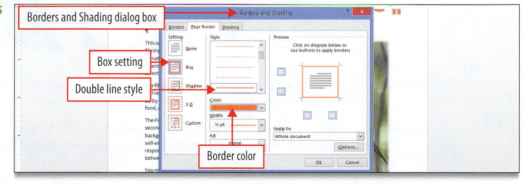

Borders and Shading dialog box

Box setting

Double line style

Border color

5 At the bottom of the **Borders and Shading** dialog box, click **OK**.

6 Press [Ctrl] + [Home] to move to the top of the document, click **Save** 💾, and then compare your screen with Figure 1.16.

FIGURE 1.16

Page border applied to document

Internships·Available¶

Objective 3 | Insert and Modify Text Boxes and Shapes

Video W1-3

Word has predefined **shapes** and **text boxes** that you can add to your documents. A shape is an object such as a line, arrow, box, callout, or banner. A text box is a movable, resizable container for text or graphics. Use these objects to add visual interest to your document.

Activity 1.11 | Inserting, Sizing, and Positioning a Shape

1 Press ↓ one time to move to the blank paragraph below the title. Press Enter four times to create additional space for a text box, and notice that the picture anchored to the paragraph moves with the text.

2 Press Ctrl + End to move to the bottom of the document, and notice that your insertion point is positioned in the empty paragraph at the end of the document. Press Delete to remove the blank paragraph.

3 Click the **INSERT tab**, and then in the **Illustrations group**, click **Shapes** to display the gallery. Compare your screen with Figure 1.17.

FIGURE 1.17

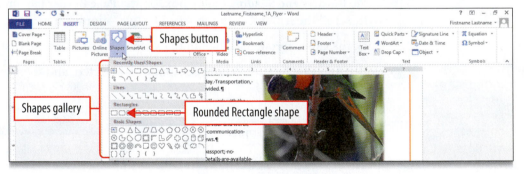

4 Under **Rectangles**, click the second shape—**Rounded Rectangle**, and then move your pointer. Notice that the ⊞ pointer displays.

5 Position the ⊞ pointer anywhere in the blank area at the bottom of the document. Click one time to insert a 1-inch by 1-inch rounded rectangle. The exact location is not important.

A blue rectangle with rounded edges displays.

6 To the right of the rectangle object, click **Layout Options** 🖼, and then at the bottom of the gallery, click **See more** to display the **Layout** dialog box.

🔄 **ANOTHER WAY**   On the FORMAT tab, in the Arrange group, click Position.

7 In the **Layout** dialog box, under **Horizontal**, click **Alignment**. To the right of **Alignment**, click the **arrow**, and then click **Centered**. To the right of **relative to**, click the **arrow**, and then click **Page**. Under **Vertical**, click in the **Absolute position** box to select the existing number, and then type **1** To the right of **below**, be sure that **Paragraph** displays. Click **OK**.

> This action centers the rectangle on the page and positions the rectangle one inch below the last paragraph.

8 On the **FORMAT tab**, click in the **Shape Height** box ⬚ Height: 0.19" ⬍ to select the existing text. Type **1.5** and then click in the **Shape Width** box ⬚ Width: 6.49" ⬍. Type **4.5** and then press Enter.

9 Compare your screen with Figure 1.18, and then **Save** 💾 your document.

FIGURE 1.18

Activity 1.12 | Typing Text in a Shape and Formatting a Shape

1 If necessary, select the rectangle shape. Type **To set up an interview, apply online at:** and then press Enter. Type **www.SturgeonPointProductions.com**

2 Press Ctrl + A to select the text you just typed. Right-click over the selected text to display the mini toolbar, and then click **Bold** **B** . With the text still selected, click **Increase Font Size** **A** three times to increase the font size to **16 pt**.

> The keyboard shortcut Ctrl + A is convenient to select all of the text in a text box.

3 With the text still selected, on the mini toolbar, click the **Font Color button arrow**. Under **Theme Colors**, click **Black, Text 1**.

4 Click outside the shape to deselect the text. Click the border of the shape to select the shape but not the text. On the **FORMAT tab**, in the **Shape Styles group**, click **Shape Fill**. In the sixth column, click the fourth color—**Orange, Accent 2, Lighter 40%**.

5 With the shape still selected, in the **Shape Styles group**, click **Shape Outline**. In the sixth column, click the first color—**Orange, Accent 2**. Compare your screen with Figure 1.19, and then **Save** 💾 your document.

FIGURE 1.19

Activity 1.13 | Inserting a Text Box

A text box is useful to differentiate portions of text from other text on the page. Because it is a *floating object*—a graphic that can be moved independently of the surrounding text characters—you can place a text box anywhere on the page.

1 Press [Ctrl] + [Home] to move to the top of the document.

2 On the **INSERT tab**, in the **Text group**, click **Text Box**. At the bottom of the gallery, click **Draw Text Box**.

3 Position the ✛ pointer over the first blank paragraph—aligned with the left margin and at approximately **1 inch on the vertical ruler**. Drag down and to the right to create a text box approximately **1.5 inches** high and **4 inches** wide—the exact size and location need not be precise.

4 With the insertion point blinking in the text box, type the following, pressing [Enter] after each line *except* the last line to create a new paragraph:

Interviews will be held:

Friday and Saturday, January 14 and 15

In the Career Services Conference Room

5 Compare your screen with Figure 1.20, and then **Save** 💾 your document

FIGURE 1.20

Activity 1.14 | Sizing and Positioning a Text Box and Formatting a Text Box Using Shape Styles

1 Point to the text box border to display the 🔩 pointer. In the space below the *Internships Available* title, by dragging, move the text box until a horizontal green alignment guide displays above the first blank paragraph mark and a vertical green alignment guide displays in the center of the page as shown in Figure 1.21.

FIGURE 1.21

2 To precisely place the text box, on the **FORMAT tab**, in the **Arrange group**, click **Position**, and then click **More Layout Options**.

3 In the **Layout** dialog box, under **Horizontal**, click **Alignment**. To the right of **Alignment**, click the **arrow**, and then click **Centered**. To the right of **relative to**, click the **arrow**, and then click **Page**.

4 Under **Vertical**, click in the **Absolute position** box, select the existing number, and then type **1.25** To the right of **below**, click the **arrow**, and then click **Margin**.

5 In the **Layout** dialog box, click the **Size tab**. Under **Height**, select the number in the **Absolute** box. Type **1.25** and then under **Width**, select the number in the **Absolute** box. Type **4** and then click **OK**.

> The text box is sized correctly, centered horizontally, and the top edge is positioned 1.25 inches below the top margin of the document.

6 Click in the text box, and then press ⌃Ctrl + Ⓐ to select all of the text. Right-click over the selected text to display the mini toolbar, change the **Font Size** to **16** and apply **Bold** Ⓑ. Press ⌃Ctrl + Ⓔ to center the text.

> ⌃Ctrl + Ⓔ is the keyboard shortcut to center text in a document or object.

7 On the ribbon, under **DRAWING TOOLS**, click the **FORMAT tab**. In the **Shape Styles group**, click **More** ⏷, and then in the first row, click the third style—**Colored Outline – Orange, Accent 2**.

8 On the **FORMAT tab**, in the **Shape Styles group**, click **Shape Effects**. Point to **Shadow**, and then under **Outer**, in the first row, click the first effect—**Offset Diagonal Bottom Right**.

9 Click anywhere in the document to deselect the text box. Compare your screen with Figure 1.22, and then **Save** 🖫 your document.

FIGURE 1.22

Text formatted and centered, text box sized and positioned, Shape Style and Shadow effect applied

---

Objective 4 | Preview and Print a Document

Video W1-4

While you are creating your document, it is useful to preview your document periodically to be sure that you are getting the result you want. Then, before printing, make a final preview to be sure the document layout is what you intend.

Activity 1.15 | Adding a File Name to the Footer by Inserting a Field

Information in headers and footers helps to identify a document when it is printed or displayed electronically. Recall that a header is information that prints at the top of every page; a footer is information that prints at the bottom of every page. In this textbook, you will insert the file name in the footer of every Word document.

1 Click the **INSERT tab**, and then in the **Header & Footer group**, click **Footer**.

2 At the bottom of the gallery, click **Edit Footer**.

The footer area displays with the insertion point blinking at the left edge, and on the ribbon, the Header & Footer Tools display.

🔄 **ANOTHER WAY**   At the bottom edge of the page, right-click, and then on the shortcut menu, click Edit Footer.

3 On the ribbon, under the **HEADER & FOOTER TOOLS**, on the **DESIGN tab**, in the **Insert group**, click **Document Info**, and then click **File Name**. Compare your screen with Figure 1.23.

FIGURE 1.23

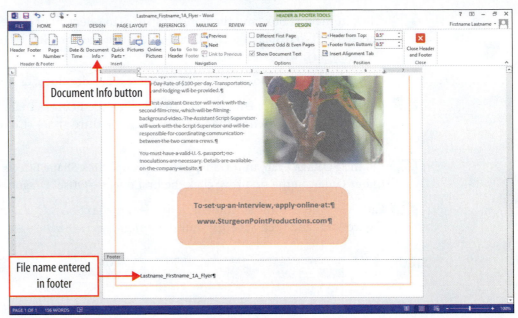

4 On the **DESIGN tab**, click **Close Header and Footer**, and then **Save** 💾 your document.

When the body of the document is active, the footer text is dimmed—displays in gray. Conversely, when the footer area is active, the footer text is not dimmed; instead, the document text is dimmed.

🔄 **ANOTHER WAY**   Double-click in the document outside of the footer area to close the footer and return to the document.

Activity 1.16 | Adding Document Properties and Previewing and Printing a Document

1 Press Ctrl + Home to move the insertion point to the top of the document. In the upper left corner of your screen, click the **FILE tab** to display **Backstage** view. On the right, at the bottom of the **Properties** list, click **Show All Properties**.

2 On the list of **Properties**, click to the right of **Tags** to display an empty box, and then type **internship, documentary**

3 Click to the right of **Subject** to display an empty box, and then type your course name and section number. Under **Related People**, be sure that your name displays as the author. If necessary, right-click the author name, click **Edit Property**, type your name, press Enter and click **OK**.

4 On the left, click **Print** to display the **Print Preview**. Compare your screen with Figure 1.24.

Here you can select any printer connected to your system and adjust the settings related to how you want to print. On the right, Print Preview displays your document exactly as it will print; the formatting marks do not display. At the bottom of the Print Preview area, in the center, the number of pages and arrows with which you can move among the pages in Print Preview display. On the right, Zoom settings enable you to shrink or enlarge the Print Preview.

FIGURE 1.24

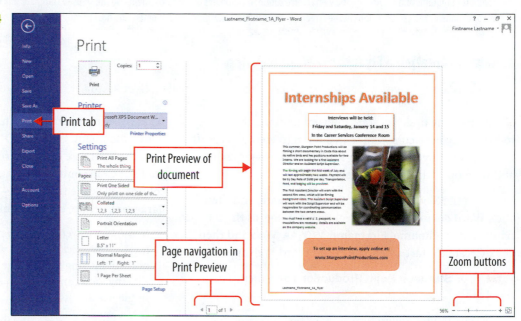

5 In the lower right corner of the window, click **Zoom In** ⊕ several times to view the document at a larger size, and notice that a larger preview is easier to read. Click **Zoom to Page** to view the entire page.

6 To submit your file electronically, skip this step and move to Step 7. To print your document on paper using the default printer on your system, in the upper left portion of the screen, click **Print**.

The document will print on your default printer; if you do not have a color printer, colors will print in shades of gray. Backstage view closes and your file redisplays in the Word window.

7 To create an electronic printout, on the left, click **Export**. On the right, click **Create PDF/XPS**. In the **Publish as PDF or XPS** dialog box, navigate to your **Word Chapter 1** folder, and then click **Publish**. If your Adobe Acrobat or Adobe Reader program displays your PDF, in the upper right corner, click **Close** ⊠.

8 Save 🖫 your document. In the upper right corner of the Word window, click **Close** ❎. If directed by your instructor to do so, submit your paper or electronic printout or your Word file.

END | You have completed Project 1A

Objective Create a Flyer in Word Web App

Build from Scratch

ALERT! **Working with Web-Based Applications and Services**

Computer programs and services on the web receive continuous updates and improvements, so the steps to complete this web-based activity may differ from the ones shown. You can often look at the screens and the information presented to determine how to complete the activity.

Activity | Creating a Flyer in the Word Web App

In this activity, you will use the Word Web App to create a flyer similar to the one you created in Project 1A.

1 From the desktop, start Internet Explorer. Navigate to **http://skydrive.com**, and then sign in to your Microsoft account. Open your **GO! Web Projects** folder—or create and then open this folder if necessary.

2 On the SkyDrive menu bar, click **Create**, and then click **Word document**. Using your own name, as the file name, type **Lastname_Firstname_WD_1A_Web** and then click **Create** to start a new file in the Word Web app.

3 Type **Sturgeon Point Productions** and then press Enter.

4 Type the following four lines of text, pressing Enter after each line *except* for the last line:

Internships Available for a Costa Rica
Native Birds Documentary
Interviews on Friday, January 14
Filming Begins the First Week of July

5 By using your I pointer, drag to select the first line in the document. On the **HOME tab**, in the **Font group**, click the **Font Size button arrow**, and then click **36**. Click the **Font Color button arrow**, and then in the fourth column, click the first color—**Blue Gray, Text 2**. In the **Paragraph group**, click **Center**.

In the Word Web App, you must drag to select text—triple-clicking a line will not select the line, nor will moving the pointer into the left margin and clicking. You can, however, double-click to select a single word.

6 Select the remaining text in the document, and then on the **HOME tab** in the **Font group**, click **Bold**. Click the **Font Size button arrow**, and then click **24**. In the **Paragraph group**, click **Center**. Compare your screen with Figure A.

FIGURE A

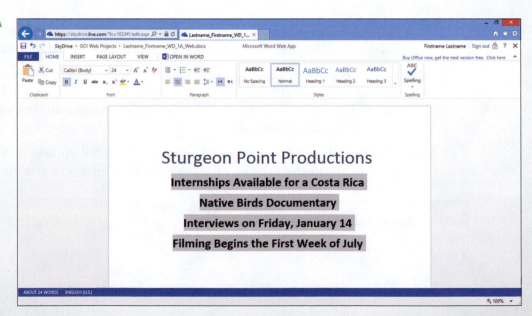

(GO! with Office Web Apps continues on the next page)

7 Click at the end of the line *Interviews on Friday, January 14,* and then press Enter to insert a blank line.

8 On the **INSERT tab**, in the **Pictures group**, click **Picture**. Navigate to the location where your student data files are stored, and then click **w01A_Bird**. Click **Open**. Notice that the picture is dimmed, indicating that it is selected.

9 Under **PICTURE TOOLS**, click the **FORMAT tab**, and then in the **Image Size group**, click **Shrink** several times until the **Scale** box displays **40.48%**. If the box does not display this exact number, click the **Shrink** or **Grow** buttons until the **Scale** is approximately this number.

10 With the picture still selected, on the **FORMAT tab**, in the **Picture Styles group**, click the sixth style—**Soft Edge Rectangle**.

11 Click anywhere in a blank area of the document so that the picture is not selected, and then compare your screen with Figure B.

12 In the upper left corner, above the **FILE tab**, click **Save** 🖫, and then submit as directed by your instructor. If you are instructed to submit an electronic printout of your file, create a PDF as indicated in the Note box that follows. Then, on the ribbon, click the **FILE tab** and click **Exit**. Sign out of your Microsoft account.

N O T E   Creating a PDF from the Word Web App

Click the FILE tab, click Print, and then click Print to PDF. In the Microsoft Word Web App message box, click Click here to view the PDF of your document. In the message bar at the bottom of your screen, click the Save arrow, and then click Save as. In the Save As dialog box, navigate to your Word Chapter 1 folder, and then save the file.

FIGURE B

PROJECT 1B | Information Handout

PROJECT ACTIVITIES

In Activities 1.17 through 1.29, you will format an information handout from Sturgeon Point Productions that describes internships available to students. Your completed document will look similar to Figure 1.25.

PROJECT FILES

For Project 1B, you will need the following files:

w01B_Programs
w01B_Web

You will save your document as:

Lastname_Firstname_1B_Programs

PROJECT RESULTS

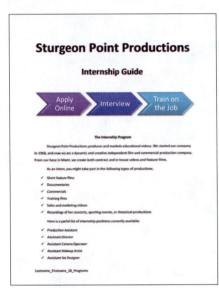

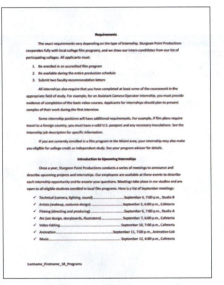

FIGURE 1.25 Project 1B Information Handout

Video W1-5

Document layout includes *margins*—the space between the text and the top, bottom, left, and right edges of the paper. Paragraph layout includes line spacing, indents, and tabs. In Word, the information about paragraph formats is stored in the paragraph mark at the end of a paragraph. When you press Enter, the new paragraph mark contains the formatting of the previous paragraph, unless you take steps to change it.

Activity 1.17 | Setting Margins

1 Start Word, and then click **Open Other Documents**. Navigate to the student files that accompany this textbook, and then open the document **w01B_Programs**. On the **HOME tab**, in the **Paragraph group**, be sure **Show/Hide** ¶ is active so that you can view the formatting marks.

2 Click the **FILE tab**, and then click **Save As**. Navigate to your **Word Chapter 1** folder, and then using your own name, **Save** the document as **Lastname_Firstname_1B_Programs**

3 Click the **PAGE LAYOUT tab**. In the **Page Setup group**, click **Margins**, and then take a moment to study the settings in the Margins gallery.

> If you have recently used custom margins settings, they will display at the top of this gallery. Other commonly used settings also display.

4 At the bottom of the **Margins** gallery, click the command followed by an ellipsis—**Custom Margins** to display the **Page Setup** dialog box.

5 In the **Page Setup** dialog box, under **Margins**, press Tab as necessary to select the value in the **Left** box, and then, with *1.25"* selected, type **1**

> This action will change the left margin to 1 inch on all pages of the document. You do not need to type the inch (") mark.

6 Press Tab to select the margin in the **Right** box, and then type **1** At the bottom of the dialog box, notice that the new margins will apply to the **Whole document**. Compare your screen with Figure 1.26.

FIGURE 1.26

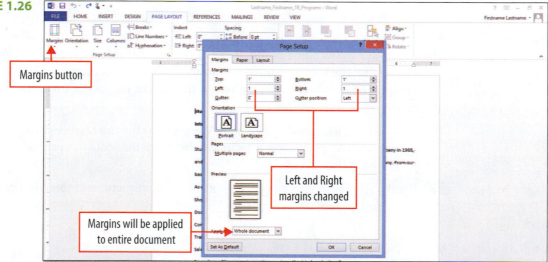

Margins button

Left and Right margins changed

Margins will be applied to entire document

1
WORD

7 Click **OK** to apply the new margins and close the dialog box. If the ruler below the ribbon is not displayed, on the **VIEW** tab, in the **Show group**, select the **Ruler** check box.

8 Scroll to position the bottom of **Page 1** and the top of **Page 2** on your screen. Notice that the page edges display, and the page number and total number of pages display on the left side of the status bar.

9 Near the bottom edge of **Page 1**, point anywhere in the bottom margin area, right-click, and then click **Edit Footer** to display the footer area.

10 On the ribbon, under the **HEADER & FOOTER TOOLS**, on the **DESIGN tab**, in the **Insert group**, click **Document Info**, and then click **File Name**.

11 Double-click anywhere in the document to close the footer area, and then **Save** 🖫 your document.

Activity 1.18 | Aligning Text

Alignment refers to the placement of paragraph text relative to the left and right margins. Most paragraph text uses *left alignment*—aligned at the left margin, leaving the right margin uneven. Three other types of paragraph alignment are: *center alignment*—centered between the left and right margins; *right alignment*—aligned at the right margin with an uneven left margin; and *justified alignment*—text aligned evenly at both the left and right margins. The table in Figure 1.27 shows examples of these alignment types.

FIGURE 1.27

TYPES OF PARAGRAPH ALIGNMENT		
ALIGNMENT	**BUTTON**	**DESCRIPTION AND EXAMPLE**
Align Left	≣	Align Left is the default paragraph alignment in Word. Text in the paragraph aligns at the left margin, and the right margin is uneven.
Center	≣	Center alignment aligns text in the paragraph so that it is centered between the left and right margins.
Align Right	≣	Align Right aligns text at the right margin. Using Align Right, the left margin, which is normally even, is uneven.
Justify	≣	The Justify alignment option adds additional space between words so that both the left and right margins are even. Justify is often used when formatting newspaper-style columns.

1 Scroll to position the middle of **Page 2** on your screen, look at the left and right margins, and notice that the text is justified—both the right and left margins of multiple-line paragraphs are aligned evenly at the margins. On the **HOME tab**, in the **Paragraph group**, notice that **Justify** ≣ is active.

To achieve a justified right margin, Word adjusts the size of spaces between words, which can result in unattractive spacing in a document that spans the width of a page. Many individuals find such spacing difficult to read.

2 Press Ctrl + A to select all of the text in the document, and then on the **HOME tab**, in the **Paragraph group**, click **Align Left** ≣.

 **ANOTHER WAY**   On the HOME tab, in the Editing group, click Select, and then click Select All.

3 Press [Ctrl] + [Home] to move to the beginning of the document. In the left margin area, point to the left of the first paragraph—*Sturgeon Point Productions*—until the pointer displays, and then click one time to select the paragraph.

Use this technique to select entire lines of text.

4 On the mini toolbar, in the **Font Size** box, select the existing number, type **40** and then press [Enter].

Use this technique to change the font size to a size that is not available on the Font Size list.

5 Select the second paragraph—*Internship Guide*—and then on the mini toolbar, change the **Font Size** to **26 pt**. Point to the left of the first paragraph—*Sturgeon Point Productions*—to display the pointer again, and then drag down to select the first two paragraphs, which form the title and subtitle of the document.

6 On the **HOME tab**, in the **Paragraph group**, click **Center** ☰ to center the title and subtitle between the left and right margins, and then compare your screen with Figure 1.28.

FIGURE 1.28

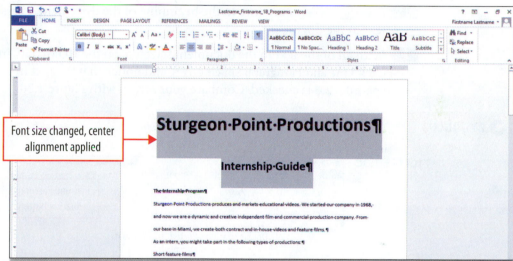

Font size changed, center alignment applied

7 Near the top of **Page 1**, locate the first bold subheading—*The Internship Program*. Point to the left of the paragraph to display the pointer, and then click one time to select this text.

8 With *The Internship Program* selected, use your mouse wheel or the vertical scroll bar to bring the bottom portion of **Page 1** into view. Locate the subheading *Requirements*. Move the pointer to the left of the paragraph to display the pointer, hold down [Ctrl], and then click one time. Scroll to the middle of **Page 2**, and then use the same technique to select the third subheading—*Introduction to Upcoming Internships*.

Three subheadings are selected; in Windows-based programs, you can hold down [Ctrl] to select multiple items.

9 Click **Center** ☰ to center all three subheadings, and then click **Save** 🖫.

Activity 1.19 | Changing Line Spacing

Line spacing is the distance between lines of text in a paragraph. Three of the most commonly used line spacing options are shown in the table in Figure 1.29.

FIGURE 1.29

LINE SPACING OPTIONS	
ALIGNMENT	**DESCRIPTION, EXAMPLE, AND INFORMATION**
Single spacing	**This text in this example uses single spacing**. Single spacing was once the most commonly used spacing in business documents. Now, because so many documents are read on a computer screen rather than on paper, single spacing is becoming less popular.
Multiple 1.08 spacing	**This text in this example uses multiple 1.08 spacing**. The default line spacing in Microsoft Word 2013 is 1.08, which is slightly more than single spacing to make the text easier to read on a computer screen. Many individuals now prefer this spacing, even on paper, because the lines of text appear less crowded.
Double spacing	**This text in this example uses double spacing**. College research papers and draft documents that need space for notes are commonly double-spaced; there is space for a full line of text between each document line.

1 Press Ctrl + Home to move to the beginning of the document. Press Ctrl + A to select all of the text in the document.

2 With all of the text in the document selected, on the **HOME tab**, in the **Paragraph group**, click **Line and Paragraph Spacing** ↕≡▾, and notice that the text in the document is double spaced—**2.0** is checked. Compare your screen with Figure 1.30.

⟳ BY TOUCH   Tap the ribbon commands.

FIGURE 1.30

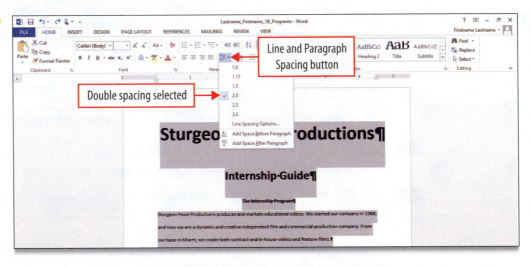

3 On the **Line Spacing** menu, click the *third* setting—**1.5**—and then click anywhere in the document to deselect the text. Compare your screen with Figure 1.31, and then **Save** 🖫 your document.

FIGURE 1.31

Activity 1.20 | Indenting Text

Indenting the first line of each paragraph is a common technique to distinguish paragraphs.

1 Below the title and subtitle of the document, click anywhere in the paragraph that begins *Sturgeon Point Productions produces*.

2 On the **HOME tab**, in the **Paragraph group**, click the **Dialog Box Launcher** [icon].

3 In the **Paragraph** dialog box, on the **Indents and Spacing tab**, under **Indentation**, click the **Special arrow**, and then click **First line** to indent the first line by 0.5", which is the default indent setting. Compare your screen with Figure 1.32.

FIGURE 1.32

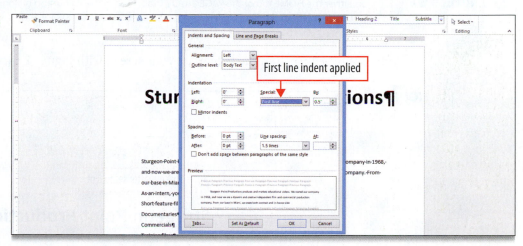

4 Click **OK**, and then click anywhere in the next paragraph, which begins *As an intern*. On the ruler under the ribbon, drag the **First Line Indent** marker [icon] to **0.5 inches on the horizontal ruler**, and then compare your screen with Figure 1.33.

FIGURE 1.33

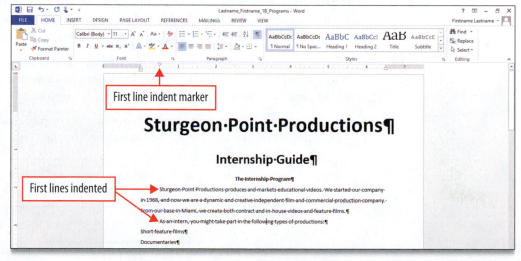

5 By using either of the techniques you just practiced, or by using the **Format Painter**, apply a first line indent of **0.5"** in the paragraph that begins *Here is a partial* to match the indent of the remaining paragraphs in the document.

6 **Save** [icon] your document.

Activity 1.21 | Adding Space Before and After Paragraphs

Adding space after each paragraph is another technique to differentiate paragraphs.

1 Press Ctrl + A to select all of the text in the document. Click the **PAGE LAYOUT tab**, and then in the **Paragraph group**, under **Spacing**, click the **After spin box up arrow** one time to change the value to **6 pt**.

To change the value in the box, you can also select the existing number, type a new number, and then press Enter. This document will use 6 pt spacing after paragraphs to add space.

> **ANOTHER WAY** On either the HOME tab or the PAGE LAYOUT tab, display the Paragraph dialog box from the Paragraph group, and then under Spacing, click the spin box arrows as necessary.

2 Press Ctrl + Home, and then compare your screen with Figure 1.34.

FIGURE 1.34

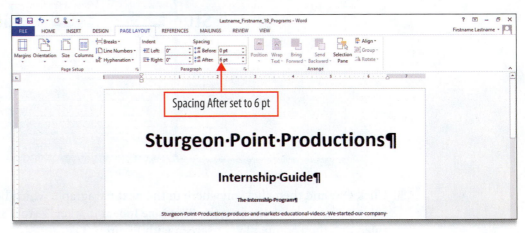

Spacing After set to 6 pt

3 Near the top of **Page 1**, select the subheading *The Internship Program*, including the paragraph mark following it, scroll down, hold down Ctrl, and then select the subheadings *Requirements* and *Introduction to Upcoming Internships*.

4 With all three subheadings selected, in the **Paragraph group**, under **Spacing**, click the **Before up spin box arrow** two times to set the **Spacing Before** to **12 pt**. Compare your screen with Figure 1.35, and then **Save** your document.

This action increases the amount of space above each of the subheadings, which will make them easy to distinguish in the document. The formatting is applied only to the selected paragraphs.

FIGURE 1.35

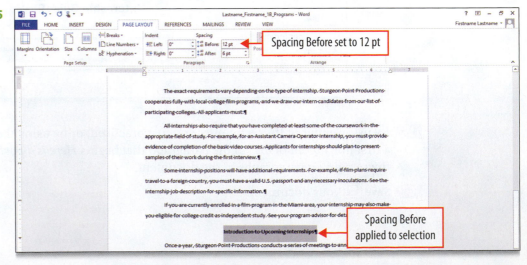

Spacing Before set to 12 pt

Spacing Before applied to selection

Video W1-6

To display a list of information, you can choose a **bulleted list**, which uses **bullets**—text symbols such as small circles or check marks—to introduce each item in a list. You can also choose a **numbered list**, which uses consecutive numbers or letters to introduce each item in a list.

Use a bulleted list if the items in the list can be introduced in any order; use a numbered list for items that have definite steps, a sequence of actions, or are in chronological order.

Activity 1.22 | Creating a Bulleted List

1 In the upper portion of **Page 1**, locate the paragraph *Short feature films*, and then point to this paragraph from the left margin area to display the [🔄] pointer. Drag down to select this paragraph and the next five paragraphs.

2 On the **HOME tab**, in the **Paragraph group**, click **Bullets** [≣ ▾] to change the selected text to a bulleted list.

> The spacing between each of the bulleted points changes to the spacing between lines in a paragraph—in this instance, 1.5 line spacing. The 6 pt. spacing after each paragraph is eliminated with the exception of the last item in the list. Each bulleted item is automatically indented.

3 On the ruler, point to **First Line Indent** [▽] and read the ScreenTip, and then point to **Hanging Indent** [⌂]. Compare your screen with Figure 1.36.

> By default, Word formats bulleted items with a first line indent of 0.25" and adds a Hanging Indent at 0.5". The hanging indent maintains the alignment of text when a bulleted item is more than one line.

> You can modify the list indentation by using Decrease Indent [≣] or Increase Indent [≣]. **Decrease Indent** moves your paragraph closer to the margin. **Increase Indent** moves your paragraph farther away from the margin.

FIGURE 1.36

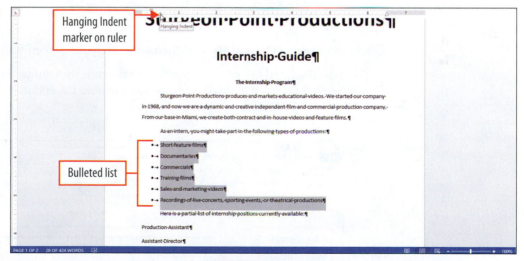

4 Scroll down slightly, and then by using the [🔄] pointer from the left margin area, select the five internship positions, beginning with *Production Assistant* and ending with *Assistant Set Designer*. In the **Paragraph group**, click **Bullets** [≣ ▾].

5 Scroll down to view **Page 2**. Apply bullets to all of the paragraphs that indicate the September meetings and meeting dates, beginning with *Technical* and ending with *Music*. **Save** [💾] your document.

Activity 1.23 │ Creating a Numbered List

1 Under the subheading *Requirements*, in the paragraph that begins *The exact requirements*, click to position the insertion point at the *end* of the paragraph, following the colon. Press Enter to create a blank paragraph. Notice that the paragraph is indented, because the First Line Indent from the previous paragraph carried over to the new paragraph.

2 To change the indent formatting for this paragraph, on the ruler, drag the **First Line Indent** marker ▽ to the left so that it is positioned directly above the lower button.

3 Being sure to include the period, type **1.** and press Spacebar. Compare your screen with Figure 1.37.

Word determines that this paragraph is the first item in a numbered list and formats the new paragraph accordingly, indenting the list in the same manner as the bulleted list. The space after the number changes to a tab, and the AutoCorrect Options button displays to the left of the list item. The tab is indicated by a right arrow formatting mark.

FIGURE 1.37

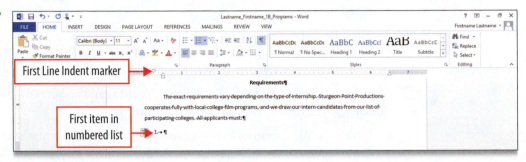

4 Click **AutoCorrect Options** ⊞▾, and then compare your screen with Figure 1.38.

From the displayed list, you can remove the automatic formatting here, or stop using the automatic numbered lists option in this document. You also have the option to open the AutoCorrect dialog box to *Control AutoFormat Options*.

FIGURE 1.38

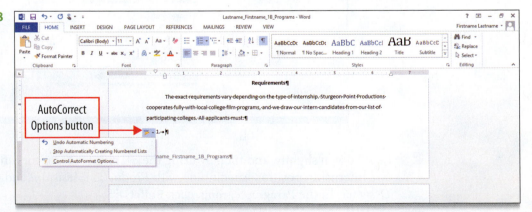

5 Click **AutoCorrect Options** ⊞▾ again to close the menu without selecting any of the commands. Type **Be enrolled in an accredited film program** and press Enter. Notice that the second number and a tab are added to the next line.

6 Type **Be available during the entire production schedule** and press Enter. Type **Submit two faculty recommendation letters** Compare your screen with Figure 1.39, and then **Save** 🖫 your document.

FIGURE 1.39

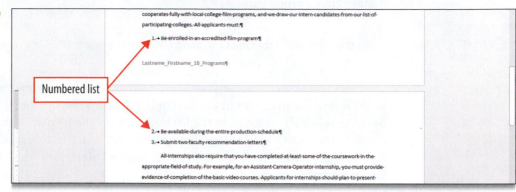

cooperates-fully-with-local-college-film-programs,-and-we-draw-our-intern-candidates-from-our-list-of-participating-colleges.·All-applicants-must:¶

1.→ Be-enrolled-in-an-accredited-film-program¶

Lastname_Firstname_1B_Programs¶

Numbered list

2.→ Be-available-during-the-entire-production-schedule¶
3.→ Submit-two-faculty-recommendation-letters¶

All·internships·also·require·that·you·have·completed·at·least·some·of·the·coursework·in·the-appropriate·field·of·study.·For·example,·for·an·Assistant·Camera·Operator·internship,·you·must·provide-evidence·of·completion·of·the·basic·video·courses.·Applicants·for·internships·should·plan·to·present-

---

More Knowledge | **To End a List**

To turn a list off, you can press Backspace, click the Numbering or Bullets button, or press Enter two times. Both list buttons—Numbering and Bullets—act as **toggle buttons**; that is, clicking the button one time turns the feature on, and clicking the button again turns the feature off.

Activity 1.24 | **Customizing Bullets**

You can use any symbol from any font for your bullet characters.

1 Press Ctrl + End to move to the end of the document, and then scroll up as necessary to display the bulleted list containing the list of meetings.

2 Point to the left of the first list item to display the 🖎 pointer, and then drag down to select all six meetings in the list—the bullet symbols are not highlighted.

3 On the mini toolbar, click the **Bullets button arrow** ▤▾ to display the **Bullet Library**, and then compare your screen with Figure 1.40.

FIGURE 1.40

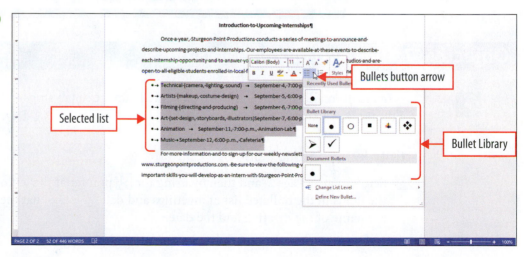

Introduction-to-Upcoming-Internships¶

Once-a-year,·Sturgeon-Point·Productions·conducts·a·series·of·meetings·to·announce·and-describe·upcoming·projects·and·internships.·Our·employees·are·available·at·these·events·to·describe-each·internship·opportunity·and·to·answer·yo...·tudios·and·are-open-to·all·eligible·students·enrolled·in·local·f...

Selected list

•→ Technical·(camera,·lighting,·sound) → September·4,·7:00·p...
•→ Artists·(makeup,·costume·design) → September·5,·6:00·p...
•→ Filming·(directing·and·producing) → September·6,·7:00·p...
•→ Art·(set-design,·storyboards,·illustrators)September·7,·6:00·p...
•→ Animation → September·11,·7:00·p.m.,·Animation·Lab¶
•→ Music→September·12,·6:00·p.m.,·Cafeteria¶

For·more·information·and·to·sign·up·for·our·weekly·newslett...
www.sturgeonpointproductions.com.·Be·sure·to·view·the·following·v...
important·skills·you·will·develop·as·an·intern·with·Sturgeon·Point·Pro...

Bullets button arrow

Recently Used Bulle...
•

Bullet Library
None • ○ ■ ▲ ❖
➤ ✓

Document Bullets
•

Bullet Library

→⌐ Change List Level
    Define New Bullet...

PAGE 2 OF 2   52 OF 446 WORDS

100%

ALERT! | **Did Your Bullet Symbols Disappear?**

If the bullet symbols no longer display, then you clicked the Bullets button. The Bullets button is a toggle button that turns the bullet symbols on and off. Click Undo to reapply the bullets, and then repeat Step 3, making sure that you click the Bullets button arrow.

4 Under **Bullet Library**, click the **check mark** symbol. If the check mark is not available, choose another bullet symbol.

5 With the bulleted list still selected, right-click over the list, and then on the mini toolbar, double-click **Format Painter** ⬝.

🔄 **ANOTHER WAY**   On the HOME tab, in the Clipboard group, click Format Painter.

6 Use the vertical scroll bar or your mouse wheel to scroll to view **Page 1**. Move the pointer to the left of the first item in the first bulleted list to display the ⬝ pointer, and then drag down to select all six items in the list and to apply the format of the third bulleted list—the check mark bullets—to this list. Repeat this procedure to change the bullets in the second list to check marks. Press ⬝Esc⬝ to turn off **Format Painter**, and then **Save** ⬝ your document. Compare your screen with Figure 1.41.

FIGURE 1.41

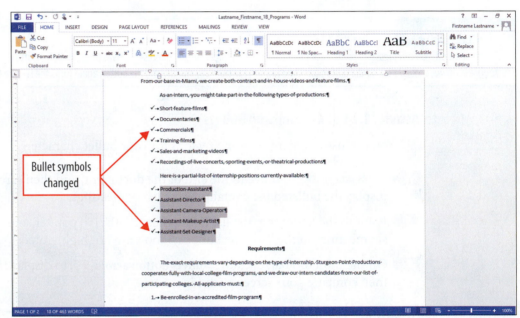

Bullet symbols changed

Objective 7 | Set and Modify Tab Stops

Video W1-7

Tab stops mark specific locations on a line of text. Use tab stops to indent and align text, and use the ⬝Tab⬝ key to move to tab stops.

Activity 1.25 | Setting Tab Stops

1 Scroll to view **Page 2**, and then by using the ⬝ pointer at the left of the first item, select all of the items in the bulleted list of meetings and dates. Notice that there is a tab mark between the name of the meeting and the date.

The arrow that indicates a tab is a nonprinting formatting mark.

2 To the left of the horizontal ruler, point to **Tab Alignment** ⬝ to display the *Left Tab* ScreenTip, and then compare your screen with Figure 1.42.

FIGURE 1.42

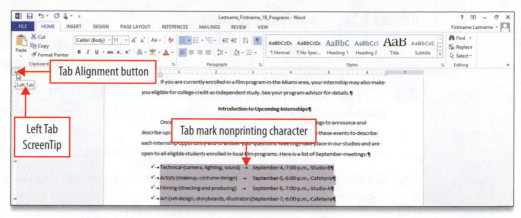

3 Click **Tab Alignment** several times to view the tab alignment options shown in the table in Figure 1.43.

FIGURE 1.43

TAB ALIGNMENT OPTIONS		
TYPE	**TAB ALIGNMENT BUTTON DISPLAYS THIS MARKER**	**RESULT OF TAB ALIGNMENT**
Left	⌐	Text is left aligned at the tab stop and extends to the right.
Center	⊥	Text is centered around the tab stop.
Right	⌐	Text is right aligned at the tab stop and extends to the left.
Decimal	⊥	The decimal point aligns at the tab stop.
Bar	▮	A vertical bar displays at the tab stop.
First Line Indent	▽	Text in the first line of a paragraph indents.
Hanging Indent	⌂	Text in all lines except the first line in the paragraph indents.

4 Display **Left Tab**. Along the lower edge of the horizontal ruler, point to and then click at **3.5 inches on the horizontal ruler**. Notice that all of the dates left align at the new tab stop location, and the right edge of the column is uneven.

5 Compare your screen with Figure 1.44, and then **Save** your document.

FIGURE 1.44

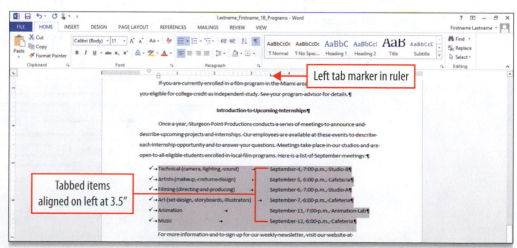

Activity 1.26 | Modifying Tab Stops

Tab stops are a form of paragraph formatting. Therefore, the information about tab stops is stored in the paragraph mark in the paragraphs to which they were applied.

1 With the bulleted list still selected, on the ruler, point to the new tab marker at **3.5 inches on the horizontal ruler**, and then when the *Left Tab* ScreenTip displays, drag the tab marker to **4 inches on the horizontal ruler**.

In all of the selected lines, the text at the tab stop left aligns at 4 inches.

2 On the ruler, point to the tab marker that you moved to display the *Left Tab* ScreenTip, and then double-click to display the **Tabs** dialog box.

ANOTHER WAY On the HOME tab, in the Paragraph group, click the Dialog Box Launcher. At the bottom of the Paragraph dialog box, click the Tabs button.

3 In the **Tabs** dialog box, under **Tab stop position**, if necessary, select *4"* and then type **6**

4 Under **Alignment**, click the **Right** option button. Under **Leader**, click the **2** option button. Near the bottom of the **Tabs** dialog box, click **Set**.

Because the Right tab will be used to align the items in the list, the tab stop at 4" is no longer necessary.

5 In the **Tabs** dialog box, in the **Tab stop position** box, click **4"** to select this tab stop, and then in the lower portion of the **Tabs** dialog box, click the **Clear** button to delete this tab stop, which is no longer necessary. Compare your screen with Figure 1.45.

FIGURE 1.45

6 Click **OK**. On the ruler, notice that the left tab marker at *4"* no longer displays, a right tab marker displays at *6"*, and a series of dots—a ***dot leader***—displays between the columns of the list. Notice also that the right edge of the column is even. Compare your screen with Figure 1.46.

A ***leader character*** creates a solid, dotted, or dashed line that fills the space to the left of a tab character and draws the reader's eyes across the page from one item to the next. When the character used for the leader is a dot, it is commonly referred to as a dot leader.

FIGURE 1.46

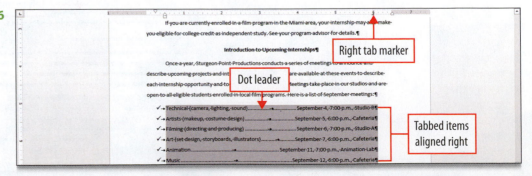

7 ▶ In the bulleted list that uses dot leaders, locate the *Art* meeting, and then click to position the insertion point at the end of that line, after the word *Cafeteria*. Press Enter to create a new blank bullet item.

8 ▶ Type **Video Editing** and press Tab. Notice that a dot leader fills the space to the tab marker location.

9 ▶ Type **September 10, 7:00 p.m., Cafeteria** and notice that the text moves to the left to maintain the right alignment of the tab stop.

10 ▶ **Save** 🖫 your document.

Objective 8 Insert a SmartArt Graphic and an Online Video

Video W1-8

SmartArt graphics are designer-quality visual representations of information, and Word provides many different layouts from which you can choose. You can also insert a link to an online video from a variety of online sources, thus enabling the reader to view the video when connected to the Internet. SmartArt graphics and videos can communicate your messages or ideas more effectively than plain text and these objects add visual interest to a document or webpage.

Activity 1.27 | Inserting a SmartArt Graphic

1 ▶ Press Ctrl + Home to move to the top of the document, and then click to the right of the subtitle *Internship Guide*.

2 ▶ Click the **INSERT tab**, and then in the **Illustrations group**, point to **SmartArt** to display its ScreenTip. Read the ScreenTip, and then click **SmartArt**.

3 ▶ In the center portion of the **Choose a SmartArt Graphic** dialog box, scroll down and examine the numerous types of SmartArt graphics available.

4 ▶ On the left, click **Process**, and then by using the ScreenTips, locate and click **Basic Chevron Process**. Compare your screen with Figure 1.47.

At the right of the dialog box, a preview and description of the SmartArt displays.

FIGURE 1.47

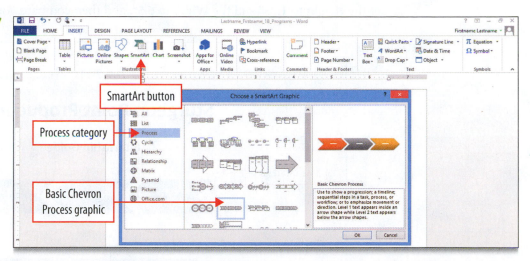

5 ▶ Click **OK** to insert the SmartArt graphic.

To the left of the inserted SmartArt graphic the text pane may display. The text pane provides one method for entering text into your SmartArt graphic. If you choose not to use the text pane to enter text, you can close it.

6 ▶ On the ribbon under **SMARTART TOOLS**, on the **DESIGN tab**, in the **Create Graphic group**, notice the **Text Pane** button. If the Text Pane button is selected, click **Text Pane** to close the pane.

7 ▶ In the SmartArt graphic, in the first blue arrow, click *[Text]*, and notice that *[Text]* is replaced by a blinking insertion point.

The word *[Text]* is called ***placeholder text***, which is non-printing text that indicates where you can type.

8 ▶ Type **Apply Online**

9 ▶ Click the placeholder text in the middle arrow. Type **Interview** and then click the placeholder text in the third arrow. Type **Train on the Job** and then compare your screen with Figure 1.48.

FIGURE 1.48

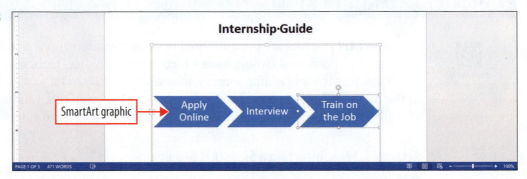

10 ▶ **Save** 🖫 your document.

Activity 1.28 | Sizing and Formatting a SmartArt Graphic

1 ▶ Click the SmartArt graphic border to select it. Be sure that none of the arrows have sizing handles around their border, which would indicate the arrow was selected, not the entire graphic.

2 ▶ Click the **FORMAT tab**, and then in the **Size group**, if necessary, click **Size** to display the **Shape Height** and **Shape Width** boxes.

3 ▶ Set the **Height** to **1.75"** and the **Width** to **6.5"**, and then compare your screen with Figure 1.49.

FIGURE 1.49

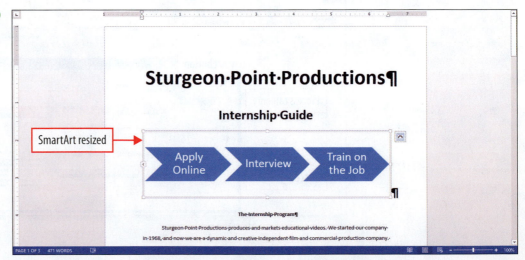

4 With the SmartArt graphic still selected, click the **SMARTART TOOLS DESIGN tab**, and then in the **SmartArt Styles group**, click **Change Colors**. Under **Colorful**, click the fourth style—**Colorful Range–Accent Colors 4 to 5**.

5 On the **SMARTART TOOLS DESIGN tab**, in the **SmartArt Styles group**, click **More** ⬇. Under **3-D**, click the second style—**Inset**. Click **Save** 💾, and then compare your screen with Figure 1.50.

FIGURE 1.50

Activity 1.29 | Inserting an Online Video

Microsoft's research indicates that two-thirds of people who open Word documents never edit them; they only read them. So with more and more documents being read online—and not on paper—it makes sense that you may want to include videos in your Word documents.

1 Press [Ctrl] + [End] to move to the end of the document.

2 On the **INSERT tab**, in the **Media group**, click **Online Video**. If the YouTube search box does not display, in the lower left corner of the Insert Video window, under Also insert from: click YouTube.

> Here you can search the web for an online video, search YouTube, or enter an *embed code* to insert a link to a video from a website. An embed code is a code that creates a link to a video, picture, or other type of *rich media* content. Rich media, also called *interactive media*, refers to computer interaction that responds to your actions; for example by presenting text, graphics, animation, video, audio, or games.

3 In the **Search YouTube** box, being sure to include the quotation marks, type **"Go 2013 1B Video"** and then press [Enter].

4 Point to the displayed thumbnail and notice the ScreenTip. Click the **1B video**, and then click **Insert**. Compare your screen with Figure 1.51.

FIGURE 1.51

5 In the center of the video, point to the **Play** button ▶ to display the 🖑 pointer, and then click. If a black screen displays, double-click one or more times until you see text on the screen, then point to the lower edge of the screen and click the Play button.

> A new window opens that contains the video and a play button. You can click the play button to view the video. When you insert an online video, the embed code is stored with the document and a link is created to the online content. In this manner, you can easily share video content that is relevant to the document without increasing the file size of the document.

6 View a few seconds of the video—more if you want—and then press Esc to return to your document.

7 Click **Save** 🖫, and then press Ctrl + Home to move to the top of your document.

8 Click the **FILE tab**, and then in the lower right portion of the screen, click **Show All Properties**. In the **Tags** box, type **internship** and in the **Subject** box, type your course name and section number. In the **Author** box, be sure your name displays; edit if necessary.

9 On the left, click **Print** to display **Print Preview**. At the bottom of the preview, click the **Previous Page** ◀ and **Next Page** ▶ buttons to move between pages. If necessary, return to the document and make any necessary changes.

10 As directed by your instructor, print your document or submit it electronically. **Save** 🖫 your document and **Close** ✕ Word.

END | You have completed Project 1B

Objective   Create a Handout in the Word Web App

You can use the Word Web App to edit your document if you are not at a computer on which Word 2013 is installed. You can change fonts and font sizes, modify paragraph alignment, and apply bullets and numbering.

> **A L E R T !**   **Working with Web-Based Applications and Services**
>
> Computer programs and services on the web receive continuous updates and improvements, so the steps to complete this web-based activity may differ from the ones shown. You can often look at the screens and the information presented to determine how to complete the activity.

Activity | Creating a Handout in the Word Web App

In this activity, you will use the Word Web App to edit a flyer similar to the one you edited in Project 1B.

1 Start Word, and then below the **Recent** list, click **Open Other Documents**. Navigate to your student data files, and then open **w01_1B_Web**. If necessary, in the upper right corner, log into Office with your Microsoft account. On the **FILE tab**, click **Save As**, and then on the right, click the name of your SkyDrive.

2 In the **Save As** dialog box, click your **GO! Web Projects** folder, and then click **Open**. In the **File name** box, type **Lastname_Firstname_WD_1B_Web** and then click **Save**.

3 Close Word, launch **Internet Explorer**, go to http://skydrive.com, sign in, and then open the file you just saved there. In the upper left, click **EDIT DOCUMENT**, and the click **Edit in Word Web App**.

4 Double-click the file that you just renamed, and then click **EDIT DOCUMENT**. On the list, click **Edit in Word Web App**.

5 Press Ctrl + A to select all the text in the document. On the **HOME tab**, in the **Paragraph group**, click **Align Text Left**.

6 Drag to select the first three lines in the document. On the **HOME tab**, in the **Paragraph group**, click **Center**. Compare your screen with Figure A.

7 Click at the beginning of the paragraph that begins *Sturgeon Point Productions produces*, and then press Tab. Click at the beginning of the paragraph that begins *As an intern*, and then press Tab.

8 Scroll the document and click at the beginning of the paragraph that begins *Here is a partial*, and then press Tab.

FIGURE A

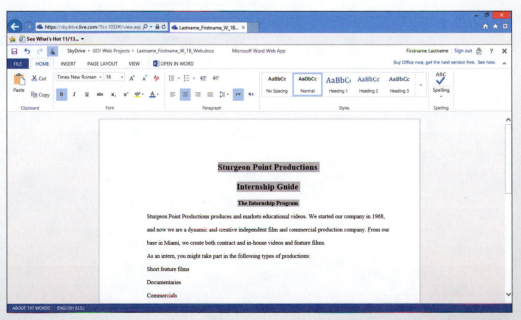

(GO! with Office Web Apps continues on the next page)

9 Click anywhere in the subheading *Introduction to Upcoming Internships*, and then on the **HOME tab**, in the **Paragraph group**, click **Center** 🗏. Click at the beginning of the paragraph that begins *Once a year*, and then press Tab.

10 Select the six paragraphs that begin with *Short feature films* and that end with *Recordings of live concerts*. On the **HOME tab**, in the **Paragraph group**, click **Bullets** ⋮ to apply round, filled bullets to the selection.

11 Select the list that begins with *Production Assistant* and ends with *Assistant Set Designer*, and then click **Bullets** ⋮ to apply bullets to the selection.

12 Select the first list to which you applied bullets. On the **HOME tab**, in the **Paragraph group**, click the **Bullets**

button arrow, and then click **Square Bullet**. Notice that the same bullet style is applied to the second list.

13 Scroll the document and then select the list that begins with *Artists* and ends with *Music*. On the **HOME tab**, in the **Paragraph group**, click **Numbering** ⋮ to apply numbers to the list.

14 Press Ctrl + A to select the entire document. On the **HOME tab**, in the **Paragraph group**, click **Line Spacing** ⋮, and then click **1.5** to change the line spacing for the entire document. Press Ctrl + Home to move to the top of the document and then compare your screen with Figure B.

15 **Save** your file and submit as directed by your instructor. Then, on the ribbon, click the **FILE tab** and click **Exit**.

FIGURE B

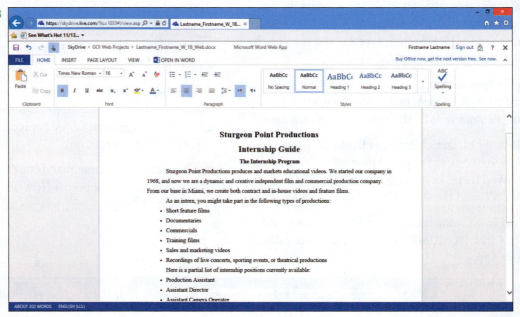

In every job, you must work and communicate with other people. A group of workers tasked with working together to solve a problem, make a decision, or create a work product is referred to as a *team*. For a team to succeed, the team members must be able to communicate with one another easily.

If all the team members work at the same location and work the same hours, communication is easy. You schedule face-to-face meetings and exchange documents and information among yourselves. But that is a rare arrangement in today's organizations. Rather, it is more likely that the members of your team work in different locations—even different countries—and work different hours or travel extensively away from the headquarters location. Also, for specific projects, teams are frequently organized across different departments of an organization or even across different organizations entirely. Then when the project is complete, the team disbands.

Collaboration is when you work together with others as a team in an intellectual endeavor to complete a shared task or achieve a shared goal; for example, when you and one or more of your classmates work together on a class project. Collaboration involves giving feedback to and receiving feedback from others on the team, and then revising the strategies to achieve the goal or produce the work product based on the feedback.

Microsoft Office 365 is a set of secure online services that enable people in an organization to communicate and collaborate by using any Internet-connected device—a computer, a tablet, or a mobile phone. Because Office 365 offers access from anywhere to email, Web conferencing, documents, and calendars, everyone on a team can work together easily. Office 365 is intended for use by multiple users in an organization.

Activity | Using the Exchange Online Outlook Meeting Tool to Collaborate

This group project relates to the **Bell Orchid Hotels**. If your instructor assigns this project to your class, you can expect to use the **Outlook Meeting tool** in **Office 365 Exchange Online** to collaborate on the following tasks for this chapter:

- If you are in the **Accounting Group**, you and your teammates will meet virtually to compose, format, proofread, and prepare a letter to send to shareholders.

- If you are in the **Engineering Group**, you and your teammates will meet virtually to compose, format, proofread, and prepare a letter to the three insurance companies that cover the hotel properties.

- If you are in the **Food and Beverage Group**, you and your teammates will meet virtually to compose, format, proofread, and finalize a letter to a customer planning a banquet.

- If you are in the **Human Resources Group**, you and your teammates will meet virtually to compose, format, proofread, and finalize a memo for employees regarding the new employee newsletter.

- If you are in the **Operations Group**, you and your teammates will meet virtually to compose, format, proofread, and finalize letters to three job applicants.

- If you are in the **Sales and Marketing Group**, you and your teammates will meet virtually to compose, edit, and finalize a letter to 20 groups of professional associations.

FIGURE A

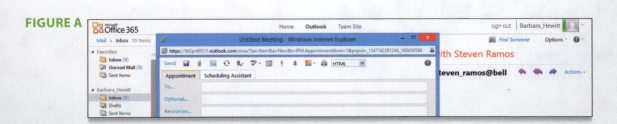

END OF CHAPTER

SUMMARY

In a document, you can type all of the text, or you can type some of the text and then insert additional text from another source such as another Word document. As you type, word wrap determines the line endings.

Graphics include pictures, shapes, and text boxes. Use graphics, text effects, and pictures to add visual appeal. When you insert pictures, Word provides many ways to position and format the pictures on the page.

SmartArt graphics visually represent your ideas and there are many SmartArt graphics from which to choose. You can also use online videos in your documents to provide visual information to the reader.

Word documents can be formatted to display your information attractively. You can add a page border, add bulleted and numbered lists, change margins and tabs, and modify paragraph and line spacing.

GO! LEARN IT ONLINE

Review the concepts and key terms in this chapter by completing these online challenges, which you can find at **www.pearsonhighered.com/go.**

Matching and Multiple Choice: Answer matching and multiple choice questions to test what you learned in this chapter. MyITLab®

Crossword Puzzle: Spell out the words that match the numbered clues, and put them in the puzzle squares.

Flipboard: Flip through the definitions of the key terms in this chapter and match them with the correct term.

GO! FOR JOB SUCCESS

Video: Personal Branding

Your instructor may assign this video to your class, and then ask you to think about, or discuss with your classmates, these questions:

FotolEdhar / Fotolia

How do you suggest job seekers communicate their unique value—their *personal brand*—to potential employers online?

What are the best ways to network online and offline?

What are some of the biggest pitfalls in using social media to communicate a personal brand?

END OF CHAPTER
REVIEW AND ASSESSMENT GUIDE FOR WORD CHAPTER 1

Your instructor may assign one or more of these projects to help you review the chapter and assess your mastery and understanding of the chapter.

	Review and Assessment Guide for Word Chapter 1		
Project	**Apply Skills from These Chapter Objectives**	**Project Type**	**Project Location**
1C	Objectives 1-4 from Project 1A	**1C Skills Review** A guided review of the skills from Project 1A.	On the following pages
1D	Objectives 5-8 from Project 1B	**1D Skills Review** A guided review of the skills from Project 1B.	On the following pages
1E	Objectives 1-4 from Project 1A	**1E Mastery (Grader Project)** A demonstration of your mastery of the skills in Project 1A with extensive decision making.	In MyITLab and on the following pages
1F	Objectives 5-8 from Project 1B	**1F Mastery (Grader Project)** A demonstration of your mastery of the skills in Project 1B with extensive decision making.	In MyITLab and on the following pages
1G	Objectives 1-8 from Projects 1A and 1B	**1G Mastery (Grader Project)** A demonstration of your mastery of the skills in Projects 1A and 1B with extensive decision making.	In MyITLab and on the following pages
1H	Combination of Objectives from Projects 1A and 1B	**1H GO! Fix It** A demonstration of your mastery of the skills in Projects 1A and 1B by creating a correct result from a document that contains errors you must find.	Online
1I	Combination of Objectives from Projects 1A and 1B	**1I GO! Make It** A demonstration of your mastery of the skills in Projects 1A and 1B by creating a result from a supplied picture.	Online
1J	Combination of Objectives from Projects 1A and 1B	**1J GO! Solve It** A demonstration of your mastery of the skills in Projects 1A and 1B, your decision-making skills, and your critical thinking skills. A task-specific rubric helps you self-assess your result.	Online
1K	Combination of Objectives from Projects 1A and 1B	**1K GO! Solve It** A demonstration of your mastery of the skills in Projects 1A and 1B, your decision-making skills, and your critical thinking skills. A task-specific rubric helps you self-assess your result.	On the following pages
1L	Combination of Objectives from Projects 1A and 1B	**1L GO! Think** A demonstration of your understanding of the chapter concepts applied in a manner that you would outside of college. An analytic rubric helps you and your instructor grade the quality of your work by comparing it to the work an expert in the discipline would create.	On the following pages
1M	Combination of Objectives from Projects 1A and 1B	**1M GO! Think** A demonstration of your understanding of the chapter concepts applied in a manner that you would outside of college. An analytic rubric helps you and your instructor grade the quality of your work by comparing it to the work an expert in the discipline would create.	Online
1N	Combination of Objectives from Projects 1A and 1B	**1N You and GO!** A demonstration of your understanding of the chapter concepts applied in a manner that you would in a personal situation. An analytic rubric helps you and your instructor grade the quality of your work.	Online
1O	Combination of Objectives from Projects 1A and 1B	**1O Cumulative Group Project for Word Chapter 1** A demonstration of your understanding of concepts and your ability to work collaboratively in a group role-playing assessment, requiring both collaboration and self-management.	Online

GLOSSARY

GLOSSARY OF CHAPTER KEY TERMS

Alignment The placement of paragraph text relative to the left and right margins.

Alignment guide Green vertical or horizontal lines that display when you are moving or sizing an object to assist you with object placement.

Artistic effects Formats applied to images that make pictures resemble sketches or paintings.

Bulleted list A list of items with each item introduced by a symbol such as a small circle or check mark, and which is useful when the items in the list can be displayed in any order.

Bullets Text symbols such as small circles or check marks that precede each item in a bulleted list.

Center alignment The alignment of text or objects that is centered horizontally between the left and right margin.

Collaboration The action of working together with others as a team in an intellectual endeavor to complete a shared task or achieve a shared goal.

Decrease Indent A command that moves your paragraph closer to the margin.

Dot leader A series of dots preceding a tab that guides the eye across the line.

Drawing objects Graphic objects, such as shapes, diagrams, lines, or circles.

Embed code A code that creates a link to a video, picture, or other type of rich media content.

Floating object A graphic that can be moved independently of the surrounding text characters.

Formatting marks Characters that display on the screen, but do not print, indicating where the Enter key, the Spacebar, and the Tab key were pressed; also called nonprinting characters.

Graphics Pictures, charts, or drawing objects.

Increase Indent A command moves your paragraph farther away from the margin.

Inline Object An object or graphic inserted in a document that acts like a character in a sentence.

Interactive media Computer interaction that responds to your actions; for example by presenting text, graphics, animation, video, audio, or games. Also referred to as rich media.

Justified alignment An arrangement of text in which the text aligns evenly on both the left and right margins.

Layout Options Picture formatting options that control the manner in which text wraps around a picture or other object.

Leader character Characters that form a solid, dotted, or dashed line that fills the space preceding a tab stop.

Left alignment An arrangement of text in which the text aligns at the left margin, leaving the right margin uneven.

Line spacing The distance between lines of text in a paragraph.

Live Layout A feature that reflows text as you move or size an object so that you can view the placement of surrounding text.

Margins The space between the text and the top, bottom, left, and right edges of the paper.

Microsoft Office 365 A set of secure online services that enable people in an organization to communicate and collaborate by using any Internet-connected device—a computer, a tablet, or a mobile phone.

Nonprinting characters Characters that display on the screen, but do not print; also called formatting marks.

Numbered list A list that uses consecutive numbers or letters to introduce each item in a list.

Object anchor The symbol that indicates to which paragraph an object is attached.

Picture Effects Formatting that enhances a picture with effects such as shadow, glow, reflection, or 3-D rotation.

Picture styles Frames, shapes, shadows, borders, and other special effects that can be added to an image to create an overall visual style for the image.

Placeholder text Non-printing text that holds a place in a document where you can type.

Rich media Computer interaction that responds to your actions; for example by presenting text, graphics, animation, video, audio, or games. Also referred to as interactive media.

Right alignment An arrangement of text in which the text aligns at the right margin, leaving the left margin uneven.

Rotation handle A symbol with which you can rotate a graphic to any angle; displays above the top center sizing handle.

Shapes Lines, arrows, stars, banners, ovals, rectangles, and other basic shapes with which you can illustrate an idea, a process, or a workflow.

SmartArt A designer-quality visual representation of your information that you can create by choosing from among many different layouts to effectively communicate your message or ideas.

Spin box A small box with an upward- and downward-pointing arrow that lets you move rapidly through a set of values by clicking.

Tab stop A specific location on a line of text, marked on the Word ruler, to which you can move the insertion point by pressing the Tab key, and which is used to align and indent text.

Team A group of workers tasked with working together to solve a problem, make a decision, or create a work product.

Template A preformatted document that you can use as a starting point and then change to suit your needs.

Text box A movable resizable container for text or graphics.

Text effects Decorative formats, such as shadowed or mirrored text, text glow, 3-D effects, and colors that make text stand out.

Text wrapping The manner in which text displays around an object.

Toggle button A button that can be turned on by clicking it once, and then turned off by clicking it again.

Wordwrap The feature that moves text from the right edge of a paragraph to the beginning of the next line as necessary to fit within the margins.

CHAPTER REVIEW

Apply 1A skills from these Objectives:

1 Create a New Document and Insert Text
2 Insert and Format Graphics
3 Insert and Modify Text Boxes and Shapes
4 Preview and Print a Document

Build from Scratch

In the following Skills Review, you will create a flyer announcing a photography internship with Sturgeon Point Productions. Your completed document will look similar to Figure 1.52.

PROJECT FILES

For Project 1C, you will need the following files:

New blank Word document
w01C_Building
w01C_Photographer

You will save your document as:

Lastname_Firstname_1C_Photography

PROJECT RESULTS

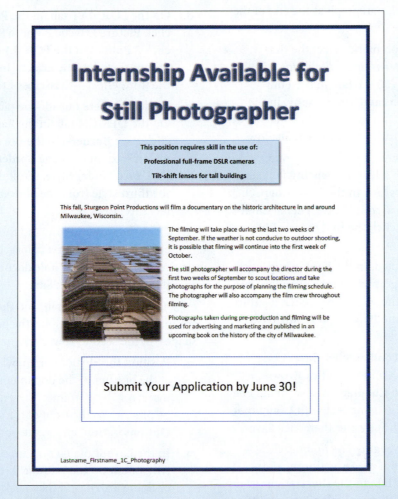

FIGURE 1.52

(Project 1C Photography continues on the next page)

1 ▶ Start Word and then click **Blank document**. On the **HOME tab**, in the **Paragraph group**, if necessary, click **Show/Hide** to display the formatting marks. If the rulers do not display, click the **VIEW tab**, and then in the **Show group**, select the **Ruler** check box.

a. Type **Internship Available for Still Photographer** and then press [Enter] two times. Type the following text: **This fall, Sturgeon Point Productions will film a documentary on the historic architecture in and around Milwaukee, Wisconsin.** Press [Enter].

b. On the ribbon, click the **INSERT tab**. In the **Text group**, click the **Object button arrow**, and then click **Text from File**. In the **Insert File** dialog box, navigate to the student files that accompany this textbook, locate and select **w01C_Photographer**, and then click **Insert**. Delete the blank paragraph at the end of the document.

c. Including the paragraph mark, select the first paragraph of text—*Internship Available for Still Photographer*. On the **HOME tab**, in the **Font group**, click **Text Effects and Typography**. In the **Text Effects** gallery, in the first row, click the fourth effect—**Fill – White, Outline – Accent 1, Shadow**.

d. With the text still selected, in the **Font group**, click in the **Font Size** box to select the existing font size. Type **44** and then press [Enter]. In the **Font group**, click the **Font Color button arrow**. Under **Theme Colors**, in the fourth column, click the first color—**Blue-Gray, Text 2**.

e. With the text still selected, in the **Font group**, click **Text Effects and Typography**. Point to **Shadow**, and then under **Outer**, in the second row, click the third style—**Offset Left**. In the **Paragraph group**, click **Center**.

f. On the **Quick Access Toolbar**, click **Save**. Under **Places**, click **Computer**, and then click **Browse**. Navigate to your **Word Chapter 1** folder. In the **File name** box, replace the existing text with **Lastname_Firstname_1C_Photography** and then click **Save**.

2 ▶ In the paragraph that begins *The filming*, click to position the insertion point at the beginning of the paragraph. On the **INSERT tab**, in the **Illustrations group**, click **Pictures**. In the **Insert Picture** dialog box, navigate to your student data files, locate and click **w01C_Building**, and then click **Insert**.

a. To the right of the selected picture, click the **Layout Options** button, and then under **With Text Wrapping**, click the first option—**Square**. **Close** the **Layout Options**.

b. On the **FORMAT tab**, in the **Size group**, click the **Shape Height spin box down arrow** as necessary to change the height of the picture to **2.7"**.

c. With the picture selected, on the **FORMAT tab**, in the **Arrange group**, click **Position**, and then click **More Layout Options**. In the **Layout** dialog box, on the **Position tab**, in the middle of the dialog box, under **Vertical**, click the **Alignment** option button. To the right of **Alignment**, click the arrow, and then click **Top**. To the right of **relative to**, click the arrow, and then click **Line**. Click **OK**.

d. On the **FORMAT tab**, in the **Picture Styles group**, click **Picture Effects**. Point to **Soft Edges**, and then click **5 Point**. On the **FORMAT tab**, in the **Adjust group**, click **Artistic Effects**. In the fourth row, click the third effect—**Crisscross Etching**.

e. Click anywhere outside the picture to deselect it. On the **DESIGN tab**, in the **Page Background group**, click **Page Borders**. In the **Borders and Shading** dialog box, on the **Page Border tab**, under **Setting**, click **Box**. Under **Style**, scroll the list and then click the third style from the bottom—a black line that fades to gray.

f. Click the **Color arrow**, and then in the next to last column, click the first color—**Blue, Accent 5**. Under **Apply to**, be sure **Whole document** is selected, and then click **OK**. Click **Save**.

3 ▶ Click the **INSERT tab**, and then in the **Illustrations group**, click **Shapes** to display the gallery. Under **Basic Shapes**, in the second row, click the fifth shape—**Frame**.

a. Position the ⊞ pointer anywhere in the blank area at the bottom of the document. Click one time to insert a 1" by 1" frame. The exact location need not be precise. To the right of the shape, click the **Layout Options** button, and at the bottom click **See more**.

b. In the **Layout** dialog box, under **Horizontal**, click the **Alignment** option button. To the right of **Alignment**, click the arrow, and then click **Centered**. To the right of **relative to**, click the arrow, and then click **Page**. Under **Vertical**, click the **Absolute position**

(Project 1C Photography continues on the next page)

option button. In the **Absolute position** box, select the existing number, and then type **1** To the right of **below**, click the arrow, and then click **Paragraph**. Click **OK**.

c. On the **FORMAT tab**, click in the **Shape Height** box. Type **1.5** and then click in the **Shape Width** box. Type **5.5** and then press Enter.

d. If necessary, select the frame shape. On the **FORMAT tab**, in the **Shape Styles group**, click **More** ⬇. In the **Shape Styles** gallery, in the first row, click the sixth style—**Colored Outline - Blue, Accent 5**. Type **Submit Your Application by June 30!** Select the text you just typed, and then on the mini toolbar, change the **Font Size** to **22**.

4 Click outside of the frame to deselect, and then press Ctrl + Home to move to the top of the document. Press ↓ two times to move to the blank paragraph below the title. Press Enter four times to make space for a text box.

a. On the **INSERT tab**, in the **Text group**, click **Text Box**. At the bottom of the gallery, click **Draw Text Box**. Position the ✛ pointer over the first blank paragraph at the left margin. Drag down and to the right to create a text box approximately 1.5 inches high and 4 inches wide—the exact size and location need not be precise.

b. With the insertion point blinking in the text box, type the following, pressing Enter after the first two lines to create a new paragraph; do *not* press Enter after the last line:

This position requires skill in the use of:

Professional full-frame DSLR cameras

Tilt-shift lenses for tall buildings

c. To precisely place the text box, on the **FORMAT tab**, in the **Arrange group**, click **Position**, and then click **More Layout Options**. In the **Layout** dialog box, under **Horizontal**, click the **Alignment** button. To the right of **Alignment**, click the arrow, and then click **Centered**. To the right of *relative to*, click the arrow, and then click **Page**.

d. Under **Vertical**, click the **Absolute position** button. In the **Absolute position** box, select the existing number. Type **2** To the right of **below**, click the **arrow**, and then click **Margin**.

e. In the **Layout** dialog box, click the **Size tab**. Under **Height**, select the number in the **Absolute** box. Type **1** and then under **Width**, select the number in the **Absolute** box. Type **3.75** and then click **OK**.

f. In the text box, select all of the text. If necessary, right-click over the selected text to display the mini toolbar. Change the **Font Size** to **12**, apply **Bold**, and then press Ctrl + E to **Center** the text.

g. On the **FORMAT tab**, in the **Shape Styles group**, click **Shape Effects**. Point to **Shadow**, and then under **Outer**, in the first row, click the first style—**Offset Diagonal Bottom Right**.

h. In the **Shape Styles group**, click **Shape Outline**. In the fifth column, click the first color—**Blue, Accent 1** to change the color of the text box border. Click **Shape Fill**, and then in the fifth column, click the second color—**Blue, Accent 1, Lighter 80%**. Click **Save**.

5 Click the **INSERT tab**, and then in the **Header & Footer group**, click **Footer**. At the bottom of the menu, click **Edit Footer**. On the **HEADER & FOOTER TOOLS DESIGN tab**, in the **Insert group**, click **Document Info**, and then click **File Name**. Double-click in the document outside of the footer area to close the footer and return to the document.

a. Press Ctrl + Home to move the insertion point to the top of the document. In the upper left corner of your screen, click the **FILE** tab to display **Backstage** view. On the right, at the bottom of the **Properties list**, click **Show All Properties**.

b. On the list of Properties, click to the right of **Tags** to display an empty box, and then type **internship, photographer** Click to the right of **Subject** to display an empty box, and then type your course name and section #. Under **Related People**, be sure that your name displays as the author. If necessary, edit the author name.

c. **Save** your file and submit as directed by your instructor. **Close** Word.

END | You have completed Project 1C

CHAPTER REVIEW

Apply 1B skills from these Objectives:

5 Change Document and Paragraph Layout

6 Create and Modify Lists

7 Set and Modify Tab Stops

8 Insert a SmartArt Graphic and an Online Video

In the following Skills Review, you will edit an information handout regarding production and development internships with Sturgeon Point Productions. Your completed document will look similar to Figure 1.53.

PROJECT FILES

For Project 1D, you will need the following file:

w01D_Internship

You will save your document as:

Lastname_Firstname_1D_Internship

PROJECT RESULTS

FIGURE 1.53

(Project 1D Internships continues on the next page)

CHAPTER REVIEW

1 Start Word, and then click **Open Other Documents**. Click **Computer**, and then click **Browse**. Navigate to your student files, and then open **w01D_Internship**. On the **HOME tab**, in the **Paragraph group**, be sure **Show/Hide** is active. Click the **FILE tab**, and then click **Save As**. Navigate to your **Word Chapter 1** folder, and then **Save** the document as **Lastname_Firstname_1D_Internship**

a. Click the **PAGE LAYOUT tab**. In the **Page Setup group**, click **Margins**, and then click **Custom Margins**. In the **Page Setup** dialog box, press Tab as necessary to select the value in the **Left** box. Type **1** and then press Tab to select the value in the **Right** box. Type **1** and then click **OK**.

b. Scroll down to view the bottom of **Page 1**, point anywhere in the bottom margin area, right-click, and then click **Edit Footer** to display the footer area. On the **HEADER & FOOTER TOOLS DESIGN tab**, in the **Insert group**, click **Document Info**, and then click **File Name**. Double-click anywhere in the document to close the footer area.

c. Press Ctrl + A to select all of the text in the document, and then on the **HOME tab**, in the **Paragraph group**, click **Align Left**.

d. Press Ctrl + Home. Select the document title, and then on the **HOME tab**, in the **Paragraph group**, click **Center**.

e. Locate the first bold subheading—*In-House Office Internships*. Point to the left of the paragraph to display the ⬚ pointer, and then click one time to select the text. With *In-House Office Internships* selected, locate the subheading *Additional Information*. Move the pointer to the left of the paragraph to display the ⬚ pointer, hold down Ctrl, and then click one time to select both paragraphs. In the **Paragraph group**, click **Center**.

f. Press Ctrl + A to select all of the text in the document. On the **HOME tab**, in the **Paragraph group**, click **Line and Paragraph Spacing**, and then click **1.5**.

2 Below the title of the document, click anywhere in the paragraph that begins *Sturgeon Point Productions is a full service*. On the **HOME tab**, in the **Paragraph group**, click the **Dialog Box Launcher** ⬚.

a. In the **Paragraph** dialog box, on the **Indents and Spacing tab**, under **Indentation**, click the **Special**

arrow, and then click **First line** to indent the first line by 0.5". Click **OK**, and then click anywhere in the paragraph that begins *Sturgeon Point Productions is looking for*. On the ruler under the ribbon, drag the **First Line Indent** marker to **0.5 inches on the horizontal ruler**.

b. Press Ctrl + A to select all of the text in the document. Click the **PAGE LAYOUT tab**, and then in the **Paragraph group**, under **Spacing**, click the **After spin box up arrow** one time to change the value to **6 pt**.

c. Select the subheading *In-House Office Internships*, including the paragraph mark following it. Scroll down, hold down Ctrl, and then select the subheading *Additional Information*. With both subheadings selected, in the **Paragraph group**, under **Spacing**, click the **Before up spin box arrow** two times to set the **Spacing Before** to **12 pt**. **Save** your document.

3 Locate the first paragraph that begins *Development Department*, and then point to this paragraph from the left margin area to display the ⬚ pointer. Drag down to select this paragraph and the next five paragraphs so that six paragraphs are selected. On the **HOME tab**, in the **Paragraph group**, click **Bullets** to change the selected text to a bulleted list.

a. Under the subheading *In-House Office Internships*, in the paragraph that begins *Sturgeon Point Productions*, click to position the insertion point at the *end* of the paragraph, following the colon. Press Enter to create a blank paragraph. On the ruler, drag the **First Line Indent** marker to the left so that it is positioned directly above the lower button. Being sure to include the period, type **1.** and then press Spacebar to create the first item in a numbered list.

b. Type **Be enrolled as a film major at a participating local college or university** and then press Enter. Type **Maintain a 3.0 GPA** and then press Enter. Type **Receive satisfactory monthly progress reports from their direct supervisor**

c. Scroll down to view the bulleted list of departments, and then select all six bulleted items in the list. On the mini toolbar, click the **Bullets button arrow**, and then under **Bullet Library**, click the **check mark** symbol. If the check mark is not available, choose another bullet symbol.

(Project 1D Internships continues on the next page)

CHAPTER REVIEW

4▸ With the list selected, move the pointer to the horizontal ruler, and then point to and click at **3.5 inches on the horizontal ruler** to insert a tab and align the job titles at the tab mark.

a. With the bulleted list still selected, on the ruler, point to the new tab marker at **3.5 inches on the horizontal ruler**, and then when the *Left Tab* ScreenTip displays, drag the tab marker to **4 inches on the horizontal ruler**.

b. On the ruler, point to the tab marker that you moved to display the *Left Tab* ScreenTip, and then double-click to display the **Tabs** dialog box.

c. In the **Tabs** dialog box, under **Tab stop position**, if necessary select *4"*, and then type **6** Under **Alignment**, click the **Right** option button. Under **Leader**, click the **2** option button. Near the bottom of the **Tabs** dialog box, click **Set**.

d. Under **Tab stop position**, select **4"**, and then click **Clear** to delete the tab stop. Click **OK**. **Save** your document.

5▸ Press Ctrl + Home to move to the top of the document, and then in the title, click to the right of the *S* in *PRODUCTIONS*.

a. Click the **INSERT tab**, and then in the **Illustrations group**, click **SmartArt**. On the left, click **Relationship**, and then scroll the list to the bottom. Locate and then click **Basic Venn**. Click **OK** to insert the SmartArt graphic. If necessary, close the Text Pane.

b. In the SmartArt graphic, click on *[Text]* in the top circle shape. Type **Film** and then click on the placeholder *[Text]* in the lower left shape. Type **Video** In the third circle, type **Internet**

c. Click the SmartArt graphic border to select it. Click the **FORMAT tab**, and then in the **Size group**, if necessary click **Size** to display the **Shape Height** and **Shape Width** boxes. Set the **Height** to **3"** and the **Width** to **6.5"**.

d. With the SmartArt graphic still selected, on the ribbon, under **SMARTART TOOLS**, click the **DESIGN tab**, and then in the **SmartArt Styles group**, click **Change Colors**. Under **Colorful**, click the third style—**Colorful Range–Accent Colors 3 to 4**. On the **DESIGN tab**, in the **SmartArt Styles group**, click **More** ▾. Under **3-D**, in the first row, click the third style—**Cartoon**. Click **Save**.

6▸ Hold down Ctrl and then press End to move to the end of the document. On the **INSERT tab**, in the **Media group**, click **Online Video**. If necessary, in the lower left corner of the Insert Video window, click YouTube. Click in the **Search YouTube** box. Including the quotation marks, type **"Go 2013 1B video"** and then press Enter. In the first row, click the first video, and then click **Insert**.

a. Click the **FILE tab**, and then on the right, click **Show All Properties**. In the **Tags** box, type **internship** and in the **Subject** box, type your course name and section number. Be sure that your name displays as the author. Click **Save**.

b. Click the **FILE tab** to display **Backstage** view. Click **Print** to display **Print Preview**. At the bottom of the preview, click the **Next Page** and **Previous Page** buttons to move between pages. If necessary, return to the document and make any necessary changes.

c. As directed by your instructor, print your document or submit it electronically. **Close** Word.

END | You have completed Project 1D

CONTENT-BASED ASSESSMENTS

MyITLab®
grader

Apply 1A skills from these Objectives:

1 Create a New Document and Insert Text

2 Insert and Format Graphics

3 Insert and Modify Text Boxes and Shapes

4 Preview and Print a Document

Build from Scratch

In the following Mastery project, you will create a flyer announcing a special event being hosted by Sturgeon Point Productions. Your printed results will look similar to those in Figure 1.54.

PROJECT FILES

For Project 1E, you will need the following files:

New blank Word document

w01E_Antarctica

w01E_Filmmaker

You will save your document as:

Lastname_Firstname_1E_Documentary

PROJECT RESULTS

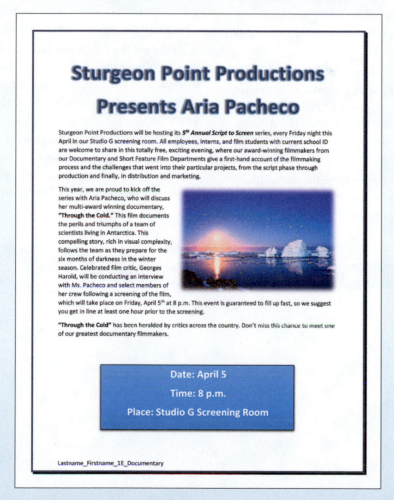

FIGURE 1.54

(Project 1E Documentary continues on the next page)

1 **Start** Word and display a **Blank document** with the ruler and formatting marks displayed. Type **Sturgeon Point Productions Presents Aria Pacheco** and then press Enter. From your student data files, insert the text file **w01E_Filmmaker**. Using your own name, **Save** the document in your **Word Chapter 1** folder as **Lastname_Firstname_1E_Documentary**

2 To the document title, apply the **Fill – White, Outline – Accent 1, Glow – Accent 1** text effect, and then change the **Font Size** to **36**. Change the **Font Color** to **Blue-Gray, Text 2**—in the fourth column, the first color. Apply an **Outer Shadow** using **Offset Left**—in the second row, the third style. **Center** the title.

3 Position the insertion point at the beginning of the paragraph that begins with *This year*, and then from your student data files, insert the picture **w01E_Antarctica**. Change the **Layout Options** to **Square** and then change the **Height** of the picture to **2.5**

4 Using the **Position** command, display the **Layout** dialog box, and then change the **Horizontal Alignment** to **Right relative to** the **Margin**. Apply a **10 Point Soft Edges** picture effect to the image, and then display the **Artistic Effects** gallery. In the third row, apply the fourth effect—**Mosaic Bubbles**.

5 Deselect the picture. Apply a **Page Border** to the document using the **Shadow** setting. Select the first style, and change the **Color** to **Blue-Gray, Text 2**. Change the **Width** to **3 pt**.

6 Below the last paragraph, draw a **Text Box** that is approximately 1.5 inches high and 4 inches wide—the exact size and location need not be precise. In the text box, type the following text:

> **Date: April 5**
>
> **Time: 8 p.m.**
>
> **Place: Studio G Screening Room**

7 Change the **Height** of the text box to **1.5** and the **Width** to **4.5** and then change the font size to **18**. Apply **Bold** and **Center**. To precisely place the text box, display the **Layout** dialog box. Change the **Horizontal Alignment** to **Centered**, **relative to** the **Page**, and then change the **Vertical Absolute position** to **0.5** below the **Paragraph**.

8 Apply a **Shape Style** to the text box—in the last row, select the second style—**Intense Effect – Blue, Accent 1**. Change the **Shape Outline** to **Black, Text 1**.

9 Insert the **File Name** in the footer, and then display the document properties. As the **Tags**, type **documentary, interview** As the **Subject**, type your course and section #. Be sure your name is indicated as the **Author**. **Save** your file.

10 Display the **Print Preview** and if necessary, return to the document and make any necessary changes. As directed by your instructor, print your document or submit it electronically. **Close** Word.

END | You have completed Project 1E

CONTENT-BASED ASSESSMENTS

Mastering Word Project 1F Pitch Festival

In the following Mastery project, you will edit a document with information regarding an event that Sturgeon Point Productions is holding for college students. Your printed results will look similar to those in Figure 1.55.

Apply 1B skills from these Objectives:

5 Change Document and Paragraph Layout

6 Create and Modify Lists

7 Set and Modify Tab Stops

8 Insert a SmartArt Graphic and an Online Video

PROJECT FILES

For Project 1F, you will need the following file:

w01F_Pitch_Festival

You will save your document as:

Lastname_Firstname_1F_Pitch_Festival

PROJECT RESULTS

Pitch Festival!

Do you have a story that must be told? Pitch us your project during the Sturgeon Point Productions annual Pitch Festival! We're setting up several days of conference video calls for college students that are currently enrolled in an accredited film production program anywhere in the United States. If your idea is selected, you will be flown to our studios In Miami, Florida to pitch your idea to our staff of producers and development executives. The following video provides additional information:

Sturgeon Point Productions is one of the leading independent film and video companies in the Miami area. We are currently looking for new, fresh, exciting ideas for short and full-length feature films and documentaries. We like character driven stories that can be shot on an independent budget within one or two locations, preferably either in our studios or in the Miami area. We are currently looking for scripts, ideas, and concepts that are in one of the following categories:

1. Human interest or educational
2. Political or journalistic
3. Biographical or documentary

The Pitch Festival will take place at our secure website on the following dates and times. There are no entry fees to pitch; this unique opportunity to pitch to our staff of professional filmmakers is absolutely free for college film students. Sign up now at www.sturgeonpointproductions.com/pitchfest for one of the following pitch sessions:

- September 12, 11 a.m...Short and Feature Film Pitches
- September 13, 8 p.m. ....Biographical and Documentary Film Pitches
- September 14, 7 p.m. ....Educational Series Pitches

Lastname_Firstname_1F_Pitch_Festival

FIGURE 1.55

(Project 1F Pitch Festival continues on the next page)

CONTENT-BASED ASSESSMENTS

1 Start Word, and then from your student files, open **w01F_Pitch_Festival**. Display formatting marks, and then **Save** the file in your **Word Chapter 1** folder as **Lastname_Firstname_1F_Pitch_Festival**

2 Insert the **File Name** in the footer. Select all the document text, and then change the **Line Spacing** for the entire document to **1.5**. **Center** the document title, and then change the title font size to **24**. Change the **Top** and **Bottom** margins to **0.5**

3 Select the three paragraphs below the title, and then apply a **First line** indent of 0.5". Select the entire document, and then change the **Spacing Before** to **6 pt** and the **Spacing After** to **6 pt**.

4 Select the last three paragraphs containing the dates, and then apply filled square bullets. If the bullets are not available, choose another bullet style. With the bulleted list selected, set a **Right** tab with **dot leaders** at **6"**.

5 Locate the paragraph that begins *Sturgeon Point Productions*, and then click at the end of the paragraph, after the colon. Press [Enter]. Create a numbered list with the following three numbered items; be sure to remove the first line indent before creating the numbered list:

Human interest or educational

Political or journalistic

Biographical or documentary

6 Position the insertion point at the end of the document after the word *Pitches*. Do *not* insert a blank line. Insert a **SmartArt** graphic from the **Process** category. Toward the bottom of the gallery, select the **Equation** SmartArt. Select the outside border of the SmartArt, and then change the **Height** of the SmartArt to **1** and the **Width** to **6.5**

7 With the SmartArt selected, change the layout to **Square**, and change the **Horizontal Alignment** to **Centered relative to** the **Page**. Change the **Vertical Alignment** to **Bottom relative to** the **Margin**.

8 In the first circle type **Your Ideas** and in the second circle type **Our Experts** In the third circle type **Pitch Festival!** Change the SmartArt color to **Colorful Range – Accent Colors 4 to 5**. Apply the **3-D Polished** style.

9 Click at the end of the paragraph below the title. Press [Enter], remove the first line indent, and then center the blank line. Insert an **Online Video**. In the **Search YouTube** box, type, including the quotations marks, **"Go 2013 1F Video"** and then insert the video with the cube on a black background. Change the height of the video to **1.5**.

10 Display the document properties. In the **Tags** box, type **pitch festival** and in the **Subject** box, type your course name and section number. Be sure your name displays as the author.

11 Display the **Print Preview** and if necessary, return to the document and make any necessary changes. As directed by your instructor, print your document or submit it electronically. **Close** Word.

END | You have completed Project 1F

CONTENT-BASED ASSESSMENTS

Mastering Word Project 1G Educational Website

In the following Mastery project, you will create a flyer that details a new educational website that Sturgeon Point Productions has developed for instructors. Your printed results will look similar to those in Figure 1.56.

PROJECT FILES

For Project 1G, you will need the following files:

New blank Word document
w01G_Education
w01G_Media

You will save your document as:

Lastname_Firstname_1G_Educational_Website

Build from Scratch

PROJECT RESULTS

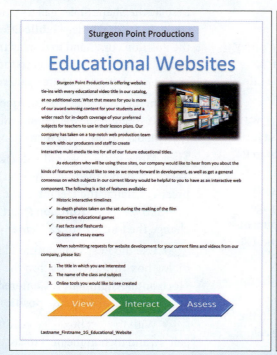

FIGURE 1.56

(Project 1G Educational Website continues on the next page)

CONTENT-BASED ASSESSMENTS

1 Start Word and display a blank document. Display formatting marks and the ruler. Type **Educational Websites** and then press Enter. Type **Sturgeon Point Productions is offering website tie-ins with every educational video title in our catalog, at no additional cost.** Press Spacebar, and then **Save** the document in your **Word Chapter 1** folder as **Lastname_Firstname_1G_Educational_Website**

2 With the insertion point positioned at the end of the sentence that you typed, insert the text from your student data file **w01G_Education**. Change the **Line Spacing** for the entire document to **1.5** and the spacing **After** to **6 pt**. To each of the four paragraphs that begin *Sturgeon Point Productions*, *As educators*, *When submitting*, and *The video*, apply a **First Line** indent of **0.5"**.

3 Change the font size of the title to **50** and then display the **Text Effects and Typography** gallery. Apply the second effect to the title—**Fill – Blue, Accent 1, Shadow**, and then **Center** the title. With only the title selected, change the **Line Spacing** to **1.0**.

4 Click at the beginning of the paragraph below the title, and then from your student data files, insert the picture **w01G_Media**. Change the picture **Height** to **2** and the **Layout Options** to **Square**. Format the picture with **Soft Edges** in **10 Point**, and then use the **Position** command to display the **Layout** dialog box. Change the picture position so that the **Horizontal Alignment** is **Right relative to** the **Margin**. Change the **Vertical Alignment** to **Top relative to** the **Line**.

5 Select the five paragraphs beginning with *Historic interactive timelines* and ending with *Quizzes and essay exams*, and then apply checkmark bullets. In the paragraph below the bulleted list, click after the colon. Press Enter and remove the first line indent. Type a numbered list with the following three numbered items:

The title in which you are interested

The name of the class and subject

Online tools you would like to see created

6 With the insertion point located at the end of the numbered list, insert a **SmartArt** graphic. In the **Process** category, locate and select the **Basic Chevron Process**. In the first shape type **View** In the second shape type **Interact** and in the third shape type **Assess**

7 Change the SmartArt color to **Colorful Range – Accent Colors 4 to 5**, and then apply the **3-D Flat Scene** style. Change the **Height** of the SmartArt to **1** and the **Width** to **6.5** Change the **Layout Options** to **Square**, the **Horizontal Alignment** to **Centered relative to** the **Page**, and the **Vertical Alignment** to **Bottom relative to** the **Margin**.

8 Select the days and times at the end of the document, and then set a **Right** tab with **dot leaders** at **6"**. Click in the blank line below the tabbed list, and **Center** the line. Insert an **Online Video**. In the **Search YouTube** box, type **Pearson Higher Education Learning**, and then insert the first video that displays. Change the video **Height** to **1.5**

9 In the space below the video, insert a **Rounded Rectangle** shape. The exact location need not be precise. Change the **Shape Height** to **1.5** and the **Shape Width** to **6.5** Display the **Shape Styles** gallery, and then in the fourth row, apply the second style—**Subtle Effect - Blue, Accent 1**. Use the **Position** command to display the **Layout** dialog box, and then change the position so that both the **Horizontal** and **Vertical Alignment** are **Centered relative to** the **Margin**.

10 In the rectangle, type **Sturgeon Point Productions** and then press Enter. Type **Partnering with Educators to Produce Rich Media Content** and then change the font size to **16**.

11 Move to the top of the document and insert a **Text Box** above the title. The exact location need not be precise. Change the **Height** of the text box to **0.5** and the width to **3.7** Type **Sturgeon Point Productions** and then change the font size to **22 Center** the text.

12 Use the **Position** command to display the **Layout** dialog box, and then position the text box so that the **Horizontal Alignment** is **Centered relative to** the **Page** and the **Vertical Absolute position** is **0.5 below** the **Page**.

13 With the text box selected, display the **Shape Fill** gallery, and then in the next to last column, select the second color—**Blue, Accent 5, Lighter 80%**. Change the **Shape Outline** to the same color—**Blue, Accent 5, Lighter 80%**.

14 Deselect the text box. Apply a **Page Border** to the document. Use the **Box** setting, and choose the first style. Change the **Color** to **Blue, Accent 5**. Change the **Top** margin to **1.25** and insert the **File Name** in the footer.

15 Display the document properties. As the **Tags** type **website** and as the **Subject** type your course and section #. Be sure your name displays in the **Author** box, and then **Save** your file. Submit your document as directed.

END | You have completed Project 1G

CONTENT-BASED ASSESSMENTS

GO! Fix It	Project 1H Casting Call	Online
GO! Make It	Project 1I Development Team	Online
GO! Solve It	Project 1J Softball	Online
GO! Solve It	Project 1K Production	

Build from Scratch

PROJECT FILES

For Project 1K, you will need the following files:

w01K_Production
w01K_Studio

You will save your document as:

Lastname_Firstname_1K_Production

The Marketing Director for Sturgeon Point Productions is developing marketing materials aimed at filmmakers. Use the following information to format a flyer that uses text effects, an appropriately placed picture with an artistic effect and text wrapping applied, and an appropriately formatted SmartArt graphic.

From the student files that accompany this textbook, locate and open the file w01K_Production. Format the document using techniques you learned in this chapter. From your student data files, insert the picture w01K_Studio, and then format the picture with an artistic effect. Insert a **SmartArt** graphic that illustrates two or three important points about the company. Be sure the flyer is easy to read and understand and has an attractive design. Save the file in your **Word Chapter 1** folder as **Lastname_Firstname_1K_Production** and submit it as directed.

(Project 1K Production continues on the next page)

CONTENT-BASED ASSESSMENTS

GO! Solve It Project 1K Production (continued)

Performance Level

Performance Criteria	Exemplary	Proficient	Developing
Use text effects	Text effects applied to text in an attractive and appropriate manner.	Text effects applied but do not appropriately display text.	Text effects not used.
Insert and format a picture	The picture is inserted and positioned correctly; text wrapping and an artistic effect are applied.	The picture is inserted but not formatted properly.	No picture is inserted in the document.
Insert and format SmartArt	The SmartArt is inserted and appropriately formatted.	The SmartArt is inserted but no formatting is applied.	No SmartArt is inserted in the document.

END | You have completed Project 1K

OUTCOMES-BASED ASSESSMENTS

RUBRIC

The following outcomes-based assessments are *open-ended assessments*. That is, there is no specific correct result; your result will depend on your approach to the information provided. Make *Professional Quality* your goal. Use the following scoring rubric to guide you in *how* to approach the problem and then to evaluate *how well* your approach solves the problem.

The *criteria*—Software Mastery, Content, Format and Layout, and Process—represent the knowledge and skills you have gained that you can apply to solving the problem. The *levels of performance*—Professional Quality, Approaching Professional Quality, or Needs Quality Improvements—help you and your instructor evaluate your result.

	Your completed project is of Professional Quality if you:	Your completed project is Approaching Professional Quality if you:	Your completed project Needs Quality Improvements if you:
1-Software Mastery	Choose and apply the most appropriate skills, tools, and features and identify efficient methods to solve the problem.	Choose and apply some appropriate skills, tools, and features, but not in the most efficient manner.	Choose inappropriate skills, tools, or features, or are inefficient in solving the problem.
2-Content	Construct a solution that is clear and well organized, contains content that is accurate, appropriate to the audience and purpose, and is complete. Provide a solution that contains no errors in spelling, grammar, or style.	Construct a solution in which some components are unclear, poorly organized, inconsistent, or incomplete. Misjudge the needs of the audience. Have some errors in spelling, grammar, or style, but the errors do not detract from comprehension.	Construct a solution that is unclear, incomplete, or poorly organized; contains some inaccurate or inappropriate content; and contains many errors in spelling, grammar, or style. Do not solve the problem.
3-Format & Layout	Format and arrange all elements to communicate information and ideas, clarify function, illustrate relationships, and indicate relative importance.	Apply appropriate format and layout features to some elements, but not others. Overuse features, causing minor distraction.	Apply format and layout that does not communicate information or ideas clearly. Do not use format and layout features to clarify function, illustrate relationships, or indicate relative importance. Use available features excessively, causing distraction.
4-Process	Use an organized approach that integrates planning, development, self-assessment, revision, and reflection.	Demonstrate an organized approach in some areas, but not others; or, use an insufficient process of organization throughout.	Do not use an organized approach to solve the problem.

OUTCOMES-BASED ASSESSMENTS

Apply a combination of the **1A** and **1B** skills.

GO! Think   Project 1L Classes

PROJECT FILES

Build from Scratch

For Project 1L, you will need the following file:

New blank Word document

You will save your document as:

Lastname_Firstname_1L_Classes

The Human Resources Director at Sturgeon Point Productions needs to create a flyer to inform full-time employees of educational opportunities beginning in September. The courses are taught each year by industry professionals and are designed to improve skills in motion picture and television development and production. Employees who have been with Sturgeon Point Productions for at least two years are eligible to take the courses free of cost. The classes provide employees with opportunities to advance their careers, gain valuable skills, and achieve technical certification. All courses take place in Studio G and interested employees should contact Elana Springs in Human Resources to sign up. Information meetings are being held at 5:30 p.m. according to the following schedule: television development on June 15; motion picture production on June 17; and recording services on June 21.

Create a flyer with basic information about the courses and information meetings. Be sure the flyer is easy to read and understand and has an attractive design. Save the document as **Lastname_Firstname_1L_Classes** and submit it as directed.

END | You have completed Project 1L

Build from Scratch

GO! Think   Project 1M Store   Online

Build from Scratch

You and GO!   Project 1N Family Flyer   Online

Build from Scratch

GO! Cumulative Group Project   Project 1O Bell Orchid Hotels
                                                                      Online

Using Tables and Templates to Create Resumes and Cover Letters

GO! to Work
Video W2

2 WORD 2013

PROJECT 2A

OUTCOMES
Write a resume by using a Word table.

OBJECTIVES
1. Create a Table
2. Format a Table
3. Present a Word Document Online

PROJECT 2B

OUTCOMES
Write a cover letter and use a template to create a cover sheet.

OBJECTIVES
4. Create a Custom Word Template
5. Correct and Reorganize Text
6. Use the Proofing Options and Print an Envelope
7. Create a Document Using a Predesigned Microsoft Template

onewordphoto / Fotolia

In This Chapter

Tables are useful for organizing and presenting data. Because a table is so easy to use, many individuals prefer to arrange tabular information in a Word table rather than setting a series of tabs. For example, you can use a table when you want to present rows and columns of information or to create a format for a document such as a resume.

When using Word to write business or personal letters, use a commonly approved letter format, and always use a clear writing style. You will make a good impression on prospective employers if you use a standard business letter style when you are writing a cover letter for a resume.

The projects in this chapter relate to the **College Career Center at Florida Port Community College** in St. Petersburg, Florida, a coastal port city near the Florida High Tech Corridor. With 60 percent of Florida's high tech companies and a third of the state's manufacturing companies located in the St. Petersburg and Tampa Bay areas, the college partners with businesses to play a vital role in providing a skilled workforce. The College Career Center assists students in exploring careers, finding internships, and applying for jobs. The Center offers workshops for resume and cover letter writing and for practice interviews.

 **Resume**

PROJECT ACTIVITIES

In Activities 2.01 through 2.11, you will create a table to use as the format for a resume. The director of the Career Center, Mary Walker-Huelsman, will use this model when assisting students with building their resumes. Your completed document will look similar to Figure 2.1.

PROJECT FILES

For Project 2A, you will need the following files:

New blank Word document
w02A_Experience

You will save your document as:

Lastname_Firstname_2A_Resume

PROJECT RESULTS

 Build from
Scratch

Josh Hayes
1541 Dearborn Lane, St. Petersburg, FL 33713

(727) 555-0313
jhayes@alcona.net

OBJECTIVE	Technology writing and editing position in the robotics industry, using research and advanced editing skills to communicate with customers.
SUMMARY OF QUALIFICATIONS	• Two years' experience in robotics lab for Aerospace Instruction Team • Excellent interpersonal and communication skills • Proficiency using Microsoft Office • Proficiency using page layout and design software • Fluency in spoken and written Spanish
EXPERIENCE	**Instructional Lab Assistant**, Florida Port Community College, St. Petersburg, FL July 2013 to present • Assist robotics professors with sophisticated experiments • Set up robotics practice sessions for Aerospace Instruction Team **Assistant Executive Editor**, Tech Today Newsletter, St. Petersburg, FL September 2012 to June 2013 • Wrote and edited articles for popular college technology newsletter • Responsible for photo editing, cropping, and resizing photos for newsletter • Received Top College Technology Publication Award **Teacher's Assistant**, Florida Port Community College, Aerospace Department, St. Petersburg, FL July 2011 to June 2012 • Helped students with homework, explained assignments, organized materials for professor • Set up robotics lab assignments for students
EDUCATION	**University of South Florida**, Tampa, FL Bachelor of Science, Mechanical Engineering, June 2015 **Florida Port Community College**, St. Petersburg, FL Associate of Arts, Journalism, June 2013
HONORS AND ACTIVITIES	• Elected to Pi Tau Sigma, honor society for mechanical engineers • Qualified for Dean's List six semesters • Student Mentor, help other students in engineering program

Lastname_Firstname_2A_Resume

FIGURE 2.1 Project 2A Resume

Objective 1 | Create a Table

Video W2-1

A *table* is an arrangement of information organized into rows and columns. The intersection of a row and a column in a table creates a box called a *cell* into which you can type. Tables are useful to present information in a logical and orderly format.

Activity 2.01 | Creating a Table by Defining Table Dimensions

1 **Start** Word and then click **Blank document**. On the **HOME tab**, in the **Paragraph group**, if necessary click **Show/Hide** to display the formatting marks. If the rulers do not display, click the **VIEW tab**, and then in the **Show group**, select the **Ruler check box**.

2 Click the **FILE tab**, and then in **Backstage** view, click **Save As**. In the **Save As** dialog box, navigate to the location where you are storing your projects for this chapter. Create a new folder named **Word Chapter 2**

3 **Save** the file in the **Word Chapter 2** folder as **Lastname_Firstname_2A_Resume**

4 On the **INSERT tab**, in the **Header & Footer group**, click **Footer**, and then at the bottom of the list, click **Edit Footer**. On the ribbon, in the **Insert group**, click **Document Info**, click **File Name**, and then at the right end of the ribbon, click **Close Header and Footer**.

5 On the **INSERT tab**, in the **Tables group**, click **Table**. In the **Insert Table** grid, in the fourth row, point to the second square, and notice that the cells are bordered in orange and *2x4 Table* displays at the top of the grid. Compare your screen with Figure 2.2.

FIGURE 2.2

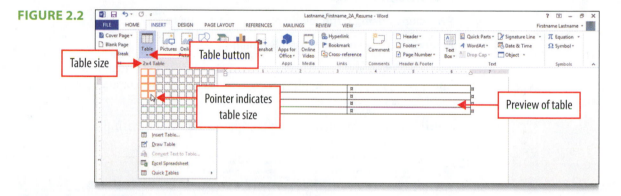

6 Click one time to create the table. Notice that formatting marks in each cell indicate the end of the contents of each cell; the mark to the right of each *row* indicates the row end. **Save** your document, and then compare your screen with Figure 2.3.

A table with four rows and two columns displays at the insertion point location, and the insertion point displays in the upper left cell. The table fills the width of the page, from the left margin to the right margin. On the ribbon, TABLE TOOLS and two additional tabs—*DESIGN* and *LAYOUT*—display. Borders display around each cell in the table.

FIGURE 2.3

Activity 2.02 | Typing Text in a Table

In a Word table, each cell behaves similarly to a document. For example, as you type in a cell, when you reach the right border of the cell, wordwrap moves the text to the next line. When you press `Enter`, the insertion point moves down to a new paragraph in the same cell. You can also insert text from another document into a table cell.

There are numerous acceptable formats for resumes, many of which can be found in Business Communications textbooks. The layout used in this project is suitable for a recent college graduate and places topics in the left column and details in the right column.

1 With the insertion point blinking in the first cell in the first row, type **OBJECTIVE** and then press `Tab`.

Pressing `Tab` moves the insertion point to the next cell in the row, or, if the insertion point is already in the last cell in the row, pressing `Tab` moves the insertion point to the first cell in the next row.

2 Type **Technology writing and editing position in the robotics industry, using research and advanced editing skills to communicate with customers.** Notice that the text wraps in the cell and the height of the row adjusts to fit the text.

3 Press `Tab` to move to the first cell in the second row. Type **SUMMARY OF QUALIFICATIONS** and then press `Tab`. Type the following, pressing `Enter` at the end of each line *except* the last line:

Two years' experience in robotics lab for Aerospace Instruction Team

Excellent interpersonal and communication skills

Proficiency using Microsoft Office

Proficiency using page layout and design software

Fluency in spoken and written Spanish

The default font and font size in a table are the same as for a document—Calibri 11 pt. The default line spacing in a table is single spacing with no space before or after paragraphs, which differs from the defaults for a document.

4 Save 💾 your document, and then compare your screen with Figure 2.4.

FIGURE 2.4

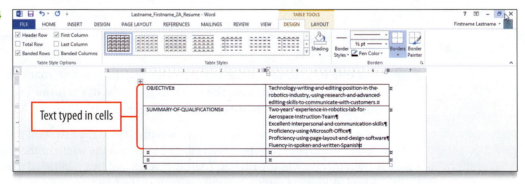

Text typed in cells

Activity 2.03 | Inserting Text from a File and Removing Blank Paragraphs

1 Press `Tab` to move to the first cell in the third row. Type **EXPERIENCE** and then press `Tab`.

2 Type the following, pressing `Enter` after each item, including the last item:

Instructional Lab Assistant, Florida Port Community College, St. Petersburg, FL July 2013 to present

Assist robotics professors with sophisticated experiments

Set up robotics practice sessions for Aerospace Instruction Team

3 Be sure your insertion point is positioned in the second column to the left of the cell marker below *Instruction Team*. Compare your screen with Figure 2.5.

FIGURE 2.5

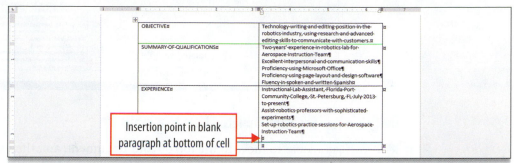

Insertion point in blank paragraph at bottom of cell

4 On the **INSERT tab**, in the **Text group**, click the **Object button arrow**, and then click **Text from File**. Navigate to your student files, select **w02A_Experience**, and then click **Insert**.

All of the text from the w02A_Experience document is added to the document at the insertion point.

 **ANOTHER WAY**   Open the second document and select the text you want. Copy the text, and then paste at the desired location.

5 Press Backspace one time to remove the blank paragraph at the end of the inserted text, and then compare your screen with Figure 2.6.

FIGURE 2.6

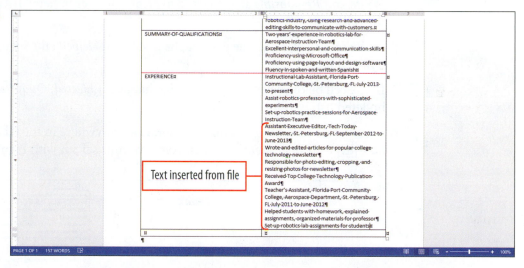

Text inserted from file

PAGE 1 OF 1   157 WORDS

6 Press Tab to move to the first cell in the fourth row. Type **HONORS AND ACTIVITIES** and then press Tab.

7 Type the following, pressing Enter at the end of each item *except* the last one:

Elected to Pi Tau Sigma, honor society for mechanical engineers

Qualified for Dean's List, six semesters

Student Mentor, help other students in engineering programs

8 **Save** 🖫 your document, and then compare your screen with Figure 2.7.

FIGURE 2.7

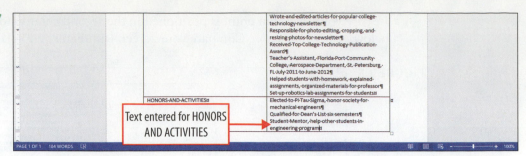

Text entered for HONORS AND ACTIVITIES

Activity 2.04 | Creating Bulleted Lists in a Table

1 Press Ctrl + Home to move to the top of your document, and then in the cell to the right of *SUMMARY OF QUALIFICATIONS*, select all of the text.

2 On the **HOME tab**, in the **Paragraph group**, click **Bullets** .

The selected text displays as a bulleted list to make each qualification more distinctive.

3 In the **Paragraph group**, click **Decrease Indent** one time to align the bullets at the left edge of the cell.

4 Scroll as necessary so that you can view the entire *EXPERIENCE* and *HONORS AND ACTIVITIES* sections on your screen. With the bulleted text still selected, in the **Clipboard group**, double-click **Format Painter**.

5 In the cell to the right of EXPERIENCE, select the second and third paragraphs—beginning *Assist* and *Set up*—to create the same style of bulleted list as you did in the previous step.

6 In the same cell, under *Assistant Executive Editor*, select the three paragraphs that begin *Wrote* and *Responsible* and *Received* to create another bulleted list aligned at the left edge of the cell.

7 In the same cell, select the paragraphs that begin *Helped* and *Set up* to create the same type of bulleted list.

8 In the cell below, select the paragraphs that begin *Elected*, *Qualified*, and *Student* to create a bulleted list.

9 Press Esc to turn off the **Format Painter**. Click anywhere in the table to deselect the text, **Save** your document, and then compare your screen with Figure 2.8.

FIGURE 2.8

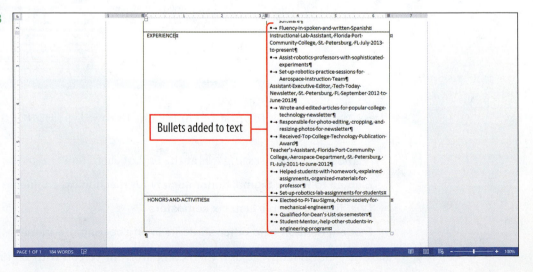

Bullets added to text

Video W2-2

Use Word's formatting tools to make your tables attractive and easy to read. Types of formatting you can add to a table include changing the row height and the column width, removing or adding borders, increasing or decreasing the paragraph or line spacing, and enhancing the text.

Activity 2.05 | Changing the Width of Table Columns and Using AutoFit

When you create a table, all of the columns are of equal width. In this activity, you will change the width of the columns.

1 Press Ctrl + Home. Click anywhere in the first column, and then on the ribbon, under **TABLE TOOLS**, click the **LAYOUT tab**. In the **Cell Size group**, notice the **Width** box, which displays the width of the active column.

2 Look at the horizontal ruler and locate the **1.5-inch mark**. Then, in the table, in any row, point to the vertical border between the two columns to display the  pointer.

3 Hold down the left mouse button and drag the column border to the left until the white arrow on the ruler is at approximately **1.5 inches on the horizontal ruler** and then release the left mouse button.

4 In the **Cell Size group**, click the **Width box down spin arrow** as necessary to set the column width to **1.4"** and notice that the right border of the table moves to the right.

Adjusting column width by dragging a column border adjusts only the width of the column; adjusting column width with the Width box simultaneously adjusts the right border of the table.

5 In the **Cell Size group**, click **AutoFit**, and then click **AutoFit Window** to stretch the table across the page within the margins so that the right border of the table is at the right margin. **Save** and then compare your screen with Figure 2.9.

> 🔄 **ANOTHER WAY**   You can adjust column widths by dragging the Move Table Column markers on the ruler. To maintain the right border of the table at the right margin, hold down Shift while dragging. To display measurements on the ruler, hold down Alt while dragging the marker.

FIGURE 2.9

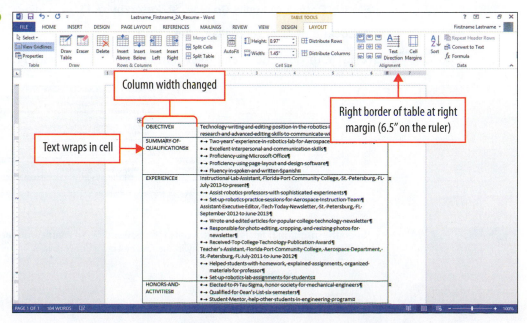

Activity 2.06 | Using One-Click Row/Column Insertion to Modify Table Dimensions

One of the most common actions you will take in a table is adding another row or another column. By using *One-click Row/Column Insertion* you can do so in context by pointing to the left or top edge where you want the row or column to appear and then clicking the ⊕ button to add it.

1 Scroll to view the lower portion of the table. On the left border of the table, *point to* the upper left corner of the cell containing the text *HONORS AND ACTIVITIES* to display the **One-click Row/Column Insertion** button ⊕. Compare your screen with Figure 2.10.

FIGURE 2.10

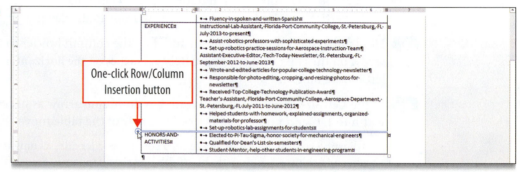

2 Click ⊕ one time to insert a new row above the HONORS AND ACTIVITIES row.

3 Click in the left cell of the new row, type **EDUCATION** and then press Tab.

4 Type the following, pressing Enter at the end of each item *except* the last one:

University of South Florida, Tampa, FL

Bachelor of Science, Mechanical Engineering, June 2015

Florida Port Community College, St. Petersburg, FL

Associate of Arts, Journalism, June 2013

5 **Save** 🖫 your document, and then compare your screen with Figure 2.11.

FIGURE 2.11

🔁 **ANOTHER WAY**   When the insertion point is in the last cell in the bottom row of a table, you can add a row by pressing the Tab key; the insertion point will display in the first cell of the new row.

Activity 2.07 | Merging Table Cells

The title of a table typically spans all of the columns. In this activity, you will merge cells so that you can position the personal information across both columns.

1 Press `Ctrl` + `Home` to move to the top of your document, and then click anywhere in the top row of the table.

2 On the **LAYOUT tab**, in the **Rows & Columns group**, click **Insert Above**.

A new row displays above the row that contained the insertion point, and the new row is selected. This is another method to insert rows and columns in a table; use this method to insert a new row at the top of a table.

> **ANOTHER WAY** Right-click in the top row, point to Insert, and then click Insert Rows Above.

3 Be sure the two cells in the top row are selected; if necessary, drag across both cells to select them.

4 On the **LAYOUT tab**, in the **Merge group**, click **Merge Cells**.

The cell border between the two cells no longer displays.

> **ANOTHER WAY** Right-click the selected row and click Merge Cells on the shortcut menu.

Activity 2.08 | Setting Tabs in a Table

1 With the merged cell still selected, on the **HOME tab**, in the **Paragraph group**, click the **Dialog Box Launcher** to display the **Paragraph** dialog box.

2 On the **Indents and Spacing tab**, in the lower left corner, click **Tabs** to display the **Tabs** dialog box.

3 Under **Tab stop position**, type **6.5** and then under **Alignment**, click the **Right** option button. Click **Set**, and then click **OK** to close the dialog box.

4 Type **Josh Hayes** Hold down `Ctrl` and then press `Tab`. Notice that the insertion point moves to the right-aligned tab stop at 6.5".

In a Word table, you must use `Ctrl` + `Tab` to move to a tab stop, because pressing `Tab` is reserved for moving the insertion point from cell to cell.

5 Type **(727) 555-0313** and then press `Enter`.

6 Type **1541 Dearborn Lane, St. Petersburg, FL 33713** Hold down `Ctrl` and then press `Tab`.

7 Type **jhayes@alcona.net** Save your document, and then compare your screen with Figure 2.12.

FIGURE 2.12

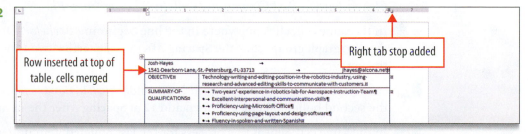

Activity 2.09 | Modifying Fonts in a Table and Using Spacing After

1 In the first row of the table, select the name *Josh Hayes*, and then on the mini toolbar, apply **Bold** B and change the **Font Size** to **16**.

2 Under *Josh Hayes*, click anywhere in the second line of text, which contains the address and email address.

3 On the **PAGE LAYOUT tab**, in the **Paragraph group**, click the **Spacing After up spin arrow** three times to add **18 pt** spacing between the first row of the table and the second row. Compare your screen with Figure 2.13.

> This action separates the personal information from the body of the resume and adds focus to the name.

FIGURE 2.13

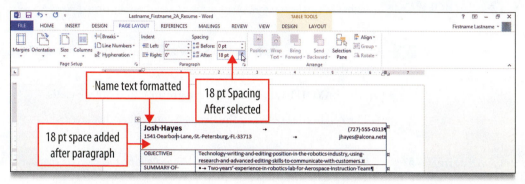

4 Using the technique you just practiced, in the second column, click in the last paragraph of *every cell* and add **18 pt Spacing After** including the last row; a border will be added to the bottom of the table, and spacing will be needed between the last row and the border.

5 In the second row, point to the word *OBJECTIVE*, hold down the left mouse button, and then drag downward in the first column to select all the headings in uppercase letters. On the mini toolbar, click **Bold** B.

NOTE | **Selecting Only One Column**

When you drag downward to select the first column, a fast mouse might also begin to select the second column when you reach the bottom. If this happens, drag upward slightly to deselect the second column and select only the first column.

---

6 In the cell to the right of *EXPERIENCE*, without selecting the following comma, select *Instructional Lab Assistant* and then on the mini toolbar, click **Bold** B.

7 In the same cell, apply **Bold** B to the other job titles—*Assistant Executive Editor* and *Teacher's Assistant*.

8 In the cell to the right of *EDUCATION*, apply **Bold** B to *University of South Florida, Tampa, FL* and *Florida Port Community College, St. Petersburg, FL*.

9 In the same cell, click anywhere in the line beginning *Bachelor*. On the **PAGE LAYOUT tab**, in the **Paragraph group**, click the **Spacing After up spin arrow** two times to add **12 pt** spacing after the paragraph.

10 In the cell to the right of *EXPERIENCE*, under *Instructional Lab Assistant*, click anywhere in the second bulleted item, and then add **12 pt Spacing After** the item.

11 In the same cell, repeat this process for the last bulleted item under *Assistant Executive Editor*.

12 ▶ Scroll to view the top of your document, **Save** 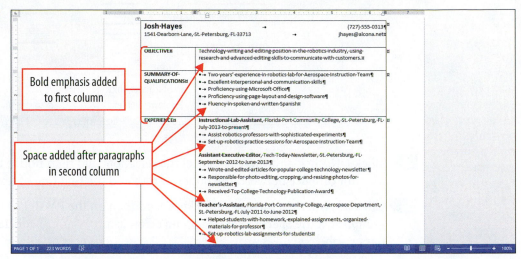 your document, and then compare your screen with Figure 2.14.

FIGURE 2.14

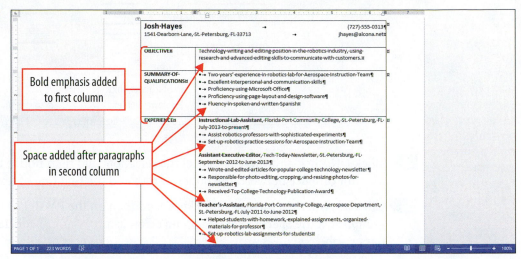

Activity 2.10 | Modifying Table Borders and Using Spacing Before

When you create a table, all of the cells have black 1/2-point, single-line, solid-line borders that print unless you remove them. Most resumes do not display any cell borders. A border at the top and bottom of the resume, however, is attractive and adds a professional look to the document.

1 ▶ Scroll as necessary to view the top margin area above the table, and then point slightly outside of the upper left corner of the table to display the **table move handle** ⊞.

2 ▶ With the pointer, click one time to select the entire table, and notice that the row markers at the end of each row are also selected.

Shaded row markers indicate that the entire row is selected. Use this technique to select the entire table.

3 ▶ On the ribbon, under **TABLE TOOLS**, click the **DESIGN tab**. In the **Borders group**, click the **Borders button arrow**, and then click **No Border**.

The black borders no longer display.

4 ▶ Press Ctrl + P, which is the keyboard shortcut to view the Print Preview, and notice that no borders display in the preview. Then, press **Back** ⬅ to return to your document.

5 ▶ With the table still selected, on the **DESIGN tab**, in the **Borders group**, click the **Borders button arrow**, and then at the bottom of the **Borders** gallery, click **Borders and Shading**.

6 ▶ In the **Borders and Shading** dialog box, on the **Borders tab**, under **Setting**, click **Custom**. Under **Style**, scroll down about one-third of the way, and then click the style with a **thick upper line and a thin lower line**.

7 ▶ In the **Preview** box at the right, point to the *top* border of the small preview and click one time.

🔄 **ANOTHER WAY**   Click the top border button, which is one of the buttons that surround the Preview.

8 ▶ Under **Style**, scroll down if necessary, click the opposite style—with the **thin upper line and the thick lower line**, and then in the **Preview** box, click the *bottom* border of the preview. Compare your screen with Figure 2.15.

FIGURE 2.15

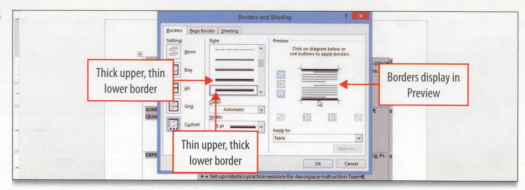

9 ▸ Click **OK**, click anywhere to cancel the selection, and then notice that there is only a small amount of space between the upper border and the first line of text.

10 ▸ Click anywhere in the text *Josh Hayes*, and then on the **PAGE LAYOUT tab**, in the **Paragraph group**, click the **Spacing Before up spin arrow** as necessary to add **18 pt** spacing before the first paragraph.

11 ▸ Press Ctrl + P to display **Print Preview**. Compare your screen with Figure 2.16.

FIGURE 2.16

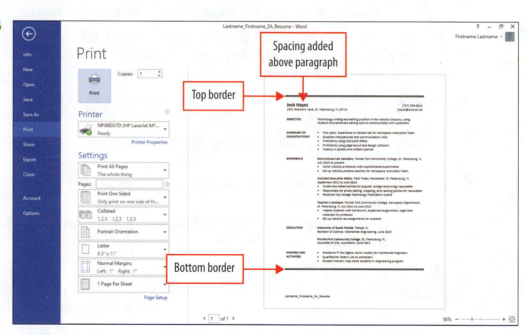

12 ▸ Press **Back** ◀ to return to your document, and then on the Quick Access Toolbar, click **Save** 🖫.

More Knowledge | **View Gridlines in a Table**

After you remove borders from a table, you can still view nonprinting gridlines, which show the cell boundaries of a table whenever the table does not have borders applied. Some people find this a useful visual aid. If you cannot see the gridlines, on the ribbon, under TABLE TOOLS, on the DESIGN tab, in the Borders group, click the Borders button arrow, and then click View Gridlines.

More Knowledge | **Convert Text to a Table**

To convert paragraphs or lists to a table, insert separator characters such as commas or tabs to show where to divide the text into columns. Then insert paragraph marks (press ENTER) to show where to begin the rows. Select the text, and then on the INSERT tab, in the Table group, click Convert Text to Table. In the Convert Text to Table dialog box, choose the options you want, and then click OK.

Video W2-3

Office Presentation Service enables you to present your Word document to others who can watch in a web browser. No preliminary setup is necessary; Word creates a link to your document that you can share with others via email or instant message. Anyone to whom you send the link can see your document while you are presenting online.

Individuals watching your presentation can navigate within the document independently of you or others in the presentation, so they can use a mouse, keyboard, or touch input to move around in the document while you are presenting it. If an individual is viewing a different portion of the document than the presenter, an alert displays on his or her screen. To return to the portion of the document that the presenter is showing, a Follow Presenter button displays.

While you are presenting, you can make minor edits to the document. If you want to share a copy of the document to the presentation attendees, you can select *Enable remote viewers to download the document* when you start the presentation. You can also share any meeting notes that you or others created in OneNote.

Activity 2.11 | Presenting a Word Document Online

If you are creating your own resume, it will be valuable to get feedback from your friends, instructors, or Career Center advisors before you submit your resume for a job application. In this Activity, you will present the resume document online for others to look at.

> **NOTE** **You May Be Asked to Sign in with Your Microsoft Account**
>
> You may be asked to sign in with your Microsoft account, even if you are already signed in, to present your document online.

1 With your resume document displayed, click **Save** 🖫.

2 Click the **FILE tab**, on the left click **Share**, and then under **Share**, click **Present Online**.

3 On the right, under **Present Online**, be sure **Office Presentation Service** displays; if necessary, click the arrow on the right to select it. Click the **Present Online** button. Wait a moment for the service to connect, and then compare your screen with Figure 2.17.

There are several methods to send your meeting invitation to others. You can click Copy Link to copy and paste the hyperlink; for example, you could copy the link into a *Skype* window. Skype is a Microsoft product with which you can make voice calls, make video calls, transfer files, or send messages—including instant messages and text messages—over the Internet.

You can also select Send in Email, which will open your Outlook email window if you use Outlook as your mail client.

> **NOTE** **Other Presentation Services May Display**
>
> Under Present Online, you might have other services displayed. For example, if you are using Office 365, Microsoft Lync may display as the default presentation service.

FIGURE 2.17

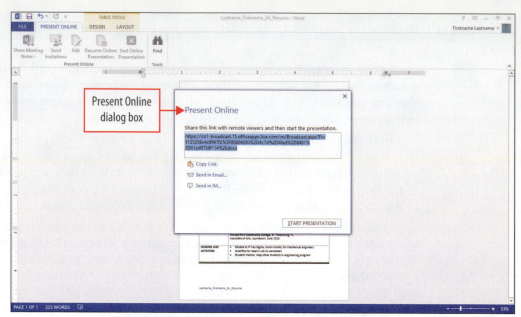

4 If you want to do so, identify a classmate or friend who is at a computer and available to view your presentation, select one of the methods to share, click **START PRESENTATION**, and when you are finished, on the ribbon, click **End Online Presentation**. Otherwise, **Close** ☒ the **Present Online** dialog box.

If you present online, you will need to initiate voice communication using Skype or by simply phoning the other person.

5 Be sure you have closed the **Present Online** dialog box. On the ribbon, on the **PRESENT ONLINE tab**, click **End Online Presentation**, and then in the message, click **End Online Presentation**.

6 Press Ctrl + Home to move to the top of your document. In the lower right corner, click **Zoom In** ➕ as necessary to set the Zoom level to **100%**. On the **HOME tab**, redisplay the formatting marks by clicking **Show/Hide**.

7 Click the **FILE tab**, and then in the lower right portion of the screen, click **Show All Properties**. In the **Tags** box, type **resume, Word table** and in the **Subject** box, type your course name and section number. In the **Author** box, be sure your name is indicated and edit if necessary.

8 On the left, click **Print** to display **Print Preview**. If necessary, return to the document and make any necessary changes.

9 As directed by your instructor, print your document or submit it electronically. **Save** 🖫 your document and **Close** ☒ Word.

More Knowledge | **Convert a Table to Text**

To convert a table to text, select the rows or table you want to convert to paragraphs, and then on the LAYOUT tab, in the Data group, click Convert to Text. In the Convert to Text dialog box, under Separate text at, click the separator character to use in place of the column boundaries, and then click OK.

END | You have completed Project 2A

Objective   Edit a Resume in Word Web App

You can create and edit tables in the Word Web App if you are not at a computer on which Word 2013 is installed.

> **ALERT!**   **Working with Web-Based Applications and Services**
>
> Computer programs and services on the web receive continuous updates and improvements, so the steps to complete this web-based activity may differ from the ones shown. You can often look at the screens and the information presented to determine how to complete the activity.

Activity   Editing a Resume in Word Web App

In this activity, you will use the Word Web App to edit a Word table containing a resume similar to the resume you created in Project 1A.

1 From the desktop, start Internet Explorer. Navigate to **http://skydrive.com** and then sign in to your Microsoft account. Click your **GO! Web Projects** folder to open it— or create and then open this folder if necessary.

2 On the SkyDrive menu bar, click **Upload**. In the **Choose File to Upload** dialog box, navigate to your student data files, click **w02_2A_Web**, and then click **Open**.

3 Point to the uploaded file **w02_2A_Web**, and then right-click. On the shortcut menu, scroll down as necessary and then click **Rename**. Using your own last name and first name, type **Lastname_Firstname_WD_2A_ Web** and then press [Enter] to rename the file.

4 Click the file that you just renamed, and then in the upper left, click **EDIT DOCUMENT**. On the list, click **Edit in Word Web App**.

5 If necessary, click to place the insertion point in the cell *OBJECTIVE*. On the ribbon, under **TABLE TOOLS**, click the **LAYOUT tab**, and then in the **Insert group**, click **Insert Above**.

6 In the first cell of the new row, type **Daniela Frank** press [Enter], select the text you just typed, and then on the **HOME tab**, in the **Styles group**, click the **More Styles arrow**, and then click **Title**. With the text selected, change the **Font** to **Calibri (Body)**.

7 Click in the second cell of the new row, and then type **1343 Siena Lane, Deerfield, WI 53531** and press [Enter]. Type **(608) 555-0588** and press [Enter]. Type **dfrank@alcona.net** and press [Enter]. Right-click the email address, and then click **Remove Link**. Select all the text in the second cell that you just typed, and then on the **HOME tab**, in the **Paragraph group**, click **Align Text Right** [≡]. Click anywhere to deselect, and then compare your screen with Figure A.

FIGURE A

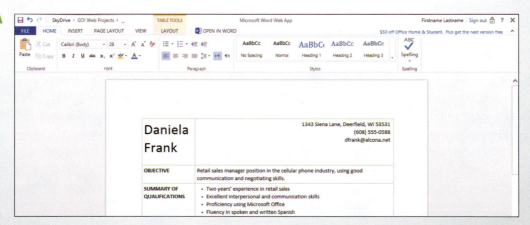

(GO! with Office Web Apps continues on the next page)

8 ▸ Scroll down and click anywhere in the *EXPERIENCE* cell. On the ribbon, under **TABLE TOOLS**, click the **LAYOUT tab**, and then in the **Insert group**, click **Insert Below**. In the first cell of the new row, press Backspace one time to move the insertion point to the left edge of the cell. Type **EDUCATION** Select the text you just typed, and then from the **HOME tab**, apply **Bold** B.

9 ▸ Press Tab to move to the second cell in the new row, press Backspace one time to move to the left edge of the cell, and then type **Madison Area Technical College, Madison, WI** and press Enter.

10 ▸ Type **Associate of Arts in Information Systems, June 2014** and press Enter. Select the upper line of text with the college information, and then press Ctrl + B to apply **Bold**. Click anywhere to deselect, and then compare your screen with Figure B.

11 ▸ On the ribbon, above the **FILE tab**, click Save 💾. Click the **FILE tab** and then click **Exit**. Submit the file as directed by your instructor. In the upper right, click your user name, and then click **Sign out**. **Close** ❌ Internet Explorer.

FIGURE B

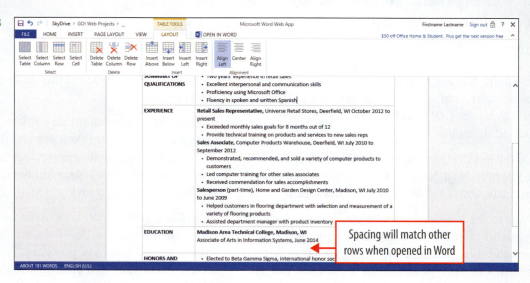

Cover Letter, Reference List, and Envelope

PROJECT ACTIVITIES

In Activities 2.12 through 2.24, you will create a letterhead, save the letterhead as a custom Word template, and then use the letterhead to create a cover letter to accompany a resume. You will also create a list of references from a Microsoft predesigned template and, if you have an envelope and printer available, format and print an envelope. Your completed documents will look similar to Figure 2.18.

PROJECT FILES

For Project 2B, you will need the following files:

You will save your documents as:

New blank Word document
w02B_Cover_Letter_Text

Lastname_Firstname_2B_Cover_Letter
Lastname_Firstname_2B_Reference_List

PROJECT RESULTS

ld from
cratch

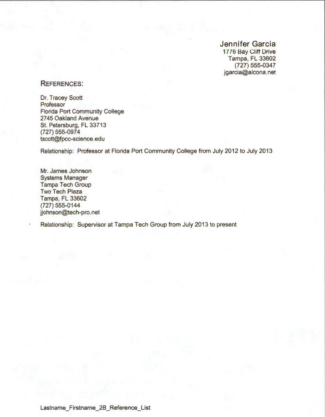

FIGURE 2.18 Project 2B Cover Letter and Reference List

Video W2-4

A *template* is a file you use as a starting point for a *new* document. A template has a predefined document structure and defined settings, such as font, margins, and available styles. On Word's opening screen, you can select from among many different templates—or you can create your own custom template.

When you open a template as the starting point for a new document, the template file opens a copy of itself, unnamed, and then you use the structure—and possibly some content, such as headings—as the starting point for a new document.

All documents are based on a template. When you create a new blank document, it is based on Word's *Normal template*, which serves as the starting point for all blank Word documents.

Activity 2.12 | Changing the Document Style Set for Paragraph Spacing and Applying a Bottom Border to a Paragraph

A *letterhead* is the personal or company information that displays at the top of a letter, and which commonly includes a name, address, and contact information. The term also refers to a piece of paper imprinted with such information at the top. In this activity, you will create a custom template for a personal letterhead.

1 Start Word and display a blank document; be sure that formatting marks and rulers display.

2 On the **DESIGN tab**, in the **Document Formatting group**, click **Paragraph Spacing**.

The Paragraph Spacing command offers various options for setting the line and paragraph spacing of your entire document. A gallery of predefined values displays; or you can create your own custom paragraph spacing.

3 On the list *point* to **Default** and notice the settings in the ScreenTip.

Recall that the default spacing for a new Word document is 0 points of blank space before a paragraph, 8 points of blank space following a paragraph, and line spacing of 1.08.

4 Point to **No Paragraph Space** and notice the settings in the ScreenTip.

The *No Paragraph Space* style inserts *no* extra space before or after a paragraph and uses line spacing of 1. This is the same format used for the line spacing commonly referred to as *single spacing*.

5 Click **No Paragraph Space**.

By using the No Paragraph Space style, you will be able to follow the prescribed format of a letter, which Business Communications texts commonly describe in terms of single spacing.

 **ANOTHER WAY**   On Word's opening screen, select the Single spaced (blank) document; or, in a blank document, select the entire document, and then on the HOME tab, in the Styles group, click No Spacing. Also, so long as you leave an appropriate amount of space between the elements of the letter, you can use Word's default spacing. Finally, you could use one of Word's predesigned templates for a cover letter and observe all spacing requirements for a letter.

---

6 Type **Jennifer Garcia** and then press Enter.

7 Type **1776 Bay Cliff Drive, Tampa, FL 33602** and then press Enter.

8 Type **(727) 555-0347 jgarcia@alcona.net** and then press Enter. If the web address changes to blue text, right-click the web address, and then, click **Remove Hyperlink**.

9 Select the first paragraph—*Jennifer Garcia*—and then on the mini toolbar, apply **Bold** B and change the **Font Size** to **16**.

10 Select the second and third paragraphs. On the mini toolbar, apply **Bold** $\boxed{\text{B}}$ and change the **Font Size** to **12**.

11 With the two paragraphs still selected, on the **HOME tab**, in the **Paragraph group**, click **Align Right** $\boxed{\equiv}$.

🔄 **ANOTHER WAY**   Press $\boxed{\text{Ctrl}}$ + $\boxed{\text{R}}$ to align text to the right.

12 Click anywhere in the first paragraph—*Jennifer Garcia*. In the **Paragraph group**, click the **Borders button arrow** $\boxed{⊞ ▾}$, and then at the bottom, click **Borders and Shading**.

13 In the **Borders and Shading** dialog box, on the **Borders tab**, under **Style**, be sure the first style—a single solid line—is selected.

14 Click the **Width arrow**, and then click **3 pt**. To the right, under **Preview**, click the bottom border of the diagram. Under **Apply to**, be sure *Paragraph* displays. Compare your screen with Figure 2.19.

FIGURE 2.19

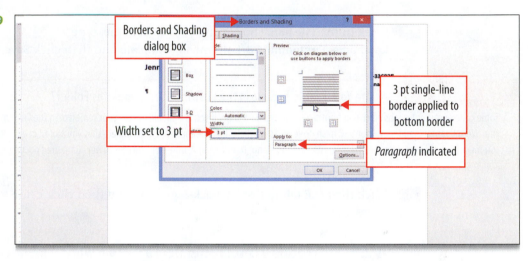

Borders and Shading dialog box

Width set to 3 pt

3 pt single-line border applied to bottom border

Paragraph indicated

🔄 **ANOTHER WAY**   Alternatively, under Preview, click the bottom border button $\boxed{⊞ ▾}$.

15 Click **OK** to display a 3 pt line below *Jennifer Garcia*, which extends from the left margin to the right margin.

The border is a paragraph command and uses the same margins of the paragraph to which it is applied.

Activity 2.13 | Saving a Document as a Custom Word Template

After you create a document format that you like and will use again, for example, a letterhead for personal letters during a job search, you can save it as a template and then use it as the starting point for any letter.

1 Press $\boxed{\text{F12}}$ to display the **Save As** dialog box. In the lower portion of the dialog box, in the **Save as type** box, at the right edge, click the arrow, and then click **Word Template**.

ALERT!   **Are You Using a Laptop Computer?**

On some laptop computers, you might have to hold down the key labeled FN while pressing the F12 key in order to display the Save As dialog box.

2 At the top of the **Save As** dialog box, notice the path, and then compare your screen with Figure 2.20.

By default, Word stores template files on your hard drive in your user folder, in a folder named Custom Word Templates. By doing so, the template is available to you from the Word opening screen.

FIGURE 2.20

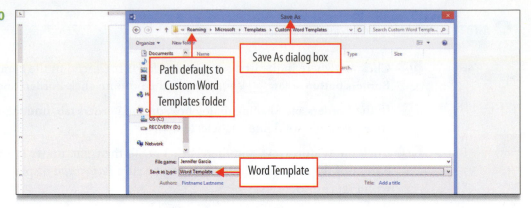

3 Click in the **File name** box, using your own name, type **Lastname_Firstname_2B_Letterhead_Template** and then click **Save**.

> **ALERT!** **Are You Unable to Save in the Custom Word Templates Folder?**
>
> Some college computer labs block you from saving on the hard drive. If you are unable to save your template in the Custom Word Templates folder, navigate to your Word Chapter 2 folder on your USB flash drive and save there. If you want to open a template that you stored in a location other than Word's default path, you must open the template directly from File Explorer—not from within Word—for it to open a new unnamed document based on the template.

4 Click the **FILE tab** to display **Backstage** view, and then click **Close** to close the file but leave Word open.

Activity 2.14 | Creating a Cover Letter from a Custom Word Template

A *cover letter* is a document that you send with your resume to provide additional information about your skills and experience. An effective cover letter includes specific information about why you are qualified for the job for which you are applying. Use the cover letter to explain your interest in the position and the organization.

> **ALERT!** **Were You Unable to Save in the Custom Word Templates Folder?**
>
> If you saved your template file on your USB flash drive because you were blocked from saving in the default folder on the hard drive, open your saved document, press F12 to display the Save As dialog box, and then in your storage location, save the document—using your own name—as Lastname_ Firstname_2B_Cover_Letter. Then move to Activity 2.15.

1 With Word open but no documents displayed, click the **FILE tab** to display **Backstage** view, and click **New** to display the new document options. Compare your screen with Figure 2.21.

Here you can create a new document from a blank document or from one of Word's many built-in or online templates.

FIGURE 2.21

FIGURE 2.22

2 Under **Suggested searches**, click **PERSONAL**, *point* to the name of your letterhead template, and then compare your screen with Figure 2.22.

> Custom templates that you create and that are stored in the Custom Word Templates folder on your hard drive are accessible to you here whenever you want to create a new document from your stored template.

3 Click your letterhead template.

> Word opens a copy of your 2B_Letterhead_Template in the form of a new Word document—the title bar indicates *Document* followed by a number. You are not opening the original template file, and changes that you make to this new document will not affect the contents of your 2B_Letterhead_Template file.

4 Press F12 to display the **Save As** dialog box, and then navigate to your **Word Chapter 2** folder. **Save** the file as **Lastname_Firstname_2B_Cover_Letter**

5 On the **INSERT tab**, in the **Header & Footer** group, click **Footer**, click **Edit Footer**, and then in the **Insert group**, click **Document Info**. Click **File Name**, and then click **Close Header and Footer**.

6 Save 💾 your document.

Video W2-5

Business letters follow a standard format and contain the following parts: the current date, referred to as the *dateline*; the name and address of the person receiving the letter, referred to as the *inside address*; a greeting, referred to as the *salutation*; the text of the letter, usually referred to as the *body* of the letter; a closing line, referred to as the *complimentary closing*; and the *writer's identification*, which includes the name or job title (or both) of the writer and which is also referred to as the *writer's signature block*.

Some letters also include the initials of the person who prepared the letter, an optional *subject line* that describes the purpose of the letter, or a list of *enclosures*—documents included with the letter.

Activity 2.15 | Adding AutoCorrect Entries

Word's *AutoCorrect* feature corrects commonly misspelled words automatically; for example *teh* instead of *the*. If you have words that you frequently misspell, you can add them to the list for automatic correction.

1 Click the **FILE tab** to display **Backstage** view. On the left, click **Options** to display the **Word Options** dialog box.

2 On the left side of the **Word Options** dialog box, click **Proofing**, and then under **AutoCorrect options**, click the **AutoCorrect Options** button.

3 In the **AutoCorrect** dialog box, click the **AutoCorrect tab**. Under **Replace**, type **resumee** and under **With**, type **resume**

> If another student has already added this AutoCorrect entry, a Replace button will display.

4 Click **Add**. If the entry already exists, click **Replace** instead, and then click **Yes**.

5 In the **AutoCorrect** dialog box, under **Replace**, type **computr** and under **With**, type **computer** Compare your screen with Figure 2.23.

FIGURE 2.23

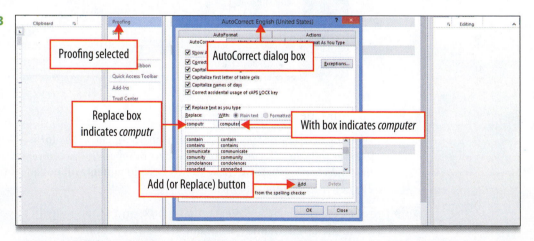

6 Click **Add** (or **Replace**) and then click **OK** two times to close the dialog boxes.

Activity 2.16 | Inserting the Current Date and Creating a Cover Letter

By using the **Date & Time** command, you can select from a variety of formats to insert the current date and time in document.

For cover letters, there are a variety of accepted letter formats that you will see in reference manuals and Business Communications texts. The one used in this chapter is a block style cover letter following the style in Courtland Bovee and John Thill, *Business Communication Today*, Eleventh Edition, Pearson Prentice Hall, 2012, p. A-2.

1 Press Ctrl + End to move the insertion point to the blank line below the letterhead, and then press Enter three times.

2 On the **INSERT tab**, in the **Text group**, click **Date & Time**, and then click the third date format. Click **OK** to create the dateline.

> Most Business Communication texts recommend that the dateline be positioned at least 0.5 inch (3 blank lines) below the letterhead; or, position the dateline approximately 2 inches from the top edge of the paper.

3 Press Enter four times, which leaves three blank lines. Type the following inside address on four lines, but do *not* press Enter following the last line:

Ms. Mary Walker-Huelsman, Director

Florida Port Community College Career Center

2745 Oakland Avenue

St. Petersburg, FL 33713

The recommended space between the dateline and inside address varies slightly among experts in Business Communication texts and office reference manuals. However, all indicate that the space can be from 1 to 10 blank lines depending on the length of your letter.

4 Press Enter two times to leave one blank line, and then compare your screen with Figure 2.24.

FIGURE 2.24

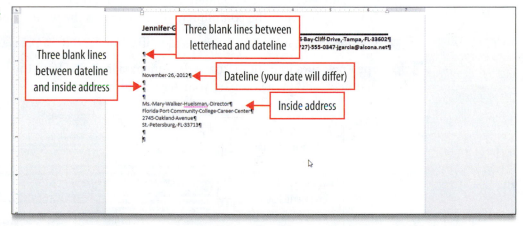

5 Type the salutation **Dear Ms. Walker-Huelsman:** and then press Enter two times.

> Always leave one blank line above and below the salutation.

6 Type, exactly as shown, the following opening paragraph that includes an intentional word usage error: **I am seeking a position in witch I can use my** and press Spacebar. Type, exactly as shown, **computr** and then watch *computr* as you press Spacebar.

> The AutoCorrect feature recognizes the misspelled word, and then changes *computr* to *computer* when you press Spacebar, Enter, or a punctuation mark.

7 Type the following, including the misspelled last word: **and communication skills. My education and experience, outlined on the enclosed resumee** and then type **,** (a comma). Notice that when you type the comma, AutoCorrect replaces *resumee* with *resume*.

8 Press Spacebar, and then complete the paragraph by typing **includes a Business Software Applications Specialist certificate from FPCC.** Compare your screen with Figure 2.25.

FIGURE 2.25

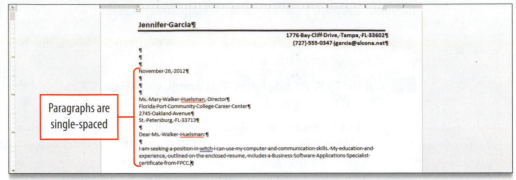

9 Press Enter two times. On the **INSERT tab**, in the **Text group**, click the **Object button arrow**, and then click **Text from File**. From your student files, locate and **Insert** the file **w02B_Cover_Letter_Text**.

Some of the words in the cover letter text display red or blue wavy underlines. These indicate potential spelling, grammar, or word usage errors, and will be addressed before the end of this project.

10 Scroll as necessary to display the lower half of the letter on your screen, and be sure your insertion point is positioned in the blank paragraph at the end of the document.

11 Press Enter one time to leave one blank line between the last paragraph of the letter and the complimentary closing.

12 Type **Sincerely,** as the complimentary closing, and then press Enter four times to leave three blank lines between the complimentary closing and the writer's identification.

13 Type **Jennifer Garcia** as the writer's identification, and then press Enter two times.

14 Type **Enclosure** to indicate that a document is included with the letter. **Save** 🖫 your document, and then compare your screen with Figure 2.26.

FIGURE 2.26

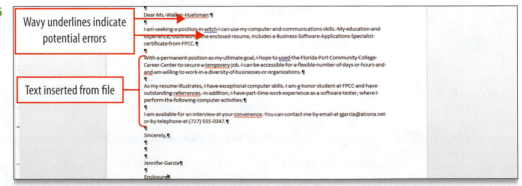

Activity 2.17 | Finding and Replacing Text

Use the Find command to locate text in a document quickly. Use the Find and Replace command to make the same change, or to make more than one change at a time, in a document.

1 Press Ctrl + Home to position the insertion point at the beginning of the document.

Because a find operation—or a find and replace operation—begins from the location of the insertion point and proceeds to the end of the document, it is good practice to position the insertion point at the beginning of the document before initiating the command.

2 On the **HOME tab**, in the **Editing group**, click **Find**.

The navigation pane displays on the left side of the screen with a search box at the top of the pane.

**ANOTHER WAY**   Hold down Ctrl and press F.

3 In the **navigation** pane, in the search box, type **ac** If necessary, scroll down slightly in your document to view the entire body text of the letter, and then compare your screen with Figure 2.27.

In the document, the search letters *ac* are selected and highlighted in yellow for both words that begin with the letters *ac* and also for the word *contact* which contains this letter combination. In the navigation pane, the three instances are shown in context—*ac* displays in bold.

FIGURE 2.27

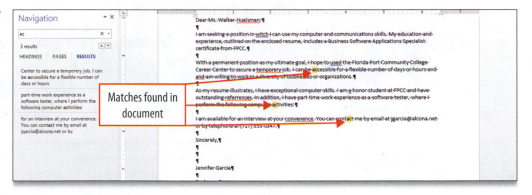

4 Click in the search box again, and type as necessary to display the word *accessible* in the search box.

One match for the search term displays in context in the navigation pane and is highlighted in the document.

5 In the document, double-click the yellow highlighted word *accessible*, and then type **available** to replace the word.

6 **Close** [**x**] the **navigation** pane, and then on the **HOME tab**, in the **Editing group**, click **Replace**.

7 In the **Find and Replace** dialog box, in the **Find what** box, replace the existing text by typing **FPCC** and in the **Replace with** box, type **Florida Port Community College** and then compare your screen with Figure 2.28.

FIGURE 2.28

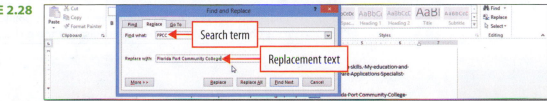

8 In the lower left corner of the dialog box, click **More** to expand the dialog box, and then under **Search Options**, select the **Match case** check box.

The acronym *FPCC* appears in the document two times. In a formal letter, the reader may not know what the acronym means, so you should include the full text instead of an acronym. In this instance, you must select the *Match case* check box so that the replaced text will match the case you typed in the Replace with box, and *not* display in all uppercase letters in the manner of *FPCC*.

9 In the **Find and Replace** dialog box, click **Replace All** to replace both instances of *FPCC*. Click **OK** to close the message box.

10 In the **Find and Replace** dialog box, clear the **Match case** check box, click **Less**, and then **Close** the dialog box. **Save** 🖫 your document.

The Find and Replace dialog box opens with the settings used the last time it was open. Therefore, it is good practice to reset this dialog box to its default settings each time you use it.

Activity 2.18 | Selecting and Moving Text to a New Location

By using Word's ***drag-and-drop*** feature, you can use the mouse to drag selected text from one location to another. This method is most useful when the text you are moving is on the same screen as the destination location.

1 Take a moment to study the table in Figure 2.29 to become familiar with the techniques you can use to select text in a document quickly.

FIGURE 2.29

SELECTING TEXT IN A DOCUMENT	
TO SELECT THIS:	**DO THIS:**
A portion of text	Click to position the insertion point at the beginning of the text you want to select, hold down Shift, and then click at the end of the text you want to select. Alternatively, hold down the left mouse button and drag from the beginning to the end of the text you want to select.
A word	Double-click the word.
A sentence	Hold down Ctrl and click anywhere in the sentence.
A paragraph	Triple-click anywhere in the paragraph; or, move the pointer to the left of the line, into the margin area. When the ⧄ pointer displays, double-click.
A line	Point to the left of the line. When the ⧄ pointer displays, click one time.
One character at a time	Position the insertion point to the left of the first character, hold down Shift, and press ← or → as many times as desired.
A string of words	Position the insertion point to the left of the first word, hold down Shift and Ctrl, and then press ← or → as many times as desired.
Consecutive lines	Position the insertion point to the left of the first word, hold down Shift and press ↑ or ↓.
Consecutive paragraphs	Position the insertion point to the left of the first word, hold down Shift and Ctrl and press ↑ or ↓.
The entire document	Hold down Ctrl and press A. Alternatively, move the pointer to the left of any line in the document. When the ⧄ pointer displays, triple-click.

2   Be sure you can view the entire body of the letter on your screen. In the paragraph that begins *With a permanent position*, in the second line, locate and double-click *days*.

3   Point to the selected word to display the ⍐ pointer.

4   Drag to the right until the dotted vertical line that floats next to the pointer is positioned to the right of the word *hours* in the same line, as shown in Figure 2.30.

FIGURE 2.30

5   Release the mouse button to move the text. Select *hours* and drag it to the left of the word *or*—the previous location of the word *days*. Click anywhere to deselect the text.

6   Examine the text that you moved, and add or remove spaces as necessary.

7   Hold down [Ctrl], and then in the paragraph that begins *I am available*, click anywhere in the first sentence to select the entire sentence.

8   Drag the selected sentence to the end of the paragraph by positioning the small vertical line that floats with the pointer to the left of the paragraph mark. **Save** 🖫 your document, and then compare your screen with Figure 2.31.

FIGURE 2.31

Activity 2.19 | Inserting a Table into a Document and Applying a Table Style

1   Locate the paragraph that begins *You can contact me*, and then click to position the insertion point in the blank line above that paragraph. Press [Enter] one time.

2   On the **INSERT tab**, in the **Tables group**, click **Table**. In the **Table** grid, in the third row, click the second square to insert a 2 × 3 table.

3   In the first cell of the table, type **Microsoft Access** and then press [Tab]. Type **Test database queries** and then press [Tab]. Complete the table using the following information:

Microsoft Excel	Enter software test data
Microsoft Word	Create and mail form letters

4   Point slightly outside of the upper left corner of the table to display the **table move handle** button ⊞. With the ⍁ pointer, click one time to select the entire table.

5   On the **LAYOUT tab**, in the **Cell Size group**, click **AutoFit**, and then click **AutoFit Contents** to have Word choose the best column widths for the two columns based on the text you entered.

6 With the table still selected, on the **DESIGN tab**, in the **Table Styles group**, click **More** ⊡. Under **Plain Tables**, click the second style—**Table Grid Light**.

Use Table Styles to change the visual style of a table.

7 With the table still selected, on the **HOME tab**, in the **Paragraph group**, click **Center** ▤ to center the table between the left and right margins. Click anywhere to deselect the table.

8 **Save** 🖫 and then compare your screen with Figure 2.32.

FIGURE 2.32

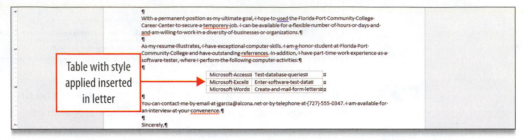

Table with style applied inserted in letter

> ### *More* Knowledge | Configure Cell Margins in a Table
>
> You can modify the margins of a cell to increase or decrease the distance between the cell border and the text in the cell. To do so, on the LAYOUT tab, in the Alignment group, click Cell Margins, and then enter the new margins.

Objective 6 | Use the Proofing Options and Print an Envelope

Video W2-6

Word compares your typing to words in the Office dictionary and compares your phrases and punctuation to a list of grammar rules. This automatic proofing is set by default. Words that are not in the dictionary and words, phrases, and punctuation that differ from the grammar rules are marked with wavy underlines; for example, the misuse of *their*, *there*, and *they're*.

Word will not flag the word *sign* as misspelled even though you intended to type *sing a song* rather than *sign a song*, because both are words contained within Word's dictionary. Your own knowledge and proofreading skills are still required, even when using a sophisticated word processing program like Word.

Activity 2.20 | Checking for Spelling and Grammar Errors

There are two ways to respond to spelling and grammar errors flagged by Word. You can right-click a flagged word or phrase, and then from the shortcut menu choose a correction or action. Or, you can initiate the Spelling & Grammar command to display the Spelling and Grammar pane, which provides more options than the shortcut menus.

> ### ALERT! | Activating Spelling and Grammar Checking
>
> If you do not see any wavy red or blue lines under words, the automatic spelling or grammar checking has been turned off on your system. To activate the spelling and grammar checking, display Backstage view, click Options, click Proofing, and then under *When correcting spelling in Microsoft Office programs*, select the first four check boxes. Under *When correcting spelling and grammar in Word*, select the first four check boxes, and then click the Writing Style arrow and click Grammar Only. Under *Exceptions for*, clear both check boxes. To display the flagged spelling and grammar errors, click the Recheck Document button, and then close the dialog box.

---

1 Position the body of the letter on your screen, and then examine the text to locate wavy underlines.

A list of grammar rules applied by a computer program like Word can never be exact, and a computer dictionary cannot contain all known words and proper names. Therefore, you will need to check any words flagged by Word with wavy underlines, and you will also need to proofread for content errors.

2 In the lower left corner of your screen, in the status bar, locate and point to the 🔲 icon to display the ScreenTip *Proofing errors were found. Click to correct.* Compare your screen with Figure 2.33.

If this button displays, you know there are potential errors identified in the document.

FIGURE 2.33

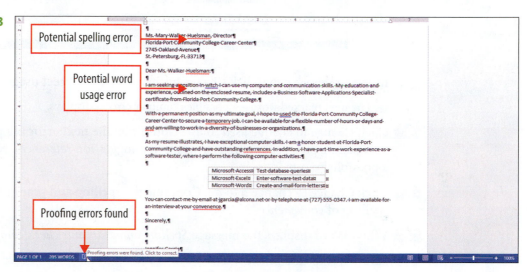

3 In the paragraph that begins *With a permanent*, in the second line, locate the word *temporery* with the wavy red underline. Point to the word and right-click, and then click **temporary** to correct the spelling error.

4 In the next line, locate the word *and* that displays with a wavy red underline, point to the word and right-click, and then on the shortcut menu, click **Delete Repeated Word** to delete the duplicate word.

5 Press [Ctrl] + [Home] to move the insertion point to the beginning of the document. Click the **REVIEW tab**, and then in the **Proofing group**, click **Spelling & Grammar** to check the spelling and grammar of the text in the document.

The Spelling pane displays on the right, and the proper name *Huelsman* is flagged. Word's dictionary contains only very common proper names—unusual names like this one will typically be flagged as a potential spelling error. If this is a name that you frequently type, consider adding it to the dictionary.

🔄 **ANOTHER WAY**   Press [F7] to start the Spelling & Grammar command.

6 In the **Spelling** pane, click **Ignore All**. Compare your screen with Figure 2.34.

The word *witch* is highlighted as a grammar error, and in the Grammar pane, *which* is suggested.

FIGURE 2.34

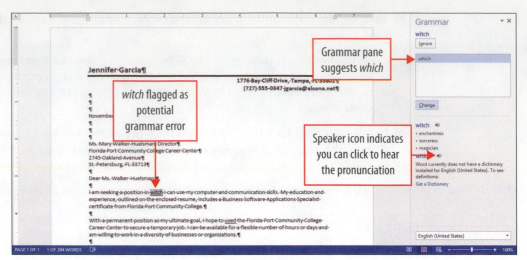

7 In the **Grammar** pane, click **Change** to change to the correct usage *which*.

The next marked word—a possible grammar error—displays.

8 Click **Change** to change *used* to *use*. Notice that the next error is a potential spelling error. In the **Spelling** pane, change *referrences* to the suggestion *references*. Notice that the next error is a possible grammar error.

9 Click **Change** to change *a* to *an*. Continue the spelling and grammar check and correct the spelling of *convenence*.

10 When Word displays the message *Spelling and grammar check complete*, click **OK**.

11 **Save** your document.

Activity 2.21 | Using the Thesaurus

A ***thesaurus*** is a research tool that lists ***synonyms***—words that have the same or similar meaning to the word you selected.

1 Scroll so that you can view the body of the letter. In the paragraph that begins *With a permanent*, at the end of the second line, double-click to select the word *diversity*, and then in the **Proofing** group, click **Thesaurus**.

The Thesaurus pane displays on the right a list of synonyms; the list will vary in length depending on the selected word.

ANOTHER WAY   Right-click the word, on the shortcut menu, point to Synonyms, and then click Thesaurus.

2 In the **Thesaurus** pane, point to the word *variety*, and then click the arrow that displays. Click **Insert** to change *diversity* to *variety*.

3 In the paragraph that begins *As my resume*, double-click the word *exceptional*, and then on the ribbon, click **Thesaurus** again.

4 In the **Thesaurus** pane, point to *excellent*, click the **arrow**, and then click **Insert**. Compare your screen with Figure 2.35.

FIGURE 2.35

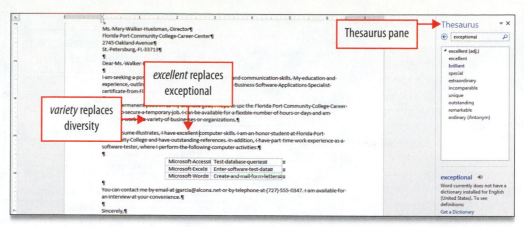

5 Close ☒ the **Thesaurus** pane.

6 Click the **FILE tab** to display **Backstage** view, and then on the **Info tab**, in the lower right portion of the screen, click **Show All Properties**. If you used your template, notice that it is indicated to the right of *Template*.

7 In the **Tags** box, type **cover letter** and in the **Subject** box, type your course name and section number. In the **Author** box, be sure your name is indicated and edit if necessary.

8 On the left, click **Print** to display **Print Preview**. If necessary, return to the document and make any necessary changes.

9 As directed by your instructor, print your document or submit it electronically. **Save** 🖫 your document and **Close** ☒ Word.

Activity 2.22 | Addressing and Printing an Envelope

Use Word's Envelopes command on the Mailings label to format and print an envelope.

> **NOTE** **This Is an Optional Activity**
>
> This activity is optional. If you do not have an envelope and printer, or do not want to complete the activity at this time, move to Activity 2.23.

1 Display your **2B_Cover_Letter**, and then select the four lines that comprise the inside address.

2 On the **MAILINGS tab**, in the **Create group**, click **Envelopes**. Notice that the **Delivery address** contains the selected inside address.

3 Click in the **Return address** box, and then type **Jennifer Garcia** and press Enter. Type **1776 Bay Cliff Drive** and then press Enter. Type **Tampa, FL 33602**

4 In the lower portion of the **Envelopes and Labels** dialog box, click **Options**, and then compare your screen with Figure 2.36.

> The default envelope size is a standard business envelope referred to as a Size 10.

FIGURE 2.36

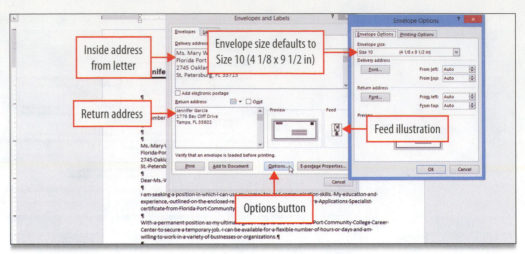

Inside address from letter

Envelope size defaults to Size 10 (4 1/8 x 9 1/2 in)

Return address

Feed illustration

Options button

---

5 Click **OK** to close the **Envelope Options** dialog box. As shown under **Feed**, insert an envelope in your printer and then click **Print**.

> Depending on the type and brand of printer you are using, your feed area may vary.

6 Close your **2B_Cover_Letter**, and then **Close** Word.

Objective 7   Create a Document Using a Predesigned Microsoft Template

Video W2-7

Microsoft provides predesigned templates for letters, calendars, invoices, and other types of documents. Recall that when you open a template, it opens unnamed so that you can reuse it as often as you need to do so.

Activity 2.23 | Locating and Opening a Template

In this activity, you will use a predesigned template to create a list of references to accompany a resume. References are not included on a resume, because you want to use the resume space for personal information. Most employers do not check references until after the first interview and when they have decided to consider you for a position. Be sure that you have already notified these individuals, asked their permission to use their name as a reference, and then contact them to tell them that a specific employer may be contacting them.

1 **Start** Word, and then on the opening screen, in the **Search for online templates** box, type **resume references** and press Enter.

2 Locate the reference list that contains three left-aligned reference items as shown in Figure 2.37.

FIGURE 2.37

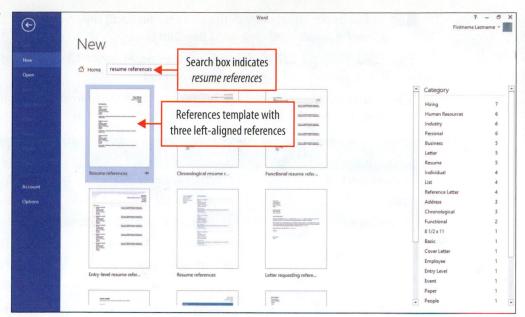

3 Click the three-item reference template, and then click **Create**. Compare your screen with Figure 2.38.

The template opens a copy of itself in the form of a new Word document—the title bar indicates *Document* followed by a number. Recall that you are not opening the template itself, and that changes you make to this new document will not affect the contents of the template file.

FIGURE 2.38

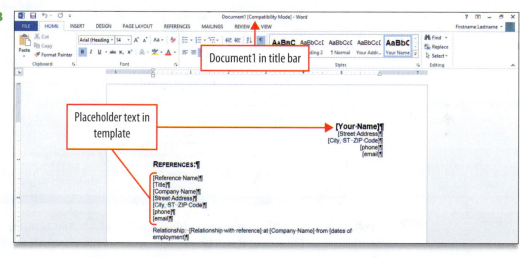

4 Press F12 to display the **Save As** dialog box. **Save** the document in your **Word Chapter 2** folder as **Lastname_Firstname_2B_Reference_List** and click **Save**. If a message indicates that you will be upgraded to the newest file format, click **OK**.

5 Add the file name to the footer, and then **Save** your document.

Activity 2.24 | Replacing Template Placeholder Text and Removing Controls

After you save the template file as a Word document, you can begin to substitute your own information in the indicated locations. *Placeholder text* is text that indicates the type of information to be entered. Text surrounded by brackets is called a *content control*. There are several different types of content controls, including date, picture, and *text controls*. All of the controls in this template are text controls.

1 In the upper right, click in the placeholder text *[Your Name]* and type **Jennifer Garcia** Click *[Street Address]* and type **1776 Bay Cliff Drive**

2 Click *[City, ST ZIP Code]* and type **Tampa, FL 33602** Click *[phone]* and type **(727) 555-0347** Click *[email]* and type **jgarcia@alcona.net**

3 Under **References**, enter two references using the following information, and then compare your screen with Figure 2.39.

TEMPLATE FIELD	REFERENCE 1	REFERENCE 2
Reference Name	Dr. Tracey Scott	Mr. James Johnson
Title	Professor	Systems Manager
Company Name	Florida Port Community College	Tampa Tech Group
Street Address	2745 Oakland Avenue	Two Tech Plaza
City, ST ZIP Code	St. Petersburg, FL 33713	Tampa, FL 33602
phone	(727) 555-0974	(727) 555-0144
email	tscott@fpcc-science.edu	jjohnson@tech-pro.net
Relationship with reference	Professor	Supervisor
Company Name	Florida Port Community College	Tampa Tech Group
dates of employment	July 2012 to July 2013	July 2013 to present

FIGURE 2.39

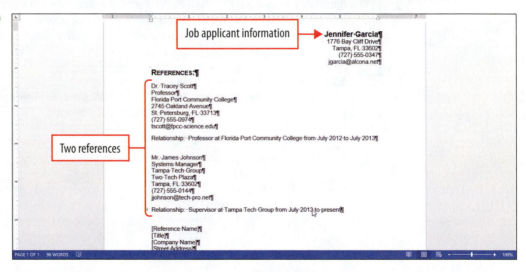

4 Scroll down to the third reference block. Select all the paragraphs of placeholder text, and then press ⌷Del⌷ to delete these unneeded controls; this list will contain only two references.

🔄 **ANOTHER WAY** Point to a content control, right-click, and then on the shortcut menu, click Remove Content Control.

5 Click **Save** 💾. Click the **FILE tab**, and then in the lower right portion of the screen, click **Show All Properties**. In the **Tags** box, type **reference list** and in the **Subject** box, type your course name and section number. In the **Author** box, be sure your name is indicated and edit if necessary.

6 On the left, click **Print** to display **Print Preview**. If necessary, return to the document and make any necessary changes.

7 As directed by your instructor, print your document or submit it electronically. **Save** 💾 your document and **Close** ✖ Word.

END | You have completed Project 2B

Objective | Create a Table in Word Web App

You can create and edit tables in the Word Web App if you are not at a computer on which Word 2013 is installed.

A L E R T ! | **Working with Web-Based Applications and Services**

Computer programs and services on the web receive continuous updates and improvements, so the steps to complete this web-based activity may differ from the ones shown. You can often look at the screens and the information presented to determine how to complete the activity.

Activity | Creating a Table in Word Web App

In this activity, you will use the Word Web App to create a Word table within a document similar to Project 2B.

1 From the desktop, start Internet Explorer. Navigate to **http://skydrive.com** and then sign in to your Microsoft account. Open your **GO! Web Projects** folder—or create and then open this folder if necessary.

2 On the SkyDrive menu bar, click **Upload**. In the **Choose File to Upload** dialog box, navigate to your student data files, click **w02_2B_Web**, and then click **Open**.

3 Point to the uploaded file **w02_2B_Web**, and then right-click. On the shortcut menu, scroll down as necessary and then click **Rename**. Using your own last name and first name, type **Lastname_Firstname_WD_2B_Web** and then press Enter to rename the file.

4 Click the file that you just renamed, and then in the upper left, click **EDIT DOCUMENT**. On the list, click **Edit in Word Web App**.

5 Press Ctrl + End to move to the end of the document, and then press Enter.

6 On the **INSERT tab**, in the **Tables group**, click **Table**, and then insert a **3 × 4 Table**.

7 Type **Position** and press Tab. Type **Type** and press Tab. Type **Location** and press Tab.

8 In the second row type **Paralegal** and press Tab. Type **Part-time** and press Tab. Type **Tampa** and press Tab. Compare your screen with Figure A.

FIGURE A

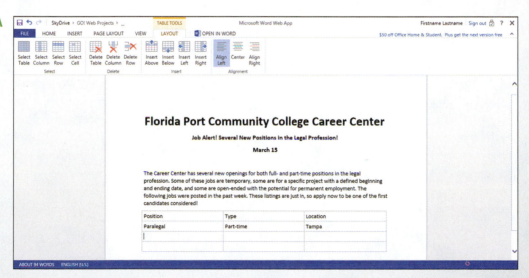

(GO! with Office Web Apps continues on the next page)

9 Type **Legal Records Clerk** and press `Tab`. Type **Full-time, 2 months** and press `Tab`. Type **North Tampa** and press `Tab`.

10 On the ribbon, under **TABLE TOOLS**, click the **LAYOUT tab**, and then in the **Delete group**, click **Delete Row**.

11 Drag to select all the cells in the first row, and then on the **HOME tab**, in the **Styles group**, click **Heading 1**.

With the three column titles still selected, in the **Paragraph group**, click **Center** . In the **Font group**, change the **Font Color** to **Black, Text 1**. Compare your screen with Figure B.

12 Above the **FILE tab**, click **Save** ⊟. Click the **FILE tab**, and then click **Exit**. Submit the file as directed by your instructor. In the upper right, click your user name, and then click **Sign out**. **Close** ❌ Internet Explorer.

FIGURE B

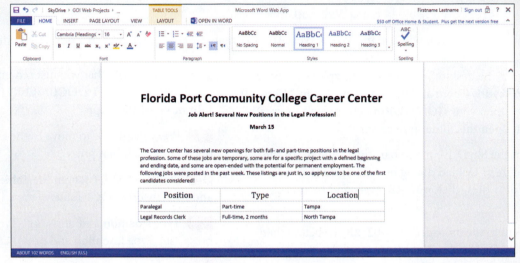

Andrew Rodriguez / Fotolia; FotolEdhar/ Fotolia; apops/ Fotolia; Yuri Arcurs/ Fotolia

Office 365 combines tools for collaboration and productivity and delivers them to multiple users in an organization by using *cloud computing*—applications and services that are accessed over the Internet with multiple devices. For example, one cloud service with which you might be familiar is *SkyDrive*, a free web-based application with which you can save, store, organize, and share files online. This cloud service is available for anyone that has a free Microsoft account.

Another cloud service from Microsoft is *Office Web Apps*. These are the online companions to the desktop versions of Microsoft Office Word, Excel, PowerPoint, and OneNote that enable you to create, access, share, and perform light editing on Microsoft Office documents from any device that connects to the Internet and uses a supported *web browser*. A web browser is software, such as Internet Explorer, Firefox, Safari, or Chrome, that displays web pages.

For an organization, cloud computing enables the addition of services without investing in additional hardware and software. For you as a team member, you can simply use your web browser to access, edit, store, and share files. You do not need to have a full version of Office installed on your computer to do this. You have all the tools and security that large organizations have!

When you use using Office 365, your email and storage servers are hosted by Microsoft. Your organization gets business-class security from Microsoft—a large, well-established company. Sophisticated security and data management features are built into Office 365 so that you can control *permissions*—access rights that define the ability of an individual or group to view or make changes to documents—and provide secure email and communications.

Activity | Using Lync to Collaborate by Using a Video Call

This group project relates to the **Bell Orchid Hotels**. If your instructor assigns this project to your class, you can expect to use **Lync** in **Office 365** to collaborate on the following tasks for this chapter:

- If you are in the **Accounting Group**, you and your teammates will conduct a video call to discuss and agree on the letter that will be sent to shareholders.
- If you are in the **Engineering Group**, you and your teammates will conduct a video call to discuss and agree on the letter that will be sent to the three insurance companies that cover the hotel properties.
- If you are in the **Food and Beverage Group**, you and your teammates will conduct a video call to discuss and agree on the letter that will be sent to a customer planning a banquet.
- If you are in the **Human Resources Group**, you and your teammates will conduct a video call to discuss and agree on the memo for employees regarding the new employee newsletter.
- If you are in the **Operations Group**, you and your teammates will conduct a video call to discuss and agree on the letter that will be sent to three job applicants.
- If you are in the **Sales and Marking Group**, you and your teammates will conduct a video call to discuss and agree on the letter that will be sent to 20 groups of professional associations.

FIGURE A

END OF CHAPTER

SUMMARY

Word tables enable you to present information in a logical and orderly format. Each cell in a Word table behaves like a document; as you type in a cell, wordwrap moves text to the next line.

A good source of information for resume formats is a business communications textbook. A simple two-column table created in Word is suitable to create an appropriate resume for a recent college graduate.

Use Word's Office Presentation Service to present a Word document to others who can watch in a web browser. Word automatically creates a link to your document that you can share with others via email.

A template is useful because it has a predefined document structure and defined settings such as font, margins, and available styles. On Word's opening screen, you can select from thousands of templates.

GO! LEARN IT ONLINE

Review the concepts and key terms in this chapter by completing these online challenges, which you can find at **www.pearsonhighered.com/go**.

Matching and Multiple Choice: Answer matching and multiple choice questions to test what you learned in this chapter. MyITLab®

Crossword Puzzle: Spell out the words that match the numbered clues, and put them in the puzzle squares.

Flipboard: Flip through the definitions of the key terms in this chapter and match them with the correct term.

GO! FOR JOB SUCCESS

Video: Cover Letter and Resume Tips

Your instructor may assign this video to your class, and then ask you to think about, or discuss with your classmates, these questions:

FotoIEdhar / Fotolia

A cover letter should contain different but complimentary information than the facts on your resume and be tailored to the specific job you are applying for. Name two different things that you could mention in a cover letter.

What type of information belongs in the Career Objective portion of your resume?

When is it best to use a chronological resume layout, and when is it appropriate to use a functional resume layout?

END OF CHAPTER

REVIEW AND ASSESSMENT GUIDE FOR WORD CHAPTER 2

Your instructor may assign one or more of these projects to help you review the chapter and assess your mastery and understanding of the chapter.

	Review and Assessment Guide for Word Chapter 2		
Project	**Apply Skills from These Chapter Objectives**	**Project Type**	**Project Location**
2C	Objectives 1-3 from Project 2A	**2C Skills Review** A guided review of the skills from Project 2A.	On the following pages
2D	Objectives 4-7 from Project 2B	**2D Skills Review** A guided review of the skills from Project 2B.	On the following pages
2E	Objectives 1-3 from Project 2A	**2E Mastery (Grader Project)** A demonstration of your mastery of the skills in Project 2A with extensive decision making.	In MyITLab and on the following pages
2F	Objectives 4-7 from Project 2B	**2F Mastery (Grader Project)** A demonstration of your mastery of the skills in Project 2B with extensive decision making.	In MyITLab and on the following pages
2G	Objectives 1-7 from Projects 2A and 2B	**2G Mastery (Grader Project)** A demonstration of your mastery of the skills in Projects 2A and 2B with extensive decision making.	In MyITLab and on the following pages
2H	Combination of Objectives from Projects 2A and 2B	**2H GO! Fix It** A demonstration of your mastery of the skills in Projects 2A and 2B by creating a correct result from a document that contains errors you must find.	Online
2I	Combination of Objectives from Projects 2A and 2B	**2I GO! Make It** A demonstration of your mastery of the skills in Projects 2A and 2B by creating a result from a supplied picture.	Online
2J	Combination of Objectives from Projects 2A and 2B	**2J GO! Solve It** A demonstration of your mastery of the skills in Projects 2A and 2B, your decision-making skills, and your critical thinking skills. A task-specific rubric helps you self-assess your result.	Online
2K	Combination of Objectives from Projects 2A and 2B	**2K GO! Solve It** A demonstration of your mastery of the skills in Projects 2A and 2B, your decision-making skills, and your critical thinking skills. A task-specific rubric helps you self-assess your result.	On the following pages
2L	Combination of Objectives from Projects 2A and 2B	**2L GO! Think** A demonstration of your understanding of the chapter concepts applied in a manner that you would outside of college. An analytic rubric helps you and your instructor grade the quality of your work by comparing it to the work an expert in the discipline would create.	On the following pages
2M	Combination of Objectives from Projects 2A and 2B	**2M GO! Think** A demonstration of your understanding of the chapter concepts applied in a manner that you would outside of college. An analytic rubric helps you and your instructor grade the quality of your work by comparing it to the work an expert in the discipline would create.	Online
2N	Combination of Objectives from Projects 2A and 2B	**2N You and GO!** A demonstration of your understanding of the chapter concepts applied in a manner that you would in a personal situation. An analytic rubric helps you and your instructor grade the quality of your work.	Online
2O	Combination of Objectives from Projects 2A and 2B	**2O Cumulative Group Project for Word Chapter 2** A demonstration of your understanding of concepts and your ability to work collaboratively in a group role-playing assessment, requiring both collaboration and self-management.	Online

GLOSSARY

GLOSSARY OF CHAPTER KEY TERMS

AutoCorrect A feature that corrects common typing and spelling errors as you type, for example changing *teh* to *the*.

Body The text of a letter.

Cell The box at the intersection of a row and column in a Word table.

Cloud computing Applications and services that are accessed over the Internet with multiple devices.

Complimentary closing A parting farewell in a business letter.

Content control In a template, an area indicated by placeholder text that can be used to add text, pictures, dates, or lists.

Cover letter A document that you send with your resume to provide additional information about your skills and experience.

Date & Time A command with which you can automatically insert the current date and time into a document in a variety of formats.

Dateline The first line in a business letter that contains the current date and which is positioned just below the letterhead if a letterhead is used.

Drag-and-drop A technique by which you can move, by dragging, selected text from one location in a document to another.

Enclosures Additional documents included with a business letter.

Inside address The name and address of the person receiving the letter and positioned below the date line.

Letterhead The personal or company information that displays at the top of a letter.

No Paragraph Style The built-in paragraph style—available from the Paragraph Spacing command—that inserts *no* extra space before or after a paragraph and uses line spacing of 1.

Normal template The template that serves as a basis for all Word documents.

Office Presentation Service A Word feature to present your Word document to others who can watch in a web browser.

One-click Row/Column Insertion A Word table feature with which you can insert a new row or column by pointing to the desired location and then clicking.

Placeholder text The text in a content control that indicates the type of information to be entered in a specific location.

Salutation The greeting line of a business letter.

Single spacing The common name for line spacing in which there is *no* extra space before or after a paragraph and that uses line spacing of 1.

Skype A Microsoft product with which you can make voice calls, make video calls, transfer files, or send messages—including instant message and text messages—over the Internet.

Subject line The optional line following the inside address in a business letter that states the purpose of the letter.

Synonyms Words with the same or similar meaning.

Table An arrangement of information organized into rows and columns.

Template An existing document that you use as a starting point for a new document; it opens a copy of itself, unnamed, and then you use the structure—and possibly some content, such as headings—as the starting point for a new document.

Text control A content control that accepts only a text entry.

Thesaurus A research tool that provides a list of synonyms.

Writer's identification The name and title of the author of a letter, placed near the bottom of the letter under the complimentary closing—also referred to as the *writer's signature block*.

Writer's signature block The name and title of the author of a letter, placed near the bottom of the letter, under the complimentary closing—also referred to as the *writer's identification*.

CHAPTER REVIEW

Apply 2A skills from these Objectives:

1 Create a Table
2 Format a Table
3 Present a Word Document Online

Build from Scratch

Skills Review | Project 2C Student Resume

In the following Skills Review, you will use a table to create a resume for Ashley Kent. Your completed resume will look similar to the one shown in Figure 2.40.

PROJECT FILES

For Project 2C, you will need the following files:

New blank Word document
w02C_Skills
w02C_Experience

You will save your document as:

Lastname_Firstname_2C_Student_Resume

PROJECT RESULTS

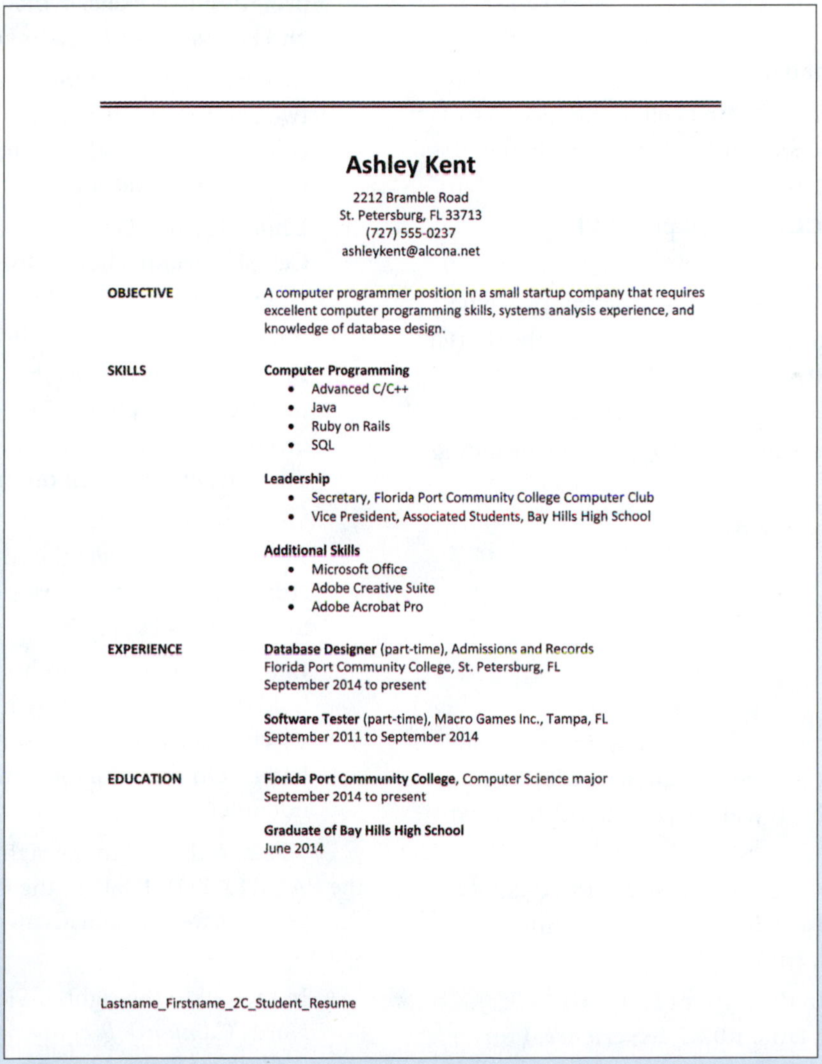

Ashley Kent

2212 Bramble Road
St. Petersburg, FL 33713
(727) 555-0237
ashleykent@alcona.net

OBJECTIVE
A computer programmer position in a small startup company that requires excellent computer programming skills, systems analysis experience, and knowledge of database design.

SKILLS

Computer Programming
- Advanced C/C++
- Java
- Ruby on Rails
- SQL

Leadership
- Secretary, Florida Port Community College Computer Club
- Vice President, Associated Students, Bay Hills High School

Additional Skills
- Microsoft Office
- Adobe Creative Suite
- Adobe Acrobat Pro

EXPERIENCE
Database Designer (part-time), Admissions and Records
Florida Port Community College, St. Petersburg, FL
September 2014 to present

Software Tester (part-time), Macro Games Inc., Tampa, FL
September 2011 to September 2014

EDUCATION
Florida Port Community College, Computer Science major
September 2014 to present

Graduate of Bay Hills High School
June 2014

Lastname_Firstname_2C_Student_Resume

FIGURE 2.40

(Project 2C Student Resume continues on the next page)

CHAPTER REVIEW

1 **Start** Word and display a blank document. Be sure that formatting marks and rulers display. **Save** the document in your **Word Chapter 2** folder as **Lastname_Firstname_2C_Student_Resume**

a. Add the file name to the footer, and then close the footer area. Click the **INSERT tab**, and then in the **Tables group**, click **Table**. In the **Table** grid, in the fourth row, click the second square to insert a **2 × 4** table.

b. In the first cell of the table, type **Ashley Kent** and then press Enter. Type the following text, pressing Enter after each line *except* the last line:

2212 Bramble Road

St. Petersburg, FL 33713

(727) 555-0237

ashleykent@alcona.net

c. Press ↓ to move to the first cell in the second row. Type **SKILLS** and then press ↓ to move to the first cell in the third row.

d. Type **EXPERIENCE** and then press ↓. Type **EDUCATION**

e. In the first cell, if the email address displays in blue, right-click the email address, and then on the shortcut menu, click **Remove Hyperlink**. **Save** your document.

2 Click in the cell to the right of *SKILLS*, and then type the following, pressing Enter after each line including the last line:

Computer Programming

Advanced C/C++

Java

Ruby on Rails

SQL

a. With the insertion point in the new line at the end of the cell, click the **INSERT tab**. In the **Text group**, click the **Object button arrow**, and then click **Text from File**.

b. Navigate to your student files, select **w02C_Skills**, and then click **Insert**. Press Backspace one time to remove the blank paragraph.

c. Click in the cell to the right of *EXPERIENCE*, and then insert the file **w02C_Experience**. Press Backspace one time to remove the blank line.

d. Click in the cell to the right of *EDUCATION*, and then type the following, pressing Enter after all lines *except* the last line:

Florida Port Community College, Computer Science major

September 2014 to present

Graduate of Bay Hills High School

June 2014

3 Point to the upper left corner of the *SKILLS* cell, and then click the **Row Insertion** button. In the first cell of the new row, type **OBJECTIVE** and then press Tab.

a. Type **A computer programmer position in a small startup company that requires excellent computer programming skills, systems analysis experience, and knowledge of database design.**

b. In any row, point to the vertical border between the two columns to display the ➕ pointer. Drag the column border to the left to approximately **1.5 inches on the horizontal ruler**.

c. Under **TABLE TOOLS**, on the **LAYOUT tab**, in the **Cell Size group**, click **AutoFit**, and then click **AutoFit Window** to be sure that your table stretches across the page within the margins.

d. In the first row of the table, drag across both cells to select them. On the **LAYOUT tab**, in the **Merge group**, click **Merge Cells**. Right-click over the selected cell, and then on the mini toolbar, click **Center**.

e. In the top row, select the first paragraph of text—*Ashley Kent*. On the mini toolbar, increase the **Font Size** to **20** and apply **Bold**.

f. In the second row, point to the word *OBJECTIVE*, hold down the left mouse button, and then drag down to select the row headings in uppercase letters. On the mini toolbar, click **Bold**. **Save** your document.

4 Click in the cell to the right of *OBJECTIVE*. On the **PAGE LAYOUT tab**, in the **Paragraph group**, click the **Spacing After up spin arrow** three times to change the spacing to **18 pt**.

a. In the cell to the right of *SKILLS*, apply **Bold** to the words *Computer Programming*, *Leadership*, and *Additional Skills*. Then, under each bold heading in

(Project 2C Student Resume continues on the next page)

the cell, select the lines of text, and create a bulleted list.

b. In the first two bulleted lists, click in the last bullet item, and then on the **PAGE LAYOUT tab**, in the **Paragraph group**, set the **Spacing After** to **12 pt**.

c. In the last bulleted list, click in the last bullet item, and then set the **Spacing After** to **18 pt**.

d. In the cell to the right of *EXPERIENCE*, apply **Bold** to *Database Designer* and *Software Tester*. Click in the line *September 2014 to present* and apply **Spacing After** of **12 pt**. Click in the line *September 2011 to September 2014* and apply **Spacing After** of **18 pt**.

e. In the cell to the right of *EDUCATION*, apply **Bold** to *Florida Port Community College* and *Graduate of Bay Hills High School*.

f. In the same cell, click in the line *September 2014 to present* and apply **Spacing After** of **12 pt**.

g. In the first row, click in the last line—*ashleykent@ alcona.net*—and then change the **Spacing After** to **18 pt**. Click in the first line—*Ashley Kent*—and set the **Spacing Before** to **30 pt** and the **Spacing After** to **6 pt**.

5 Point to the upper left corner of the table, and then click the **table move handle** ⊞ to select the entire table. Under **TABLE TOOLS**, on the **DESIGN tab**, in the **Table**

Styles group, click the **Borders button arrow**, and then click **No Border**.

a. In the **Table Styles group**, click the **Borders button arrow** again, and then at the bottom of the gallery, click **Borders and Shading**. In the **Borders and Shading** dialog box, under **Setting**, click **Custom**. Under **Style**, scroll down slightly, and then click the style with two equal lines.

b. Click the **Width arrow**, and then click **1 1/2 pt**. Under **Preview**, click the top border of the preview box, and then click **OK**.

c. Click the **FILE tab** to display **Backstage** view, and then in the lower right portion of the screen, click **Show All Properties**. In the **Tags** box, type **resume, table** and in the **Subject** box, type your course name and section number. In the **Author** box, be sure your name is indicated and edit if necessary.

d. On the left, click **Print** to display **Print Preview**. If necessary, return to the document and make any necessary changes.

e. **Save** 🖫 your document, and then if you want to do so, present your document online to a fellow classmate. Then as directed by your instructor, print your document or submit it electronically. **Close** Word.

END | You have completed Project 2C

CHAPTER REVIEW

Apply 2B skills from these Objectives:

4 Create a Custom Word Template

5 Correct and Reorganize Text

6 Use the Proofing Options and Print an Envelope

7 Create a Document Using a Predesigned Microsoft Template

In the following Skills Review, you will create a letterhead, save the letterhead as a custom Word template, and then use the letterhead to create a cover letter to accompany a resume. You will also create a list of references from a Microsoft predesigned template and, if you have an envelope and printer available, format and print an envelope. Your completed documents will look similar to Figure 2.41.

PROJECT FILES

Build from Scratch

For Project 2D, you will need the following files:

New blank Word document
w02D_Cover_Letter_Text

You will save your documents as:

Lastname_Firstname_2D_Cover_Letter
Lastname_Firstname_2D_Reference_List

PROJECT RESULTS

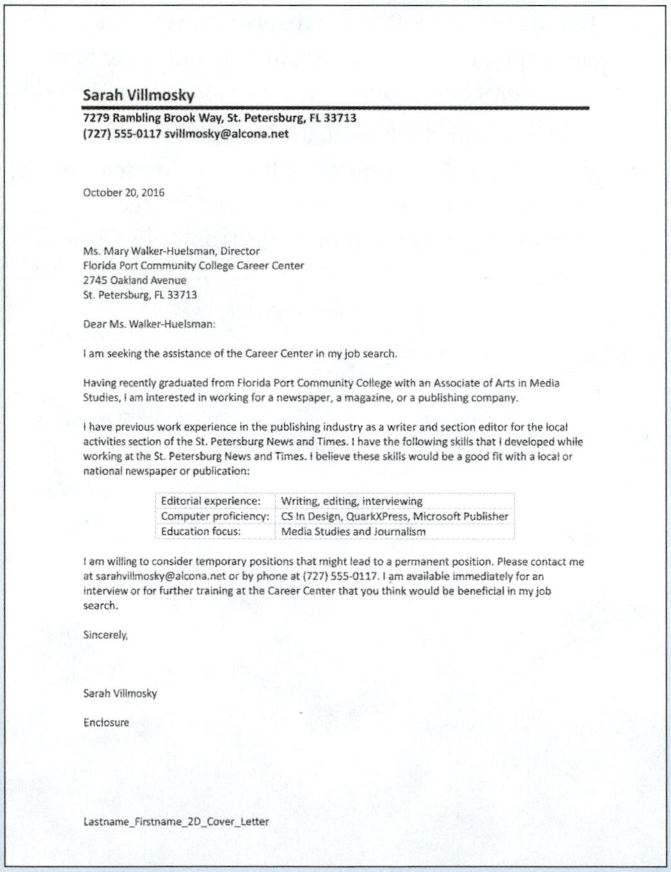

Sarah Villmosky
7279 Rambling Brook Way, St. Petersburg, FL 33713
(727) 555-0117 svillmosky@alcona.net

October 20, 2016

Ms. Mary Walker-Huelsman, Director
Florida Port Community College Career Center
2745 Oakland Avenue
St. Petersburg, FL 33713

Dear Ms. Walker-Huelsman:

I am seeking the assistance of the Career Center in my job search.

Having recently graduated from Florida Port Community College with an Associate of Arts in Media Studies, I am interested in working for a newspaper, a magazine, or a publishing company.

I have previous work experience in the publishing industry as a writer and section editor for the local activities section of the St. Petersburg News and Times. I have the following skills that I developed while working at the St. Petersburg News and Times. I believe these skills would be a good fit with a local or national newspaper or publication:

Editorial experience:	Writing, editing, interviewing
Computer proficiency:	CS In Design, QuarkXPress, Microsoft Publisher
Education focus:	Media Studies and Journalism

I am willing to consider temporary positions that might lead to a permanent position. Please contact me at sarahvillmosky@alcona.net or by phone at (727) 555-0117. I am available immediately for an interview or for further training at the Career Center that you think would be beneficial in my job search.

Sincerely,

Sarah Villmosky

Enclosure

Lastname_Firstname_2D_Cover_Letter

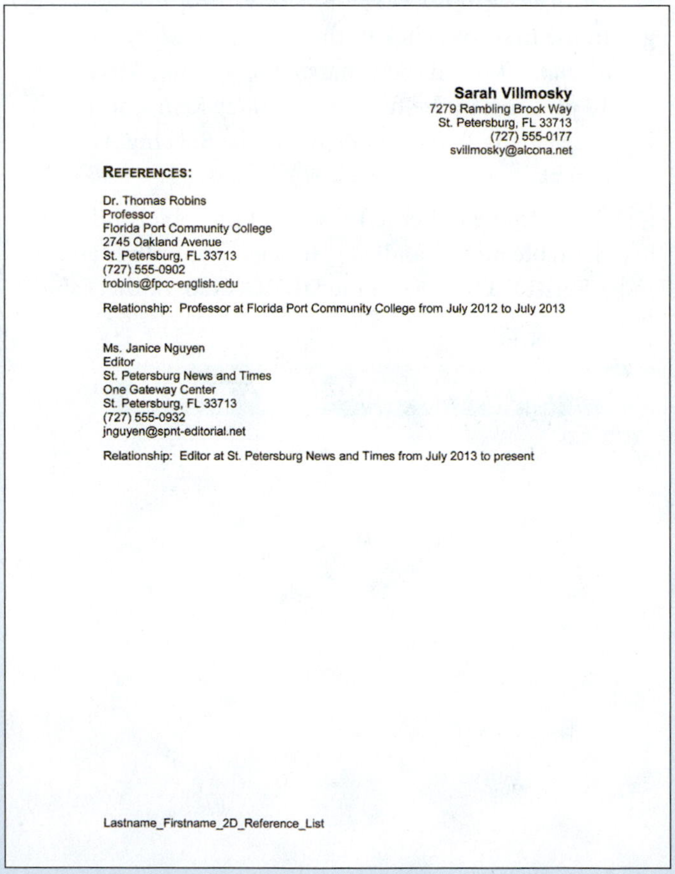

Sarah Villmosky
7279 Rambling Brook Way
St. Petersburg, FL 33713
(727) 555-0177
svillmosky@alcona.net

REFERENCES:

Dr. Thomas Robins
Professor
Florida Port Community College
2745 Oakland Avenue
St. Petersburg, FL 33713
(727) 555-0902
trobins@fpcc-english.edu

Relationship: Professor at Florida Port Community College from July 2012 to July 2013

Ms. Janice Nguyen
Editor
St. Petersburg News and Times
One Gateway Center
St. Petersburg, FL 33713
(727) 555-0932
jnguyen@spnt-editorial.net

Relationship: Editor at St. Petersburg News and Times from July 2013 to present

Lastname_Firstname_2D_Reference_List

FIGURE 2.41

(Project 2D Cover Letter and Reference List continues on the next page)

CHAPTER REVIEW

1 ▶ **Start** Word and display a blank document; be sure that formatting marks and rulers display. On the **DESIGN tab**, in the **Document Formatting group**, click **Paragraph Spacing**, and then click **No Paragraph Space**.

a. Type **Sarah Villmosky** and then press Enter. Type **7279 Rambling Brook Way, St. Petersburg, FL 33713** and then press Enter.

b. Type **(727) 555-0117 svillmosky@alcona.net** and then press Enter. If the web address changes to blue text, right-click the web address, and then click **Remove Hyperlink**.

c. Select the first paragraph—*Sarah Villmosky*—and then on the mini toolbar, apply **Bold**, and change the **Font Size** to **16**.

d. Select the second and third paragraphs, and then on the mini toolbar, apply **Bold**, and change the **Font Size** to **12**.

e. Click anywhere in the first paragraph—*Sarah Villmosky*. On the **HOME tab**, in the **Paragraph group**, click the **Borders button arrow**, and then click **Borders and Shading**. Under **Style**, click the first style—a single solid line. Click the **Width arrow**, and then click **3 pt**. In the **Preview** area, click the bottom border, and then click **OK**.

f. Press F12 to display the **Save As** dialog box. In the lower portion of the dialog box, in the **Save as type** box, click the arrow, and then click **Word Template**. In the **File name** box, type **Lastname_Firstname_2D_Letterhead_Template** and then click **Save** to save the custom Word template in the default path, which is the Templates folder on the hard drive of your computer.

g. Click the **FILE tab** to display **Backstage** view, and then click **Close** to close the file but leave Word open.

h. With Word open but no documents displayed, click the **FILE tab**, and then click **New**. Under **Suggested searches**, click **PERSONAL**, and then locate and click the letterhead template that you just created.

i. Press F12 to display the **Save As** dialog box, navigate to your **Word Chapter 2** folder, and then **Save** the file as **Lastname_Firstname_2D_Cover_Letter**

j. On the **INSERT tab**, in the **Header & Footer group**, click **Footer**, click **Edit Footer**, and then in the **Insert**

group, click **Document Info**. Click **File Name**, and then click **Close Header and Footer**. Click **Save**.

2 ▶ Click the **FILE tab**. On the left, click **Options**. On the left side of the **Word Options** dialog box, click **Proofing**, and then under **AutoCorrect options**, click the **AutoCorrect Options** button.

a. In the **AutoCorrect** dialog box, click the **AutoCorrect tab**. Under **Replace**, type the misspelled word **assistence** and under **With**, type **assistance** Click **Add**. If the entry already exists, click **Replace instead**, and then click **Yes**. Click **OK** two times to close the dialog boxes.

b. Press Ctrl + End, and then press Enter three times. On the **INSERT tab**, in the **Text group**, click **Date & Time**, and then click the third date format. Click **OK**.

c. Press Enter four times. Type the following inside address using four lines, but do *not* press Enter after the last line:

Ms. Mary Walker-Huelsman, Director

Florida Port Community College Career Center

2745 Oakland Avenue

St. Petersburg, FL 33713

d. Press Enter two times, type **Dear Ms. Walker-Huelsman:** and then press Enter two times. Type, exactly as shown with the intentional misspelling, and then watch *assistence* as you press Spacebar: **I am seeking the assistence**

e. Type **of the Career Center in my job search.** Press Enter two times.

f. On the **INSERT tab**, in the **Text Group**, click the **Object button arrow**, and then click **Text from File**. From your student files, locate and insert the file **w02D_Cover_Letter_Text**.

g. Scroll to view the lower portion of the page, and be sure your insertion point is in the empty paragraph mark at the end. Press Enter, type **Sincerely,** and then press Enter four times. Type **Sarah Villmosky** and press Enter two times. Type **Enclosure** and then **Save** your document.

h. Press Ctrl + Home. On the **HOME tab**, in the **Editing group**, click **Find**. In the **navigation** pane, click in the search box, and then type **journalism** In the letter,

(Project 2D Cover Letter and Reference List continues on the next page)

CHAPTER REVIEW

double-click the yellow highlighted word *Journalism* and type **Media Studies**

i. **Close** the **navigation** pane, and then on the **HOME tab**, in the **Editing group**, click **Replace**. In the **Find and Replace** dialog box, in the **Find what** box, replace the existing text by typing **SPNT** In the **Replace with** box, type **St. Petersburg News and Times** Click **More** to expand the dialog box, select the **Match case** check box, click **Replace All**, and then click **OK**. **Close** the **Find and Replace** dialog box.

j. In the paragraph that begins *I am available*, hold down Ctrl, and then click anywhere in the first sentence. Drag the selected sentence to the end of the paragraph by positioning the small vertical line that floats with the point to the left of the paragraph mark.

3 Below the paragraph that begins *I have previous*, click to position the insertion point in the blank paragraph, and then press Enter one time. On the **INSERT tab**, in the **Tables group**, click **Table**. In the **Table grid**, in the third row, click the second square to insert a 2 × 3 table. Type the following information in the table:

Editorial experience:	Writing, editing, interviewing
Computer proficiency:	CS In Design, QuarkXPress, Microsoft Publisher
Education focus:	Media Studies and Journalism

a. Point outside of the upper left corner of the table and click the **table move handle** button to select the entire table. On the **LAYOUT tab**, in the **Cell Size group**, click **AutoFit**, and then click **AutoFit Contents**.

b. With the table selected, on the **DESIGN tab**, in the **Table Styles group**, click **More**. Under **Plain Tables**, click the second style—**Table Grid Light**.

c. With the table still selected, on the **HOME tab**, in the **Paragraphs group**, click **Center**. **Save** your document.

4 Press Ctrl + Home. On the **REVIEW tab**, in the **Proofing group**, click **Spelling & Grammar**. For the spelling of *Villmosky*, in the **Spelling** pane, click **Ignore All**. For the spelling of *Huelsman*, click **Ignore All**.

a. For the grammar error *a*, click **Change**. Click **Change** to correct the misspelling of *intrested*. Click **Delete** to delete the duplicated word *for*. Change *activitys* to *activities*. Change *benificial* to *beneficial*. Click **OK** when the Spelling & Grammar check is complete.

b. In the paragraph that begins *I am willing*, in the third line, double-click the word *preparation*. In the **Proofing group**, click **Thesaurus**.

c. In the **Thesaurus** pane, point to *training*, click the arrow, and then click **Insert**. **Close** the **Thesaurus** pane.

d. Click **FILE tab**, and then in the lower right portion of the screen, click **Show All Properties**. In the **Tags** box, type **cover letter** and in the **Subject** box, type your course name and section number.

e. In the **Author** box, be sure your name is indicated and edit if necessary. On the left, click **Print**. If necessary, return to the document and make any necessary changes. **Save** your document, and then **Close** Word.

5 **Start** Word, and then on the opening screen, in the **Search online templates** box, type **resume references** and press Enter. Click the reference list that contains three left-aligned reference items, and then click **Create**.

a. Press F12 to display the **Save As** dialog box. **Save** the document in your **Word Chapter 2** folder as **Lastname_Firstname_2D_Reference_List** A message may indicate that the file will be upgraded to the newest file format.

b. Add the file name to the footer.

c. In the upper right, click in the placeholder text *[Your Name]* and type **Sarah Villmosky** Click *[Street Address]* and type **7279 Rambling Brook Way**

d. Click *[City, ST ZIP Code]* and type **St. Petersburg, FL 33713** Click *[phone]* and type **(727) 555-0177** Click *[email]* and type **svillmosky@alcona.net**

(Project 2D Cover Letter and Reference List continues on the next page)

Skills Review Project 2D Cover Letter and Reference List (continued)

6 Under **References**, enter two references using the information in Table 1:

a. Delete the remaining template controls.

b. Click the **FILE tab**, click **Show All Properties**, and then in the **Tags** box, type **reference list** and in the **Subject** box type your course name and section number. In the **Author** box, be sure your name is indicated and edit if necessary.

c. On the left, click **Print**. If necessary, return to the document and make any changes. Click **Save**. As directed by your instructor, print or submit electronically the two documents that are the results of this project. **Close** Word.

TABLE 1

Template Field	Reference 1	Reference 2
Reference Name	Dr. Thomas Robins	Ms. Janice Nguyen
Title	Professor	Editor
Company Name	Florida Port Community College	St. Petersburg News and Times
Street Address	2745 Oakland Avenue	One Gateway Center
City, ST ZIP Code	St. Petersburg, FL 33713	St. Petersburg, FL 33713
phone	(727) 555-0902	(727) 555-0932
email	trobins@fpcc-english.edu	jnguyen@spnt-editorial.net
Relationship with reference	Professor	Editor
Company Name	Florida Port Community College	St. Petersburg News and Times
dates of employment	July 2012 to July 2013	July 2013 to present

END | You have completed Project 2D

Return to Step 6a

CONTENT-BASED ASSESSMENTS

MyITLab® grader

Mastering Word | Project 2E Table of Job Listings

Apply 2A skills from these Objectives:

1. Create a Table
2. Format a Table
3. Present a Word Document Online

In the following Mastering Word project, you will create an announcement for new job postings at the Career Center. Your completed document will look similar to Figure 2.42.

PROJECT FILES

For Project 2E, you will need the following files:

New blank Word document

w02E_New_Jobs

Build from Scratch

You will save your document as:

Lastname_Firstname_2E_Job_Listings

PROJECT RESULTS

Florida Port Community College Career Center

Job Alert! New Positions for Computer Science Majors!

April 11

Florida Port Community College Career Center has new jobs available for both part-time and full-time positions in Computer Science. Some of these jobs are temporary, some are for a specific project with a defined beginning and ending date, and some are open-ended with the potential for permanent employment. The following jobs were posted in the past week. These listings are just in, so apply now to be one of the first candidates considered!

For further information about any of these new jobs, or a complete listing of jobs that are available through the Career Center, please call Mary Walker-Huelsman at (727) 555-0030 or visit our website at www.fpcc.pro/careers.

New Computer Science Listings for the Week of April 11

Position	Type	Location
Computer Engineer	Full-time, two months	Clearwater
Project Assistant	Full-time, three months	Coral Springs
Software Developer	Full-time, open-ended	Tampa
UI Designer	Part-time, two months	St. Petersburg

To help prepare yourself before applying for these jobs, we recommend that you review the following articles on our website at www.fpcc.pro/careers.

Topic	Article Title
Research	Working in Computer Science Fields
Interviewing	Interviewing in Startup Companies

Lastname_Firstname_2E_Job_Listings

FIGURE 2.42

(Project 2E Table of Job Listings continues on the next page)

CONTENT-BASED ASSESSMENTS

1 **Start** Word and display a blank document; display formatting marks and rulers. **Save** the document in your **Word Chapter 2** folder as **Lastname_Firstname_2E_Job_Listings** and then add the file name to the footer.

2 Type **Florida Port Community College Career Center** and press Enter. Type **Job Alert! New Positions for Computer Science Majors!** and press Enter. Type **April 11** and press Enter. **Insert** the file **w02E_New_Jobs**.

3 At the top of the document, select and **Center** the three title lines. Select the title *Florida Port Community College Career Center*, change the **Font Size** to **20 pt** and apply **Bold**. Apply **Bold** to the second and third title lines. Locate the paragraph that begins *For further*, and then below that paragraph, position the insertion point in the second blank paragraph. **Insert** a **3 × 4** table. Enter the following in the table:

Position	Type	Location
Computer Engineer	Full-time, two months	Clearwater
Software Developer	Full-time, open-ended	Tampa
UI Designer	Part-time, two months	St. Petersburg

4 In the table, point to upper left corner of the cell *Software Developer* to display the **Row Insertion** button, and then click to insert a new row. In the new row, type the following information so that the job titles remain in alphabetic order:

Project Assistant	Full-time, three months	Coral Springs

5 Select the entire table. On the **LAYOUT tab**, in the **Cell Size group**, click **AutoFit**, and then click **AutoFit Contents**. With the table still selected, on the **HOME tab**, **Center** the table. With the table still selected, on the **PAGE LAYOUT tab**, add **6 pt Spacing Before** and **6 pt Spacing After**.

6 With the table still selected, remove all table borders, and then add a **Custom 1 pt** solid line top border and bottom border. Select all three cells in the first row, apply **Bold**, and then **Center** the text. Click anywhere in the first row, and then on the **LAYOUT tab**, in the **Rows & Columns group**, insert a row above. Merge the three cells in the new top row, and then type **New Computer Science Listings for the Week of April 11** Notice that the new row keeps the formatting of the row from which it was created.

7 At the bottom of the document, **Insert** a **2 × 3** table. Enter the following:

Topic	Article Title
Research	Working in Computer Science Fields
Interviewing	Interviewing in Startup Companies

8 Select the entire table. On the **LAYOUT tab**, in the **Cell Size group**, use the **AutoFit** button to **AutoFit Contents**. On the **HOME tab**, **Center** the table. On the **PAGE LAYOUT tab**, add **6 pt Spacing Before** and **6 pt Spacing After**. With the table still selected, remove all table borders, and then add a **Custom 1 pt** solid line top border and bottom border. Select the cells in the first row, apply **Bold**, and then **Center** the text.

9 Click the **FILE tab** to display **Backstage** view, and then in the lower right portion of the screen, click **Show All Properties**. In the **Tags** box, type **new listings, computer science** and in the **Subject** box, type your course name and section number. In the **Author** box, be sure your name is indicated and edit if necessary.

10 On the left, click **Print** to display **Print Preview**. If necessary, return to the document and make any necessary changes. **Save** your document, and then if you want to do so, present your document online to a fellow classmate. Then as directed by your instructor, print your document or submit it electronically. **Close** Word.

END | You have completed Project 2E

CONTENT-BASED ASSESSMENTS

Mastering Word	Project 2F Career Tips Memo and Fax Cover Sheet

Apply 2B skills from these Objectives:

4 Create a Custom Word Template

5 Correct and Reorganize Text

6 Use the Proofing Options and Print an Envelope

7 Create a Document Using a Predesigned Microsoft Template

In the following Mastering Word project, you will create a memo and fax cover sheet that includes job tips for students and graduates using the services of the Florida Port Community College Career Center. Your completed documents will look similar to Figure 2.43.

PROJECT FILES

For Project 2F, you will need the following files:

w02F_Memo_Template
w02F_Memo_Text
Equity Fax template from Microsoft's installed templates

You will save your documents as:

Lastname_Firstname_2F_Career_Tips
Lastname_Firstname_2F_Fax

PROJECT RESULTS

Florida Port Community College Career Center

Memo

DATE: January 12, 2016

TO: Florida Port Community College Students and Graduates

FROM: Mary Huelsman-Walker, Director

SUBJECT: Using the Career Center

Tips for Students and Recent Graduates of Florida Port Community College

It is no surprise that after you leave college, you will be entering one of the most competitive job markets on record. That doesn't mean it's impossible to get your dream job. It does, however, mean that it's critical that you know how to put your best self forward to job interviewers and that you highlight all of your academic, personal, and professional achievements in a way that will help you stand out from the crowd. An Associate degree from Florida Port Community College is just the first step on your journey to getting the professional career that you want.

Give 100 Percent to Every Job

Treat every job as a career. Be willing to go beyond your assignment and complete tasks not delegated to you. Take the initiative to see ways to contribute to the company. Be willing to stay if there is unfinished work. You never know who you will meet on any job. Making a positive impression every time will give you a network of people who may help you down the road. Networking is an established means professionals use to further their careers. You can always benefit from networking. You will distinguish yourself from potential competitors if you truly give 100 percent to each job. Always remember these job basics:

Job Item	Tip for Success
Time Management	Show up on time and don't hurry to leave
Attire	Dress appropriately for the job
Work Area	Keep your work area neat and organized

Use the Career Center

Here at the Career Center and on our website, we offer tips on how to write a stellar resume and a cover letter that puts your hard work up front and center. Have you volunteered somewhere? Have you participated at a club at school? Were you a TA or a tutor? Did you make the Dean's list or graduate with honors? These are the kinds of achievements interviewers want to see. Meet with your career guidance counselor and together, come up with a plan to find the jobs that you want and get the important interview.

Lastname_Firstname_2F_Career_Tips

FAX

To:	Jane Westerfield	From:	Mary Huelsman-Walker
Fax:	(727) 555-0048	Pages:	1
Phone:	(727) 555-0047	Date:	1.12.2016
Re:	Career Tips for Students and Graduates	CC:	President Schultz

☐ Urgent   ☐ For Review   ☐ Please Comment   ☐ Please Reply   ☐ Please Recycle

Comments:

Jane: I know you are on leave, so I thought I would fax this Job Tips memo to you. We look forward to your return.

1.12.2016

Lastname_Firstname_2F_Fax

FIGURE 2.43

(Project 2F Career Tips Memo and Fax Cover Sheet continues on the next page)

CONTENT-BASED ASSESSMENTS

1 Be sure that Word is *closed*. On the taskbar, click **File Explorer**. Navigate to your student files and open **w02F_Memo_Template**. Notice that *Document1* displays in the title bar. (Recall that custom templates stored in a location other than the Templates folder on your hard drive must be opened directly from File Explorer in order for you to create and open a new document based on the template.)

2 Press F12. Navigate to your **Word Chapter 2** folder, and then in the **File name** box, using your own name, type **Lastname_Firstname_2F_Career_Tips**

3 Add the file name to the footer. At the top of your document, in the *DATE* paragraph, click to the right of the tab formatting mark, and then type **January 12, 2016** Use a similar technique to add the following information:

TO:	Florida Port Community College Students and Graduates
FROM:	Mary Huelsman-Walker, Director
SUBJECT:	Using the CC

4 Position the insertion point in the blank paragraph below the memo heading. **Insert** the file **w02F_Memo_Text**, and then press Backspace one time to remove the blank line at the end of the inserted text.

5 Select and **Center** the title *Tips for Students and Recent Graduates of Florida Port Community College*. By using either the **Spelling & Grammar** command on the **REVIEW** tab or by right-clicking words that display blue or red wavy underlines, correct or ignore words flagged as spelling, grammar, or word usage errors. Note: If you are checking an entire document, it is usually preferable to move to the top of the document, and then use the **Spelling & Grammar** command so that you do not overlook any flagged words.

6 In the paragraph that begins *Treat every job*, in the second line of the paragraph, locate and double-click *donate*. On the **REVIEW tab**, in the **Proofing group**, click **Thesaurus**, and then from the **Thesaurus** pane, change the word to *contribute*. In the last line of the same paragraph, point to *fundamentals*, right-click, point to **Synonyms**, and then click *basics*.

7 Using Match Case, replace all instances of *CC* with *Career Center*, and then in the paragraph that begins *An Associate degree*, move the first sentence to the end of the paragraph.

8 At the end of the paragraph that begins *Treat every job*, create a blank paragraph. **Insert** a 2 × 4 table, and then type the following information:

Job Item	Tip for Success
Time Management	Show up on time and don't hurry to leave
Attire	Dress appropriately for the job
Work Area	Keep your work area neat and organized

9 Select the entire table. **AutoFit Contents**, and then apply the **Grid Table 1 Light – Accent 1** table style—under **Grid Tables**, in the first row, the second style. **Center** the table.

10 Click the **FILE tab**, and then click **Show All Properties**. As the **Tags**, type **memo, job tips** and as the **Subject**, type your course name and section number. Be sure your name is indicated as the **Author**, and edit if necessary. **Save** and **Close** the document but leave Word open. Hold this file until you complete this project.

11 With Word open but no documents displayed, click the **FILE tab**, and then click **New**. In the **Search for online templates** box, type **fax (equity)** and press Enter, and then click the first **Fax (Equity theme)** template. Click **Create**. Press F12. Save the document in your **Word Chapter 2** folder, using your own name, as **Lastname_Firstname_2F_Fax** and then insert the file name in the footer. You may see a message indicating that the file will be upgraded to the newest format.

12 Use the following information to type in each control:

To:	Jane Westerfield
From:	Mary Huelsman-Walker
Fax:	(727) 555-0048
Pages:	1
Phone:	(727) 555-0047
Date:	1/12/2016
Re:	Career Tips for Students and Graduates
CC:	President Schultz
COMMENTS:	Jane: I know you are on leave, so I thought I would fax this Job Tips memo to you. We look forward to your return.

(Project 2F Career Tips Memo and Fax Cover Sheet continues on the next page)

CONTENT-BASED ASSESSMENTS

13 Click the **FILE tab**, and then click **Show All Properties**. As the **Tags**, type **memo, job tips** and as the **Subject**, type your course name and section number. The author will indicate *Mary Huelsman-Walker*. **Save** and

Close the document. As directed by your instructor, print or submit electronically the two files that are the results of this project. **Close** Word.

END | You have completed Project 2F

CONTENT-BASED ASSESSMENTS

Mastering Word	Project 2G Application Letter, Resume, and Fax Cover Sheet

In the following Mastering Word project, you will create a letter from a custom template, a resume, and a fax cover sheet from a Microsoft predesigned template. Your completed documents will look similar to Figure 2.44.

Apply 2A and 2B skills from these Objectives:

1 Create a Table
2 Format a Table
3 Present a Word Document Online
4 Create a Custom Word Template
5 Correct and Reorganize Text
6 Use the Proofing Options and Print an Envelope
7 Create a Document Using a Predesigned Microsoft Template

PROJECT FILES

For Project 2G, you will need the following files:

w02G_Letter_Text

w02G_Letterhead_Template

w02G_Resume

Equity Fax template from Microsoft's installed templates

You will save your documents as:

Lastname_Firstname_2G_Letter

Lastname_Firstname_2G_Resume

Lastname_Firstname_2G_Fax

PROJECT RESULTS

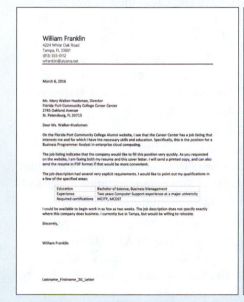

FIGURE 2.44

(Project 2G Application Letter, Resume, and Fax Cover Sheet continues on the next page)

CONTENT-BASED ASSESSMENTS

1 Be sure that Word is *closed*. On the taskbar, click **File Explorer**. Navigate to your student files and open **w02G_Letterhead_Template**. Notice that *Document1* displays in the title bar. (Recall that custom templates stored in a location other than the Templates folder on your hard drive must be opened directly from File Explorer in order for you to create and open a new document based on the template.)

2 Press [F12]. Navigate to your **Word Chapter 2** folder, and then in the **File name** box, using your own name, type **Lastname_Firstname_2G_Letter**

3 Add the file name to the footer. Be sure that rulers and formatting marks display. Move to the end of the document, and then press [Enter] three times. Use the **Date & Time** command to insert the current date using the third format, and then press [Enter] four times. Type the following:

> **Ms. Mary Walker-Huelsman, Director**
>
> **Florida Port Community College Career Center**
>
> **2745 Oakland Avenue**
>
> **St. Petersburg, FL 33713**

4 Press [Enter] two times, type **Dear Ms. Walker-Huelsman:** and press [Enter] two times. **Insert** the text from the file **w02G_Letter_Text** and press [Backspace] one time to remove the blank paragraph at the bottom of the selected text.

5 By using either the **Spelling & Grammar** command on the **REVIEW tab** or by right-clicking words that display blue or red wavy underlines, correct or ignore words flagged as spelling, grammar, or word usage errors. Hint: If you are checking an entire document, it is usually preferable to move to the top of the document, and then use the **Spelling & Grammar** command so that you do not overlook any flagged words.

6 Replace all instances of **posting** with **listing**. In the paragraph that begins *The job description*, use the **Thesaurus** pane or the **Synonyms** command on the shortcut menu to change *specific* to *explicit* and *credentials* to *qualifications*.

7 In the paragraph that begins *I currently live in Tampa*, select the first sentence of the paragraph and drag it to the end of the same paragraph. Click in the blank paragraph below the paragraph that begins *The job*

description, and then press [Enter] one time. **Insert** a 2 × 3 table, and then type the text shown in Table 1.

TABLE 1

Education	**Bachelor of Science, Business Management**
Experience	**Two years Computer Support experience at a major university**
Required Certifications	**MCITP, MCDST**

8 Select the entire table. **AutoFit Contents**, and then apply the **Table Grid Light** table style—under **Plain Tables**, in the first row, the first style. **Center** the table.

9 Click the **FILE tab**, and then click **Show All Properties**. As the **Tags**, type **letter, alumni website** and as the **Subject**, type your course name and section number. Be sure your name is indicated as the **Author**, and edit if necessary. **Save** and **Close** the document but leave Word open. Hold this file until you complete this project.

10 From your student files, open **w02G_Resume**. Press [F12], and then **Save** the document in your **Word Chapter 2** folder as **Lastname_Firstname_2G_Resume** Add the file name to the footer.

11 **Insert** a new second row in the table. In the first cell of the new row, type **OBJECTIVE** and then press [Tab]. Type **To obtain a Business Programmer Analyst position that will use my technical and communication skills and computer support experience.** In the same cell, add **12 pt Spacing After**.

12 Select the entire table. On the **LAYOUT tab**, **AutoFit Contents**. Remove the table borders, and then display the **Borders and Shading** dialog box. With the table selected, create a **Custom** single solid line **1 1/2 pt** top border.

13 In the first row of the table, select both cells and then **Merge Cells**. **Center** the five lines and apply **Bold**. In the first row, select *William Franklin* and change the **Font Size** to **20 pt** and add **24 pt Spacing Before**. In the email address at the bottom of the first row, add **24 pt Spacing After**.

14 In the first column, apply **Bold** to the four headings. In the cell to the right of *EDUCATION*, apply **Bold** to the

(Project 2G Application Letter, Resume, and Fax Cover Sheet continues on the next page)

name and address of the two colleges. Add **12 pt Spacing After** to the two lines that begin *September*. In the cell to the right of *RELEVANT EXPERIENCE*, apply **Bold** to the names of the two jobs—*IT Analyst* and *Computer Technician*. In the same cell, below the line that begins *January 2014*, apply bullets to the six lines that comprise the job duties. Create a similar bulleted list for the duties as a Computer Technician. Add **12 pt Spacing After** to the last line of each of the bulleted lists.

15 In the cell to the right of *CERTIFICATIONS*, select all four lines and create a bulleted list. Click the **FILE tab**, and then click **Show All Properties**. As the **Tags**, type **resume, business programmer analyst** and as the **Subject**, type your course name and section number. Be sure your name is indicated as the **Author**, and edit if necessary. **Save** and **Close** the document but leave Word open. Hold this file until you complete this project.

16 In Word's templates, search for **personal fax** and then select the second (shorter) template named **Fax cover sheet (informal)**. Click **Create**. **Save** the document in your **Word Chapter 2** folder as **Lastname_Firstname_2G_Fax** and then add the file name to the footer.

17 Type the text shown in Table 2 for the content controls.

TABLE 2

Subject:	**Application for Job Listing on Alumni Website**
Date:	**March 6, 2016**
To:	**Mary Walker-Huelsman**
From:	**William Franklin**
Phone number:	**(727) 555-0056**
Phone number:	**(813) 555-0122**
Fax number:	**(727) 555-0057**
No. of Pages	1
Comments:	**Two pages to follow that include my resume and a cover letter for the position of Business Programmer Analyst.**

18 Click the **FILE tab**, and then click **Show All Properties**. As the **Tags**, type **fax cover page** and as the **Subject**, type your course name and section number. Be sure your name is indicated as the **Author**, and edit if necessary. Click **Save**. As directed by your instructor, print or submit electronically the three files that are the results of this project. **Close** Word.

END | You have completed Project 2G

CONTENT-BASED ASSESSMENTS

GO! Fix It	Project 2H New Jobs	Online

Build from Scratch

GO! Make It	Project 2I Training	Online

Build from Scratch

GO! Solve It	Project 2J Job Postings	Online

Build from Scratch

GO! Solve It	Project 2K Agenda	

PROJECT FILES

For Project 2K, you will need the following file:

Agenda template from Word's Online templates

You will save your document as:

Lastname_Firstname_2K_Agenda

On Word's opening screen, search for an online template using the search term **formal meeting agenda**. Create the agenda and then save it in your Word Chapter 2 folder as **Lastname_Firstname_2K_Agenda** Use the following information to prepare an agenda for an FPCC Career Center meeting.

The meeting will be chaired by Mary Walker-Huelsman. It will be the monthly meeting of the Career Center's staff—Kevin Rau, Marilyn Kelly, André Randolph, Susan Nguyen, and Charles James. The meeting will be held on March 15, 2016, at 3:00 p.m. The old business agenda items (open issues) include (1) seeking more job listings related to the printing and food service industries, (2) expanding the alumni website, and (3) the addition of a part-time trainer. The new business agenda items will include (1) writing a grant so the center can serve more students and alumni, (2) expanding the training area with 20 additional workstations, (3) purchase of new computers for the training room, and (4) renewal of printing service contract.

Add the file name to the footer, add your name, your course name, the section number, and then add the keywords **agenda, monthly staff meeting** to the Properties area. Submit as directed.

Performance Level

Performance Criteria		Exemplary: You consistently applied the relevant skills	Proficient: You sometimes, but not always, applied the relevant skills	Developing: You rarely or never applied the relevant skills
	Select an agenda template	Agenda template is appropriate for the information provided for the meeting.	Agenda template is used, but does not fit the information provided.	No template is used for the agenda.
	Add appropriate information to the template	All information is inserted in the appropriate places.	All information is included, but not in the appropriate places.	Information is missing.
	Format template information	All text in the template is properly aligned and formatted.	All text is included, but alignment or formatting is inconsistent.	No additional formatting has been added.

END | You have completed Project 2K

OUTCOMES-BASED ASSESSMENTS

RUBRIC

The following outcomes-based assessments are *open-ended assessments*. That is, there is no specific correct result; your result will depend on your approach to the information provided. Make *Professional Quality* your goal. Use the following scoring rubric to guide you in *how* to approach the problem and then to evaluate *how well* your approach solves the problem.

The *criteria*—Software Mastery, Content, Format and Layout, and Process—represent the knowledge and skills you have gained that you can apply to solving the problem. The *levels of performance*—Professional Quality, Approaching Professional Quality, or Needs Quality Improvements—help you and your instructor evaluate your result.

	Your completed project is of Professional Quality if you:	Your completed project is Approaching Professional Quality if you:	Your completed project Needs Quality Improvements if you:
1-Software Mastery	Choose and apply the most appropriate skills, tools, and features and identify efficient methods to solve the problem.	Choose and apply some appropriate skills, tools, and features, but not in the most efficient manner.	Choose inappropriate skills, tools, or features, or are inefficient in solving the problem.
2-Content	Construct a solution that is clear and well organized, contains content that is accurate, appropriate to the audience and purpose, and is complete. Provide a solution that contains no errors in spelling, grammar, or style.	Construct a solution in which some components are unclear, poorly organized, inconsistent, or incomplete. Misjudge the needs of the audience. Have some errors in spelling, grammar, or style, but the errors do not detract from comprehension.	Construct a solution that is unclear, incomplete, or poorly organized; contains some inaccurate or inappropriate content; and contains many errors in spelling, grammar, or style. Do not solve the problem.
3-Format & Layout	Format and arrange all elements to communicate information and ideas, clarify function, illustrate relationships, and indicate relative importance.	Apply appropriate format and layout features to some elements, but not others. Overuse features, causing minor distraction.	Apply format and layout that does not communicate information or ideas clearly. Do not use format and layout features to clarify function, illustrate relationships, or indicate relative importance. Use available features excessively, causing distraction.
4-Process	Use an organized approach that integrates planning, development, self-assessment, revision, and reflection.	Demonstrate an organized approach in some areas, but not others; or, use an insufficient process of organization throughout.	Do not use an organized approach to solve the problem.

OUTCOMES-BASED ASSESSMENTS

Apply a combination of the **2A** and **2B** skills.

GO! Think   Project 2L Workshops

PROJECT FILES

Build from Scratch

For Project 2L, you will need the following files:

New blank Word document
w02L_Workshop_Information

You will save your document as:

Lastname_Firstname_2L_Workshops

The Florida Port Community College Career Center offers a series of workshops for both students and alumni. Any eligible student or graduate can attend the workshops, and there is no fee. Currently, the Career Center offers a three-session workshop covering Excel and Word, a two-session workshop covering Business Communication, and a one-session workshop covering Creating a Resume.

Print the w02L_Workshop_Information file and use the information to complete this project. Create an announcement with a title, an introductory paragraph, and a table listing the workshops and the topics covered in each workshop. Use the file w02L_Workshop_Information for help with the topics covered in each workshop. Format the table cells appropriately. Add an appropriate footer and document properties. Save the document as **Lastname_Firstname_2L_Workshops** and submit it as directed.

END | You have completed Project 2L

Build from Scratch

GO! Think!   Project 2M Planner   Online

Build from Scratch

You and GO!   Project 2N Personal Resume   Online

Build from Scratch

GO! Cumulative Group Project   Project 2O Bell Orchid Hotels
                                                                       Online

Creating Research Papers, Newsletters, and Merged Mailing Labels

GO! to Work
Video W3

PROJECT 3A

OUTCOMES
Create a research paper that includes citations and a bibliography.

PROJECT 3B

OUTCOMES
Create a multiple-column newsletter and merged mailing labels.

OBJECTIVES

1. Create a Research Paper
2. Insert Footnotes in a Research Paper
3. Create Citations and a Bibliography in a Research Paper
4. Use Read Mode and PDF Reflow

OBJECTIVES

5. Format a Multiple-Column Newsletter
6. Use Special Character and Paragraph Formatting
7. Create Mailing Labels Using Mail Merge

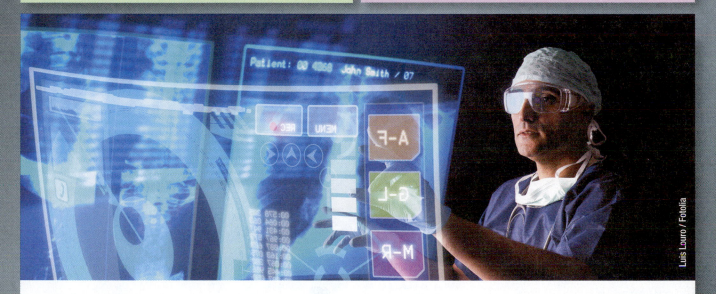

Luis Louro / Fotolia

In This Chapter

Microsoft Word provides many tools for creating complex documents. For example, Word has tools that enable you to create a research paper that includes citations, footnotes, and a bibliography. You can also create multiple-column newsletters, format the nameplate at the top of the newsletter, use special character formatting to create distinctive title text, and add borders and shading to paragraphs to highlight important information.

In this chapter, you will edit and format a research paper, create a two-column newsletter, and then create a set of mailing labels to mail the newsletter to multiple recipients.

The projects in this chapter relate to **University Medical Center**, which is a patient-care and research institution serving the metropolitan area of Memphis, Tennessee. Because of its outstanding reputation in the medical community and around the world, University Medical Center is able to attract top physicians, scientists, and researchers in all fields of medicine and achieve a level of funding that allows it to build and operate state-of-the-art facilities. A program in biomedical research was recently added. Individuals throughout the eastern United States travel to University Medical Center for diagnosis and care.

Research Paper

PROJECT ACTIVITIES

In Activities 3.01 through 3.14, you will edit and format a research paper that contains an overview of a new area of study. This paper was created by Gerard Foster, a medical intern at University Medical Center, for distribution to his classmates studying various physiologic monitoring devices. Your completed document will look similar to Figure 3.1.

PROJECT FILES

For Project 3A, you will need the following file: You will save your document as:

w03A_Quantitative_Technology   **Lastname_Firstname_3A_Quantitative_Technology**

PROJECT RESULTS

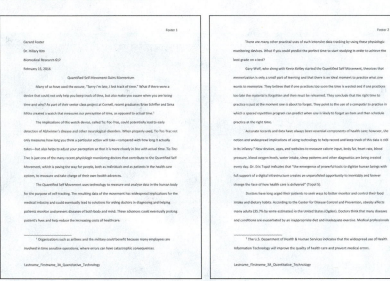

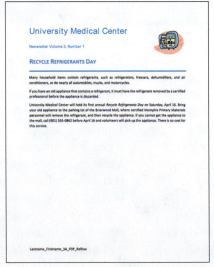

FIGURE 3.1 Project 3A Research Paper

Video W3-1

When you write a research paper or a report for college or business, follow a format prescribed by one of the standard *style guides*—a manual that contains standards for the design and writing of documents. The two most commonly used styles for research papers are those created by the *Modern Language Association (MLA)* and the *American Psychological Association (APA)*; there are several others.

N O T E **If You Are Using a Touchscreen**

- Tap an item to click it.
- Press and hold for a few seconds to right-click; release when the information or commands displays.
- Touch the screen with two or more fingers and then pinch together to zoom in or stretch your fingers apart to zoom out.
- Slide your finger on the screen to scroll—slide left to scroll right and slide right to scroll left.
- Slide to rearrange—similar to dragging with a mouse.
- Swipe from edge: from right to display charms; from left to expose open apps, snap apps, or close apps; from top or bottom to show commands or close an app.
- Swipe to select—slide an item a short distance with a quick movement—to select an item and bring up commands, if any.

Activity 3.01 | Formatting the Spacing and First-Page Information for a Research Paper

When formatting the text for your research paper, refer to the standards for the style guide that you have chosen. In this activity, you will create a research paper using the MLA style. The MLA style uses 1-inch margins, a 0.5" first line indent, and double spacing throughout the body of the document with no extra space above or below paragraphs.

1 Start Word. From your student files, locate and **Open** the document **w03A_Quantitative_Technology**. If necessary, display the formatting marks and rulers. In the location where you are storing your projects for this chapter, create a new folder named **Word Chapter 3** and then **Save** the file in the folder as **Lastname_Firstname_3A_Quantitative_Technology**

2 Press Ctrl + A to select the entire document. On the **HOME tab**, in the **Paragraph group**, click **Line and Paragraph Spacing**, and then change the line spacing to **2.0**. On the **PAGE LAYOUT tab**, in the **Paragraph group**, change the **Spacing After** to **0 pt**.

3 Press Ctrl + Home to deselect and move to the top of the document. Press Enter one time to create a blank line at the top of the document, and then click to position the insertion point in the blank line. Type **Gerard Foster** and press Enter.

4 Type **Dr. Hillary Kim** and press Enter. Type **Biomedical Research 617** and press Enter. Type **February 15, 2016** and press Enter.

5 Type **Quantified Self Movement Gains Momentum** and then press Ctrl + E, which is the keyboard shortcut to center a paragraph of text. Click **Save**, and then compare your screen with Figure 3.2.

More Knowledge **Creating a Document Heading for a Research Paper**

On the first page of an MLA-style research paper, on the first line, type the report author. On the second line, type the person for whom the report is prepared—for example, your professor or supervisor. On the third line, type the name of the class or business. On the fourth line, type the date. On the fifth line, type the report title and center it.

FIGURE 3.2

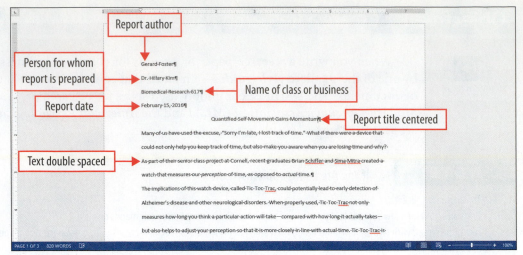

Report author

Person for whom report is prepared

Gerard·Foster¶

Dr.·Hillary·Kim¶

Name of class or business

Biomedical·Research·617¶

Report date

February·15,·2016¶

Quantified·Self·Movement·Gains·Momentum¶

Report title centered

Many·of·us·have·used·the·excuse,·"Sorry·I'm·late,·I·lost·track·of·time."·What·if·there·were·a·device·that·

could·not·only·help·you·keep·track·of·time,·but·also·make·you·aware·when·you·are·losing·time·and·why?·

Text double spaced

As·part·of·their·senior·class·project·at·Cornell,·recent·graduates·Brian·Schiffer·and·Sima·Mitra·created·a·

watch·that·measures·our·*perception*·of·time,·as·opposed·to·*actual*·time.¶

The·implications·of·this·watch·device,·called·Tic-Toc·Trac,·could·potentially·lead·to·early·detection·of·

Alzheimer's·disease·and·other·neurological·disorders.·When·properly·used,·Tic-Toc·Trac·not·only·

measures·how·long·you·think·a·particular·action·will·take—compared·with·how·long·it·actually·takes—

but·also·helps·to·adjust·your·perception·so·that·it·is·more·closely·in·line·with·actual·time.·Tic-Toc·Trac·is·

PAGE 1 OF 3   820 WORDS   100%

More Knowledge | **Creating a Bookmark**

In a document, you can mark a place you want to find again easily. Select the content to which you want to assign the bookmark. On the INSERT tab, in the Links group, click Bookmark, and assign a name. To go to the bookmark, press CTRL + G, select Bookmark, and then click the bookmark name.

Activity 3.02 | Formatting the Page Numbering and Paragraph Indents for a Research Paper

1 On the **INSERT tab**, in the **Header & Footer group**, click **Header**, and then at the bottom of the list, click **Edit Header**.

2 Type **Foster** and then press Spacebar.

Recall that the text you insert into a header or footer displays on every page of a document. Within a header or footer, you can insert many different types of information; for example, automatic page numbers, the date, the time, the file name, or pictures.

3 Under **HEADER & FOOTER TOOLS**, on the **DESIGN tab**, in the **Header & Footer group**, click **Page Number**, and then point to **Current Position**. In the gallery, under **Simple**, click **Plain Number**. Compare your screen with Figure 3.3.

Word will automatically number the pages using this number format.

FIGURE 3.3

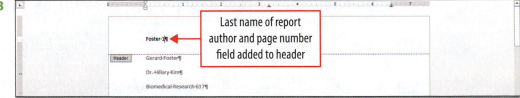

Foster·1¶

Last name of report author and page number field added to header

Header   Gerard·Foster¶

Dr.·Hillary·Kim¶

Biomedical·Research·617¶

4 On the **HOME tab**, in the **Paragraph group**, click **Align Right**. Double-click anywhere in the document to close the Header area.

5 Near the top of **Page 1**, locate the paragraph beginning *Many of us*, and then click to position the insertion point at the beginning of the paragraph. By moving the vertical scroll bar, scroll to the end of the document, hold down Shift, and then click to right of the last paragraph mark to select all of the text from the insertion point to the end of the document. Release Shift.

6 With the text selected, in the **Paragraph group**, click the **Dialog Box Launcher** button to display the **Paragraph** dialog box.

7 On the **INDENTS and SPACING tab**, under **Indentation**, click the **Special arrow**, and then click **First line**. In the **By** box, be sure **0.5"** displays. Click **OK**. Compare your screen with Figure 3.4.

The MLA style uses 0.5-inch indents at the beginning of the first line of every paragraph. *Indenting*—moving the beginning of the first line of a paragraph to the right or left of the rest of the paragraph—provides visual cues to the reader to help divide the document text and make it easier to read.

FIGURE 3.4

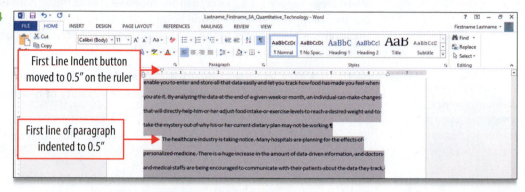

First Line Indent button moved to 0.5" on the ruler

First line of paragraph indented to 0.5"

ANOTHER WAY   On the ruler, point to the First Line Indent button, and then drag the button to 0.5" on the horizontal ruler.

8 Press Ctrl + Home to deselect and move to the top of the document. On the **INSERT tab**, in the **Header & Footer group**, click **Footer**, and then at the bottom of the list click **Edit Footer**.

9 In the **Insert group**, click **Document Info**, and then click **File Name**. On the ribbon, click **Close Header and Footer**.

The file name in the footer is *not* part of the research report format, but it is included in projects in this textbook so that you and your instructor can identify your work.

10 **Save** your document.

More Knowledge   **Suppressing the Page Number on the First Page of a Document**

Some style guidelines require that the page number and other header and footer information on the first page be hidden from view—***suppressed***. To hide the information contained in the header and footer areas on Page 1 of a document, double-click in the header or footer area. Then, under HEADER & FOOTER TOOLS, on the DESIGN tab, in the Options group, select the Different First Page check box.

Objective 2   Insert Footnotes in a Research Paper

Video W3-2

Reports and research papers typically include information that you find in other sources, and these must be credited. Within report text, numbers mark the location of ***notes***—information that expands on the topic being discussed but that does not fit well in the document text. The numbers refer to ***footnotes***—notes placed at the bottom of the page containing the note, or to ***endnotes***—notes placed at the end of a document or chapter.

Activity 3.03 | Inserting Footnotes

You can add footnotes as you type your document or after your document is complete. Word renumbers the footnotes automatically, so footnotes need not be entered in order, and if one footnote is removed, the remaining footnotes automatically renumber.

1 Scroll to view the upper portion of **Page 2**, and then locate the paragraph that begins *Accurate records*. In the third line of the paragraph, click to position the insertion point to the right of the period after *infancy*.

2 On the **REFERENCES tab**, in the **Footnotes group**, click **Insert Footnote**.

> Word creates space for a footnote in the footnote area at the bottom of the page and adds a footnote number to the text at the insertion point location. Footnote *1* displays in the footnote area, and the insertion point moves to the right of the number. A short black line is added just above the footnote area. You do not need to type the footnote number.

3 Type **The U.S. Department of Health & Human Services indicates that the widespread use of Health Information Technology will improve the quality of health care and prevent medical errors.**

> This is an explanatory footnote; the footnote provides additional information that does not fit well in the body of the report.

4 Click the **HOME tab**, and then examine the font size and line spacing settings. Notice that the new footnote displays in 10 pt font size and is single-spaced, even though the font size of the document text is 11 pt and the text is double-spaced, as shown in Figure 3.5.

FIGURE 3.5

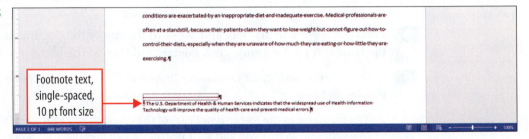

Footnote text, single-spaced, 10 pt font size

5 Scroll to view the top of **Page 1**, and then locate the paragraph that begins *Many of us*. At the end of the paragraph, click to position the insertion point to the right of the period following *time*.

6 On the **REFERENCES tab**, in the **Footnotes group**, click **Insert Footnote**. Type **Organizations such as airlines and the military could benefit because many employees are involved in time-sensitive operations, where errors can have catastrophic consequences.** Notice that the footnote you just added becomes the new footnote *1*. Click **Save** , and then compare your screen with Figure 3.6.

> The first footnote that you typed, which is on Page 2 and begins *The U.S. Department of Health*, is renumbered as footnote *2*.

FIGURE 3.6

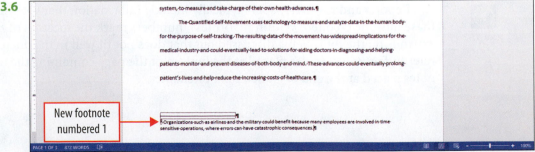

New footnote numbered 1

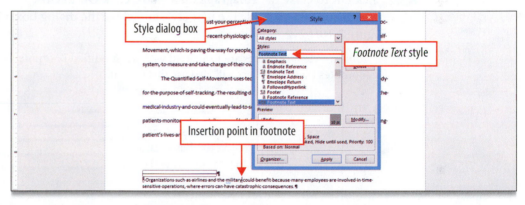
Activity 3.04 | Modifying a Footnote Style

Microsoft Word contains built-in paragraph formats called *styles*—groups of formatting commands, such as font, font size, font color, paragraph alignment, and line spacing—that can be applied to a paragraph with one command.

The default style for footnote text is a single-spaced paragraph that uses a 10-point Calibri font and no paragraph indents. MLA style specifies double-spaced text in all areas of a research paper—including footnotes. According to the MLA style, first lines of footnotes must also be indented 0.5 inch and use the same font size as the report text.

1 At the bottom of **Page 1**, point anywhere in the footnote text you just typed, right-click, and then on the shortcut menu, click **Style**. Compare your screen with Figure 3.7.

The Style dialog box displays, listing the styles currently in use in the document, in addition to some of the word processing elements that come with special built-in styles. Because you right-clicked on the footnote text, the selected style is the Footnote Text style.

FIGURE 3.7

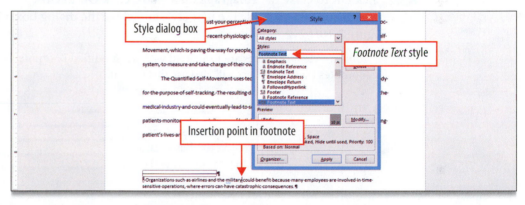

2 In the **Style** dialog box, click **Modify**, and then in the **Modify Style** dialog box, locate the small **Formatting** toolbar in the center of the dialog box. Click the **Font Size button arrow**, click **11**, and then compare your screen with Figure 3.8.

FIGURE 3.8

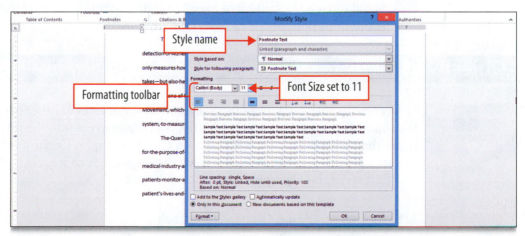

> **3** In the lower left corner of the dialog box, click **Format**, and then click **Paragraph**. In the **Paragraph** dialog box, on the **Indents and Spacing tab**, under **Indentation**, click the **Special arrow**, and then click **First line**.

> **4** Under **Spacing**, click the **Line spacing arrow**, and then click **Double**. Compare your dialog box with Figure 3.9.

FIGURE 3.9

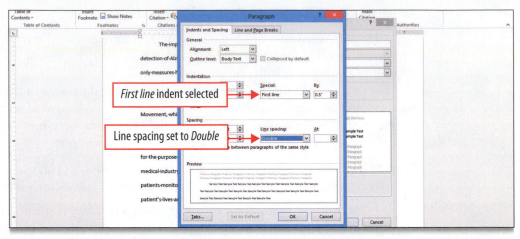

> **5** Click **OK** to close the **Paragraph** dialog box, click **OK** to close the **Modify Style** dialog box, and then click **Apply** to apply the new style and **close** the dialog box. Compare your screen with Figure 3.10.

Your inserted footnotes are formatted with the modified Footnote Text paragraph style; any new footnotes that you insert will also use this format.

FIGURE 3.10

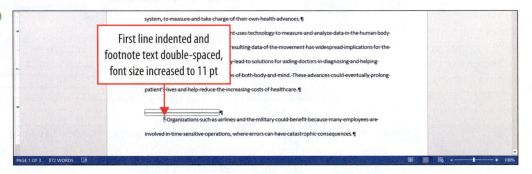

> **6** Scroll to view the bottom of **Page 2** to confirm that the new format was also applied to the second footnote, and then **Save** 💾 your document.

Objective 3   Create Citations and a Bibliography in a Research Paper

Video W3-3

When you use quotations from or detailed summaries of other people's work, you must specify the source of the information. A **_citation_** is a note inserted into the text of a report or research paper that refers the reader to a source in the bibliography. Create a **_bibliography_** at the end of a research paper to list the sources you have referenced. Such a list is typically titled **_Works Cited_** (in MLA style), _Bibliography_, _Sources_, or _References_.

Activity 3.05 | Adding Citations for a Book

When writing a long research paper, you will likely reference numerous books, articles, and websites. Some of your research sources may be referenced many times, others only one time.

References to sources within the text of your research paper are indicated in an *abbreviated* manner. However, as you enter a citation for the first time, you can also enter the *complete* information about the source. Then, when you have finished your paper, you will be able to automatically generate the list of sources that must be included at the end of your research paper.

1 Scroll to view the middle of **Page 2**. In the paragraph that begins *Accurate records*, at the end of the paragraph, click to position the insertion point to the right of the quotation mark.

The citation in the document points to the full source information in the bibliography, which typically includes the name of the author, the full title of the work, the year of publication, and other publication information.

2 On the **REFERENCES tab**, in the **Citations & Bibliography group**, click the **Style button arrow**, and then click **MLA** to insert a reference using MLA bibliography style.

3 Click **Insert Citation**, and then click **Add New Source**. Click the **Type of Source arrow**, and then click **Book**. Add the following information, and then compare your screen with Figure 3.11:

Author:	**Sopol, Eric J.**
Title:	**The Creative Destruction of Medicine**
Year:	**2012**
City:	**New York**
Publisher:	**Basic Books**
Medium	**Print**

FIGURE 3.11

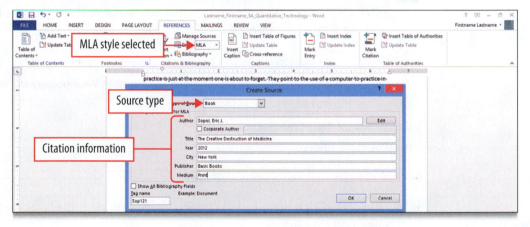

NOTE **Citing Corporate Authors and Indicating the Medium**

If the author of a document is only identified as the name of an organization, select the Corporate Author check box and type the name of the organization in the Corporate Author box.

In the Seventh edition of the *MLA Handbook for Writers of Research Papers*, the category Medium was added and must be included for any item on the Works Cited page. Entries for this category can include Print, Web, Performance, and Photograph, among many others.

---

4 Click **OK** to insert the citation. Point to *(Sopol)* and click one time to select the citation.

In the MLA style, citations that refer to items on the *Works Cited* page are placed in parentheses and are referred to as *parenthetical references*—references that include the last name of the author or authors and the page number in the referenced source, which you add to the reference. No year is indicated, and there is no comma between the name and the page number.

5 Save ⊞ the document.

Activity 3.06 | Editing Citations

1 In the lower right corner of the box that surrounds the reference, point to the small arrow to display the ScreenTip *Citation Options*. Click this **Citation Options arrow**, and then on the list of options, click **Edit Citation**.

2 In the **Edit Citation** dialog box, under **Add**, in the **Pages** box, type **5** to indicate that you are citing from Page 5 of this source. Compare your screen with Figure 3.12.

FIGURE 3.12

3 Click **OK** to display the page number of the citation. Click outside of the citation box to deselect it. Then type a period to the right of the citation, and delete the period to the left of the quotation mark.

In the MLA style, if the reference occurs at the end of a sentence, the parenthetical reference always displays to the left of the punctuation mark that ends the sentence.

4 Press Ctrl + End to move to the end of the document, and then click to position the insertion point after the letter *e* in *disease* and to the left of the period.

5 In the **Citations & Bibliography group**, click **Insert Citation**, and then click **Add New Source**. Click the **Type of Source arrow**, if necessary scroll to the top of the list, click **Book**, and then add the following information:

Author:	**Glaser, John P. and Claudia Salzberg**
Title:	**The Strategic Application of Information Technology in Health Care Organizations**
Year:	**2011**
City:	**San Francisco**
Publisher:	**Jossey-Bass**
Medium:	**Print**

6 Click **OK**. Click the inserted citation to select it, click the **Citation Options arrow**, and then click **Edit Citation**.

7 In the **Edit Citation** dialog box, under **Add**, in the **Pages** box, type **28** to indicate that you are citing from page 28 of this source. Click **OK**.

8 On the **REFERENCES tab**, in the **Citations & Bibliography group**, click **Manage Sources**, and then compare your screen with Figure 3.13.

The Source Manager dialog box displays. Other citations on your computer display in the Master List box. The citations for the current document display in the Current List box. Word maintains the Master List so that if you use the same sources regularly, you can copy sources from your Master List to the current document. A preview of the bibliography entry also displays at the bottom of the dialog box.

FIGURE 3.13

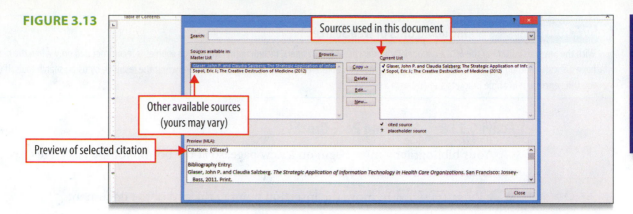

9 At the bottom of the **Source Manager** dialog box, click **Close**. Click anywhere in the document to deselect the parenthetical reference, and then **Save** 🖫 your document.

Activity 3.07 | Adding Citations for a Website

1 In the lower portion of **Page 2**, in the paragraph that begins *Doctors have long*, in the third line, click to position the insertion point after the s in *States* and to the left of the period.

2 In the **Citations & Bibliography group**, click **Insert Citation**, and then click **Add New Source**. Click the **Type of Source arrow**, scroll down as necessary, and then click **Web site**. Type the following information:

Author:	**Ogden, Cynthia L., Margaret D. Carroll, Brian K. Kit, and Katherine M. Flegal**
Name of Web Page:	**NCHS Data Brief Number 82**
Year:	**2012**
Month:	**January**
Day:	**15**
Year Accessed:	**2016**
Month Accessed:	**January**
Day Accessed:	**17**
Medium	**Web**

3 Click **OK**. Save 🖫, and then compare your screen with Figure 3.14.

A parenthetical reference is added. Because the cited web page has no page numbers, only the author name is used in the parenthetical reference.

FIGURE 3.14

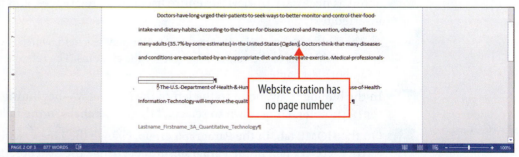

Activity 3.08 | Inserting Page Breaks

Your bibliography must begin on a new page, so at the bottom of the last page of your report, you must insert a manual page break.

1 Press Ctrl + End to move the insertion point to the end of the document.

> If there is a footnote on the last page, the insertion point will display at the end of the final paragraph, but above the footnote—a footnote is always associated with the page that contains the citation.

2 Press Ctrl + Enter to insert a manual page break.

> A *manual page break* forces a page to end at the insertion point location, and then places any subsequent text at the top of the next page. Recall that the new paragraph retains the formatting of the previous paragraph, so in this instance the first line is indented.

> A *page break indicator*, which shows where a manual page break was inserted, displays at the bottom of Page 3.

3 On the **HOME tab**, in the **Paragraph group**, click the **Dialog Box Launcher** button 🔲 to display the **Paragraph** dialog box.

4 On the **Indents and Spacing tab**, under **Indentation**, click the **Special arrow**, and then click **(none)**. Click **OK**, and then **Save** 💾 your document.

🔄 **ANOTHER WAY**   On the ruler, point to the First Line Indent button ▽, and then drag the button to 0" on the horizontal ruler.

Activity 3.09 | Creating a Reference Page

At the end of a report or research paper, include a list of each source referenced. *Works Cited* is the reference page heading used in the MLA style guidelines. Other styles may refer to this page as a *Bibliography* (Business Style) or *References* (APA Style). Always display this information on a separate page.

1 With the insertion point blinking in the first line of **Page 4**, type **Works Cited** and then press Enter. On the **REFERENCES tab**, in the **Citations & Bibliography group**, in the **Style** box, be sure *MLA* displays.

2 In the **Citations & Bibliography group**, click **Bibliography**, and then near the bottom of the list, click **Insert Bibliography**.

3 Scroll as necessary to view the entire list of three references, and then click anywhere in the inserted text.

> The bibliography entries that you created display as a field, which is indicated by the gray shading. This field links to the Source Manager for the citations. The references display alphabetically by the author's last name.

4 In the bibliography, point to the left of the first entry—beginning *Glaser, John P.*—to display the 🔄 pointer. Drag down to select all three references in the field.

5 On the **HOME tab**, in the **Paragraph group**, change the **Line spacing** to **2.0**, and then on the **PAGE LAYOUT tab**, in the **Paragraph group**, change the **Spacing After** to **0 pt**.

> The entries display according to MLA guidelines; the text is double-spaced, the extra space between paragraphs has been removed, and each entry uses a *hanging indent*—the first line of each entry extends 0.5 inch to the left of the remaining lines of the entry.

6 At the top of **Page 4**, click anywhere in the title text *Works Cited*, and then press Ctrl + E to center the title. Compare your screen with Figure 3.15, and then **Save** 🖫 your document.

In MLA style, the *Works Cited* title is centered.

FIGURE 3.15

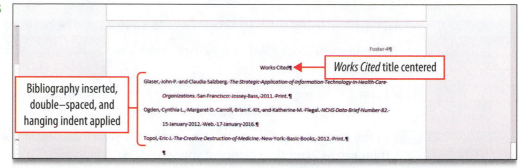

Works Cited title centered

Bibliography inserted, double–spaced, and hanging indent applied

Activity 3.10 | Managing and Modifying Sources for a Document

Use the Source Manager to organize the sources cited in your document. For example, in the Source Manager dialog box, you can copy sources from the master list to the current list, delete a source, edit a source, or search for a source. You can also display a preview of how your citations will appear in your document.

1 On the **REFERENCES tab**, in the **Citations & Bibliography group**, click **Manage Sources**.

2 On the left, in the **Master List**, click the entry for *Sopol, Eric J.* and then between the **Master List** and the **Current List**, click **Edit**.

The name of this source should be *Topol* instead of *Sopol*.

3 In the **Edit Source** dialog box, in the **Author** box, delete *S* and type **T**

4 Click **OK**. When the message box indicates *This source exists in your master list and current document. Do you want to update both lists with these changes?* click **Yes**. Compare your screen with Figure 3.16.

In the lower portion of the Source Manager dialog box, a preview of the corrected entry displays.

FIGURE 3.16

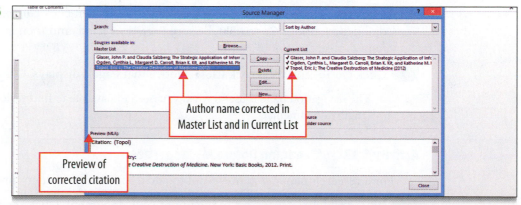

Author name corrected in Master List and in Current List

Preview of corrected citation

5 In the lower right corner, click **Close**. On your **Works Cited page**, notice that the author name is *not* corrected. Scroll to view the lower portion of **Page 2**, and notice that the author name *is* corrected and the citation is selected.

6 On the selected citation *(Topol 5)*, click the **Citation Options arrow**, and then click **Update Citations and Bibliography**. Press Ctrl + End, and notice that this action updates the **Works Cited page** with the corrected name.

> Editing a source in Source Manager updates only the sources in the document; to update the Works Cited page, use the Update Citations and Bibliography command on the citation.

7 Drag to select all the lines for the three references. On the **HOME tab**, in the **Paragraph group**, click **Line and Paragraph Spacing** ⌷▾, and then click **2.0**. Click **Save** ⌷.

Activity 3.11 | Using the Navigation Pane to Go to a Specific Page

In a multipage document, use the navigation pane to move to a specific page or to find specific objects in the document.

1 Press Ctrl + Home to move to the top of the document. Click the **VIEW tab**, and then in the **Show group**, select the **navigation pane** check box.

2 In the **navigation pane**, on the right end of the **Search document** box, click the **Search for more things arrow**, and then compare your screen with Figure 3.17.

FIGURE 3.17

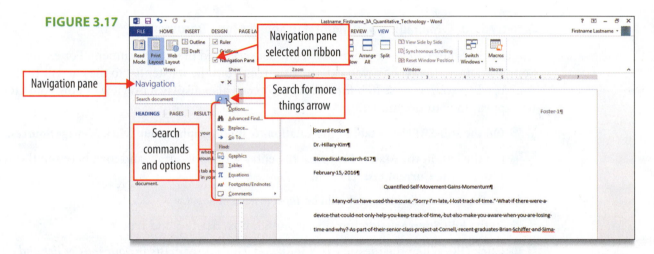

3 Under **Find**, click **Footnotes/Endnotes**. Notice that the first numbered footnote is selected.

4 In the **navigation pane**, to the right of *Result 1 of 2*, click the down arrow to move to the next numbered footnote.

5 Click the **Search for more things arrow** again, and then click **Go To**. In the **Find and Replace** dialog box, under **Go to what**, be sure **Page** is selected, and then in the **Enter page number** box, type **4**

6 Click **Go To**, and then click **Close**. Notice that **Page 4** displays. **Close** ✖ the **navigation pane**.

> The navigation pane is useful when you need to navigate to find various elements, especially in a lengthy document.

Activity 3.12 | Managing Document Properties

For a research paper, you may want to add additional document properties.

1 Press Ctrl + Home to return to the top of your document. Click the **FILE tab** to display **Backstage** view, and then in the lower right corner of the screen, click **Show All Properties**.

2 As the document **Title**, type **Quantified Self Movement Gains Momentum** and then as the **Tags**, type **quantified self, physiologic monitoring, research paper**

3 ▸ Click in the **Comments** box and type **Draft copy of a research report that will be distributed to class members** and then in the **Categories** box, type **Biomedical Research**

4 ▸ In the **Subject** box, type your course name and section number. In the **Company** box, select and delete any existing text, and then type **University Medical Center**

5 ▸ Click in the **Manager** box and type **Dr. Hillary Kim** Be sure your name displays as the **Author** and edit if necessary.

6 ▸ At the top of the **Properties** list, click the text *Properties*, and then click **Advanced Properties**. In the dialog box, click the **Summary tab**, and then compare your screen with Figure 3.18.

In the Advanced Properties dialog box, you can view and modify additional document properties.

FIGURE 3.18

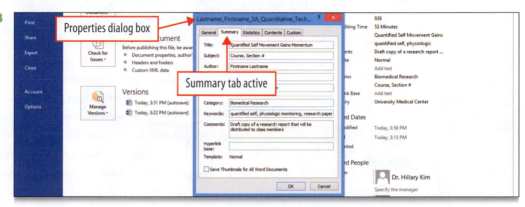

7 ▸ Click the **Statistics tab**.

The document statistics show the number of revisions made to the document, the last time the document was edited, and the number of paragraphs, lines, words, and characters in the document. Additional information categories are available by clicking the Custom tab.

8 ▸ **Close** ☒ the dialog box, and then on the left, click **Save** to save and return to your document.

Objective 4   Use Read Mode and PDF Reflow

Video W3-4

Read Mode optimizes the view of the Word screen for the times when you are *reading* Word documents on the screen and not creating or editing them. Microsoft's research indicates that two-thirds of user sessions in Word contain no editing—meaning that people are simply reading the Word document on the screen. The Column Layout feature of Read Mode reflows the document to fit the size of the device you are reading so that the text is as easy to read on a tablet device as on a 24-inch screen. The Object Zoom feature of Read Mode resizes graphics to fit the screen you are using, but you can click or tap to zoom in on the graphic.

PDF Reflow provides the ability to import PDF files into Word so that you can transform a PDF back into a fully editable Word document. This is useful if you have lost the original Word file or if someone sends you a PDF that you would like to modify. PDF Reflow is not intended to act as a viewer for PDF files—for that you will still want to use the desktop app known as Adobe Reader or the *Windows Reader app*, with which you can open a PDF or XPS file, zoom, find words or phrases, take notes, save changes, and then print or share the file.

Activity 3.13   Using Read Mode

1 ▸ If necessary, press Ctrl + Home to move to the top of your document. On the **VIEW tab**, in the **Views group**, click **Read Mode**, and notice that **Read Mode** keeps footnotes displayed on the page associated with the footnote.

🔄 **ANOTHER WAY**   On the right side of the status bar, click the Read Mode button 📖.

2 In the upper left corner, click **TOOLS**.

You can use these tools to find something within the document or jump out to Bing to conduct an Internet search.

3 Click **Find**, and then in the **Search** box, type **Topol** Notice that Word displays the first page where the search term displays and highlights the term in yellow. Compare your screen with Figure 3.19.

FIGURE 3.19

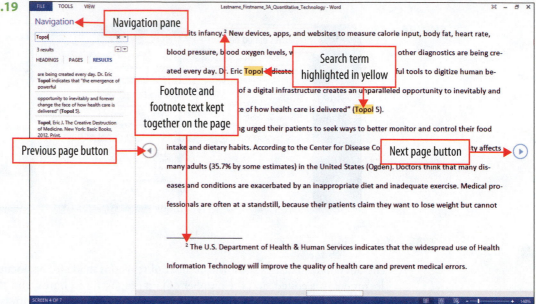

4 In the upper left corner, click **VIEW**, and then take a moment to study the table in Figure 3.20.

FIGURE 3.20

VIEW COMMANDS IN READ MODE	
VIEW COMMAND	**ACTION**
Edit Document	Return to Print Layout view to continue editing the document.
Navigation Pane	Search for specific text or click a heading or page to move to that location.
Show Comments	See comments, if any, within the document.
Column Width	Change the display of the document to fit more or less text on each line.
Page Color	Change the colors used to show the document to make it easier to read. Some readers prefer a sepia (brownish-gray) shading as the background or a black background with white text.
Layout	Read in different layouts. Select Column Layout, which is the default, or Paper Layout, which mimics the 8.5 × 11 format but without the ribbon.

5 On the **VIEW** menu, click **Edit Document** to return to **Print Layout** view. **Close** ❌ the **navigation pane**.

🔄 **ANOTHER WAY**   On the status bar on the right, click the Print Layout button 📄.

Activity 3.14 | Using PDF Reflow

1 ▶ Save 🖫 your document. Click the **FILE tab**, and then on the left, click **Close** to close your document but leave Word open.

2 ▶ Press ⌃Ctrl + F12 to display the **Open** dialog box, navigate to your student data files, and then click **w03A_PDF**. In the lower right corner, click **Open**. If a message indicates that *Word will now convert the PDF to an editable Word document…*, click **OK**.

3 ▶ If necessary, on the right side of the status bar, click **Print Layout** 🖫.

4 ▶ In the newsletter heading, change the **Volume** number to **3** Insert a footer, and then, using your own name, type **Lastname_Firstname_3A_PDF_Reflow** as shown in Figure 3.21.

FIGURE 3.21

Your first and last name in footer → Lastname_Firstname_3A_PDF_Reflow

5 ▶ Close the footer area. Press F12 to display the **Save As** dialog box, and then navigate to your **Word Chapter 3** folder. In the lower portion of the dialog box, click the **Save as type arrow**, and then click **PDF**.

6 ▶ In the **File name** box, type **Lastname_Firstname_3A_PDF_Reflow** and then in the lower right corner, click **Save** or press Enter.

This action re-saves the document as a PDF file.

> 🔄 **ANOTHER WAY**   Click the FILE tab, on the left click Export, click Create PDF/XPS, navigate to the desired folder, and then click Publish.

7 ▶ **Close** the **w03A_PDF** document without saving. **Close** ⎡ **x** ⎤ Word. Print or submit electronically the two files that are the result of this project.

More Knowledge   **Inserting Watermarks**

You can add ghost text such as *Draft* or *Confidential* behind the content of a page. To do so, on the DESIGN tab, in the Page Background group, click Watermark, and select or create the watermark you want to use.

END | You have completed Project 3A

GO! with Office Web Apps

Objective | Insert a Link and Highlight Text in a Word Web App Document

You can use the Word Web App to insert a link to a website.

> **ALERT!** **Working with Web-Based Applications and Services**
>
> Computer programs and services on the web receive continuous updates and improvements, so the steps to complete this web-based activity may differ from the ones shown. You can often look at the screens and the information presented to determine how to complete the activity.

Activity | Inserting a Link and Highlighting a Text Selection

The Word Web App does not include the commands on the REFERENCES tab, so if you open a report that contains footnotes or citations created in the Word desktop app, you cannot edit them in the Word Web App. However, you can still make common text edits as you have practiced in other Web App projects. You can also insert a link to a website. In this activity, you will use the Word Web App to insert a link in a report, which you might want to do before sharing the report electronically for review by others.

1 From the desktop, start Internet Explorer. Navigate to **http://skydrive.com**, and then sign in to your Microsoft account. Open your **GO! Web Projects** folder; or create this folder if you have not done so.

2 In the SkyDrive menu bar, click **Upload**. Navigate to your student data files, click **w03_3A_Web**, and then click **Open**.

3 Point to the uploaded file **w03_3A_Web**, and then right-click. On the shortcut menu, scroll as necessary, and then click **Rename**. Using your own last name and first name, type **Lastname_Firstname_WD_3A_Web** and then press [Enter] to rename the file.

4 Click the file that you just renamed, and then click **EDIT DOCUMENT**. On the list, click **Edit in Word Web App**.

5 In the paragraph that begins *The implications*, drag to select *Tic-Toc-Trac*, and then on the **HOME tab**, in the **Font group**, click **Text Highlight Color** [icon]. Click the **Yellow** block to highlight this text in yellow.

6 Press [Ctrl] + [End] to move to the end of the document, and then press [Enter].

7 On the **INSERT tab**, in the **Links group**, click **Link**. In the **Display text** box, type **See how Tic-Toc-Trac works!**

8 In the **Address** box, type **www.tictoctrac.com** and then click **Insert**. Compare your screen with Figure A.

9 To test the link, point to it, hold down [Ctrl] and then click one time. The site opens on a new tab.

10 In your browser, close the **TicTocTrac** tab.

11 Above the **FILE tab**, click **Save** [icon]. Click the **FILE tab**, and then click **Exit**. Submit as directed by your instructor. Sign out of your SkyDrive.

FIGURE A

graduates Brian Schiffer and Sima Mitra created a watch that measures our perception of time, as opposed to actual time.

The implications of this watch device, called Tic-Toc-Trac, could potentially lead to early detection of Alzheimer's disease and other neurological disorders. When properly used, Tic-Toc-Trac not only measures how long you think a particular action will take—compared with how long it actually takes—but also helps to adjust your perception so that it is more closely in line with actual time. The Tic-Toc-Trac is just one of the many recent physiologic monitoring devices that contribute to the Quantified Self Movement, which is paving the way for people, both as individuals and as patients in the health care system, to measure and take charge of their own health advances.

See how Tic-Toc-Trac works!

PROJECT ACTIVITIES

In Activities 3.15 through 3.29, you will edit a newsletter that University Medical Center is sending to the board of directors and create the necessary mailing labels. Your completed documents will look similar to Figure 3.22.

PROJECT FILES

For Project 3B, you will need the following files:

New blank Word document
w03B_Environment_Newsletter
w03B_Addresses

You will save your documents as:

Lastname_Firstname_3B_Mailing_Labels
Lastname_Firstname_3B_Addresses
Lastname_Firstname_3B_Environment_Newsletter

PROJECT RESULTS

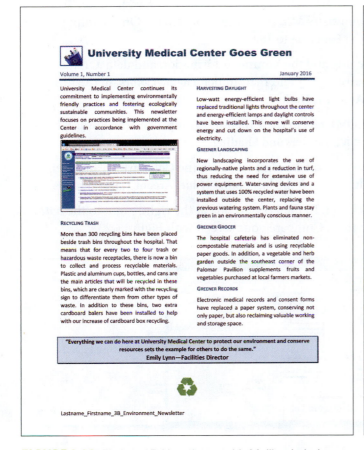

FIGURE 3.22 Project 3B Newsletter with Mailing Labels

Video W3-5

A **newsletter** is a periodical that communicates news and information to a specific group. Newsletters, as well as all newspapers and most magazines, use multiple columns for articles because text in narrower columns is easier to read than text that stretches across a page. You can create a newsletter in Word by changing a single column of text into two or more columns. If a column does not end where you want it to, you can end the column at a location of your choice by inserting a **manual column break**—an artificial end to a column to balance columns or to provide space for the insertion of other objects.

Activity 3.15 │ Changing One Column of Text to Two Columns

Newsletters are usually two or three columns wide. When using 8.5 × 11-inch paper in portrait orientation, avoid creating four or more columns because they are so narrow that word spacing looks awkward, often resulting in one long word on a line by itself.

1 Start Word. On Word's opening screen, in the lower left, click **Open Other Documents**. Navigate to your student files, and then locate and open the document **w03B_Environment_ Newsletter**. If necessary, display the formatting marks and rulers. **Save** the file in your **Word Chapter 3** folder as **Lastname_Firstname_3B_Environment_Newsletter** and then add the file name to the footer.

2 Select the first paragraph of text—*University Medical Center Goes Green*. On the mini toolbar, change the **Font** to **Arial Black** and the **Font Size** to **18**.

3 Select the first two paragraphs—the title and the Volume information and date. On the mini toolbar, click the **Font Color button arrow** , and then under **Theme Colors**, in the fifth column, click the last color—**Blue, Accent 1, Darker 50%**.

4 With the text still selected, on the **HOME tab**, in the **Paragraph group**, click the **Borders button arrow**, and then at the bottom, click **Borders and Shading**.

5 In the **Borders and Shading** dialog box, on the **Borders tab**, click the **Color arrow**, and then under **Theme Colors**, in the fifth column, click the last color—**Blue, Accent 1, Darker 50%**.

6 Click the **Width arrow**, and then click **3 pt**. In the **Preview** box at the right, point to the *bottom* border of the preview and click one time. Compare your screen with Figure 3.23.

FIGURE 3.23

> **ANOTHER WAY**   In the Preview area, click the Bottom Border button.

7 In the **Borders and Shading** dialog box, click **OK**.

The line visually defines the newsletter's **nameplate**—the banner on the front page of a newsletter that identifies the publication.

8 Below the Volume information, click at the beginning of the paragraph that begins *University Medical Center continues*. By using the vertical scroll box, scroll to view the lower portion of the document, hold down ⇧Shift, and then click after the paragraph mark at the end of the paragraph that begins *Electronic medical records* to select all of the text between the insertion point and the sentence ending with the word *space*. Be sure that the paragraph mark is included in the selection. Compare your screen with Figure 3.24.

Use ⇧Shift to define a selection that may be difficult to select by dragging.

FIGURE 3.24

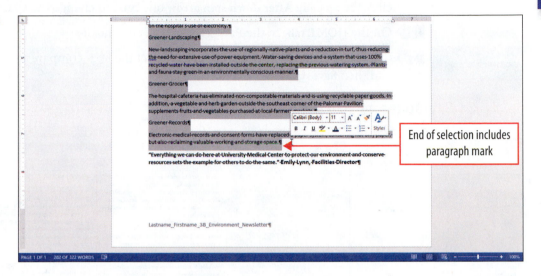

End of selection includes paragraph mark

9 On the **PAGE LAYOUT tab**, in the **Page Setup group**, click **Columns**, and then click **Two**. Compare your screen with Figure 3.25, and then **Save** 🖫 your newsletter.

Word divides the text into two columns and inserts a *section break* at the end of the selection, dividing the one-column section of the document from the two-column section of the document. A *section* is a portion of a document that can be formatted differently from the rest of the document. A section break marks the end of one section and the beginning of another section.

FIGURE 3.25

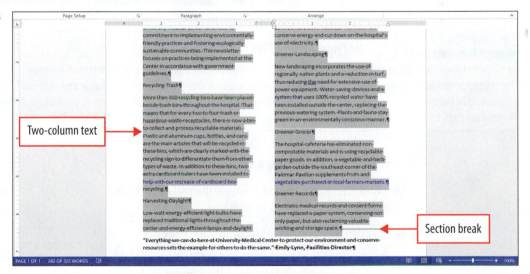

Two-column text

Section break

Activity 3.16 | Formatting Multiple Columns

The uneven right margin of a single page-width column is easy to read. When you create narrow columns, justified text is sometimes preferable. Depending on the design and layout of your newsletter, you might decide to reduce extra space between paragraphs and between columns to improve the readability of the document.

1 With the two columns of text still selected, on the **PAGE LAYOUT tab**, in the **Paragraph group**, click the **Spacing After down spin arrow** one time to change the spacing after to **6 pt**.

2 On the **HOME tab**, in the **Paragraph group**, click **Justify** ▤.

3 Click anywhere in the document to deselect the text, compare your screen with Figure 3.26, and then **Save** 🖫.

FIGURE 3.26

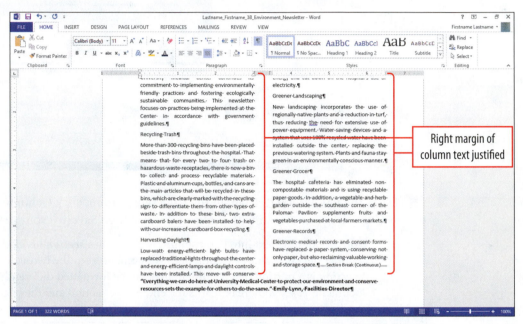

More Knowledge | **Justifying Column Text**

Although many magazines and newspapers still justify text in columns, there are a variety of opinions about whether to justify the columns, or to use left alignment and leave the right edge uneven. Justified text tends to look more formal and cleaner, but in a word processing document, it also results in uneven spacing between words. It is the opinion of some authorities that justified text is more difficult to read, especially in a page-width document. Let the overall look and feel of your newsletter be your guide.

Activity 3.17 | Inserting a Column Break

1 Near the bottom of the first column, click to position the insertion point at the beginning of the line *Harvesting Daylight*.

2 On the **PAGE LAYOUT tab**, in the **Page Setup group**, click **Breaks**. Under **Page Breaks**, click **Column**, and then if necessary, scroll to view the bottom of the first column.

A column break displays at the bottom of the first column; text to the right of the column break moves to the top of the next column.

3 Compare your screen with Figure 3.27, and then **Save** 🖫.

A *column break indicator*—a dotted line containing the words *Column Break*—displays at the bottom of the column.

FIGURE 3.27

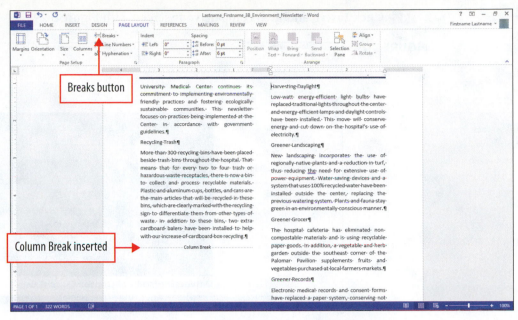

Breaks button

Column Break inserted

Activity 3.18 | Inserting an Online Picture

You can search for and insert online pictures in your document without saving the images to your computer. Pictures can make your document visually appealing and more interesting.

1 Press Ctrl + Home. On the **INSERT tab**, in the **Illustrations group**, click **Online Pictures**.

2 In the **Office.com Clip Art** search box, type **recycling bottles** so that Word can search for images that contain the keywords *recycling* and *bottles*. Press Enter.

3 Click the image of the recycle bin on a black background. If the image does not display, select a similar picture. Compare your screen with Figure 3.28.

FIGURE 3.28

Online Pictures button

Selected image

Keywords

4 Click **Insert**, and then compare your screen with Figure 3.29.

FIGURE 3.29

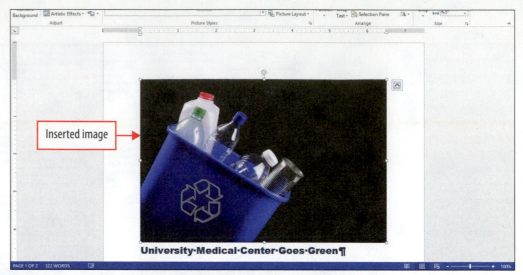

Inserted image

University·Medical·Center·Goes·Green¶

5 Press Ctrl + End to move to the end of the document. On the **INSERT tab**, in the **Illustrations group**, click **Online Pictures**. In the **Office.com Clip Art** search box, type **green recycling symbol** and then press Enter.

6 Click the first recycling symbol and then compare your screen with Figure 3.30. If the picture is not available, choose a similar picture.

FIGURE 3.30

Selected image

7 Click **Insert**. With the picture selected, on the **FORMAT tab**, in the **Size group**, click in the **Height** box. Type **0.5** and then press Enter. To the right of the picture, click **Layout Options**, and then click **Square**. At the bottom of the **Layout Options gallery**, click **See more**.

8 On the **Position tab**, under **Horizontal**, click the **Alignment** option button. Click the **Alignment arrow**, and then click **Centered**. Click the **relative to arrow** and then click **Page**. Under **Vertical**, click the **Alignment** option button. Click the **Alignment arrow**, and then click **Bottom**. Click the **relative to arrow**, and then click **Margin**. Compare your screen with Figure 3.31.

FIGURE 3.31

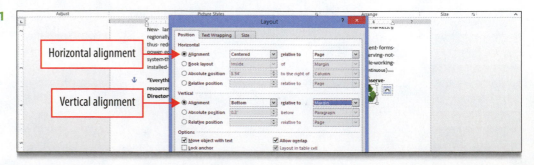

Horizontal alignment

Vertical alignment

9 Click **OK**, scroll to the bottom of the page, and then notice that the recycle image displays at the bottom of the second page. **Save**  the document.

 **ANOTHER WAY**   Drag the image to visually position the image.

Activity 3.19 | Cropping a Picture and Resizing a Picture by Scaling

In this activity, you will edit the recycle bin image by cropping and scaling the picture. When you *crop* a picture, you remove unwanted or unnecessary areas of the picture. When you *scale* a picture, you resize it to a percentage of its size.

1 Press Ctrl + Home to move to the top of the document, and then click the recycle bin picture to select it. On the **FORMAT tab**, in the **Size group**, click the upper portion of the **Crop** button to display crop handles around the picture. Compare your screen with Figure 3.32.

> *Crop handles* are used like sizing handles to define unwanted areas of the picture.

FIGURE 3.32

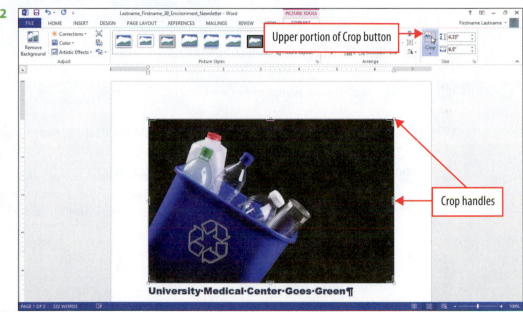

2 Point to the center right crop handle to display the pointer. Compare your screen with Figure 3.33.

> Use the *crop pointer* to crop areas of a picture.

FIGURE 3.33

3 ▶ With the crop pointer displayed, hold down the left mouse button and drag to the left to approximately **5 inches on the horizontal ruler**, and then release the mouse button. Compare your screen with Figure 3.34.

The portion of the image to be removed displays in gray.

FIGURE 3.34

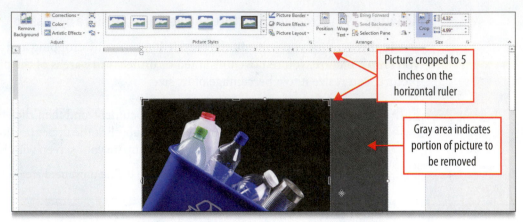

Picture cropped to 5 inches on the horizontal ruler

Gray area indicates portion of picture to be removed

4 ▶ Click anywhere in the document outside of the image to apply the crop.

🔄 **ANOTHER WAY**   Click the upper portion of the Crop button to apply the crop.

5 ▶ Click to select the picture again. On the **FORMAT tab**, in the **Size group**, click the **Dialog Box Launcher** button 🔲.

6 ▶ In the **Layout dialog box**, on the **Size tab**, under **Scale**, be sure that the **Lock aspect ratio** and **Relative to original picture size** check boxes are selected. Select the number in the **Height box**, type **10** and then press Tab. Compare your screen with Figure 3.35.

When *Lock aspect ratio* is selected, the height and width of the picture are sized proportionately and only one scale value is necessary. The second value—in this instance Width—adjusts proportionately. When *Relative to original picture size* is selected, the scale is applied as a percentage of the original picture size.

FIGURE 3.35

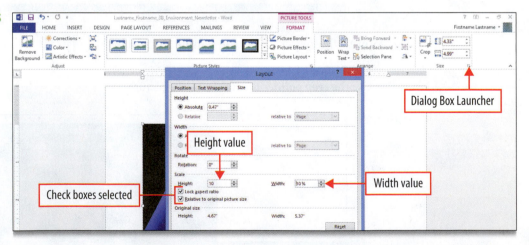

Dialog Box Launcher

Height value

Width value

Check boxes selected

7 ▶ In the **Layout** dialog box, click the **Text Wrapping tab**. Under **Wrapping style**, click **Square**.

8 ▶ Click the **Position tab**, and then under **Horizontal**, click the **Alignment** option button. Be sure that the **Alignment** indicates **Left** and **relative to Column**. Under **Vertical**, click the **Alignment** option button, and then change the alignment to **Top relative to Margin**. Click **OK**, and then compare your screen with Figure 3.36.

FIGURE 3.36

Picture cropped,
scaled, and positioned

University·Medical·Center·Goes·Green¶

Activity 3.20 | Setting Transparent Color and Recoloring a Picture

You can make one color in a picture transparent using the Set Transparent Color command. When you *recolor* a picture, you change all the colors in the picture to shades of a single color.

1 On the **VIEW tab**, in the **Zoom group**, click **Zoom**, and then click **200%**. Click **OK**. Drag the scroll bars as necessary so that you can view the recycle bin picture at the top of the document.

2 If necessary, select the recycle bin picture. On the **FORMAT tab**, in the **Adjust group**, click **Color**, and then below the gallery, click **Set Transparent Color**. Move the pointer into the document to display the ✎ pointer.

3 Point anywhere in the black background of the recycle bin picture, and then click to apply the transparent color to the background. Compare your screen with Figure 3.37.

FIGURE 3.37

Transparent color
applied to black
background

University·Medical·Center·Goes·Gr

Volume·1,·Number·1

4 Press Ctrl + End to move to the end of your document, and then select the picture of the recycle symbol. On the **FORMAT tab**, in the **Adjust group**, click **Color** to display a gallery of recoloring options. Under **Recolor**, in the last row, click the fourth option— **Olive Green, Accent color 3 Light**. Compare your screen with Figure 3.38, and then **Save** 🔲 the document.

FIGURE 3.38

Picture recolored

Lastname_Firstname_3B_Environment_Newsletter¶

Activity 3.21 | Adjusting the Brightness and Contrast of a Picture

Brightness is the relative lightness of a picture. **Contrast** is the difference between the darkest and lightest area of a picture.

1 If necessary, select the recycle symbol. On the **FORMAT tab**, in the **Adjust group**, click **Corrections**. Under **Brightness/Contrast**, point to several of the options to view the effect that the settings have on the picture.

2 Under **Brightness/Contrast**, in the last row, click the first setting—**Brightness: −40% Contrast: +40%**. Compare your screen with Figure 3.39.

FIGURE 3.39

Brightness and Contrast setting applied to picture

Lastname_Firstname_3B_Environment_Newsletter¶

3 On the **VIEW tab**, in the **Zoom group**, click **100%**, and then **Save** 🖫 the document.

Activity 3.22 | Applying a Border to a Picture and Flipping a Picture

The *flip* commands create a reverse image of a picture or object.

1 Press Ctrl + Home to move to the top of the document, and then select the picture of the recycle bin. On the **FORMAT tab**, in the **Picture Styles group**, click the **Picture Border button arrow**. Under **Theme Colors**, in the fourth column, click the first color—**Dark Blue, Text 2**.

2 Click the **Picture Border arrow** again, and then point to **Weight**. Click **1 1/2 pt** to change the thickness of the border.

3 On the **FORMAT tab**, in the **Arrange group**, click **Rotate Objects** 🔄, and then click **Flip Horizontal**. Click anywhere in the document to deselect the picture. **Save** 🖫, and then compare your screen with Figure 3.40.

FIGURE 3.40

Picture bordered and flipped

University·Medical·Center·Goes·Green¶

Volume·1,·Number·1   →   January·2016¶

Activity 3.23 | Inserting a Screenshot

A *screenshot* is an image of an active window on your computer that you can paste into a document. Screenshots are especially useful when you want to insert an image of a website into your Word document. You can insert a screenshot of any open window on your computer.

1 In the paragraph that begins *University Medical Center continues*, click after the period at the end of the paragraph. Start Internet Explorer, and then navigate to **www.epa.gov/osw /conserve** and press Enter.

2 From the taskbar, redisplay your **3B_Environment_Newletter** document.

3 With the insertion point positioned at the end of the paragraph, on the **INSERT tab**, in the **Illustrations group**, click **Screenshot**.

All of your open windows display in the Available Windows gallery and are available to paste into the document.

4 In the **Screenshot** gallery, click the browser window that contains the EPA site to insert the screenshot at the insertion point. If a message box displays asking if you want to hyperlink the screenshot, click No, and then notice that the image is inserted and is sized to fit between the margins of the first column. Compare your screen with Figure 3.41.

By selecting No in the message box, you are inserting a screenshot without links to the actual website. Choose Yes, if you want to link the image to the website.

FIGURE 3.41

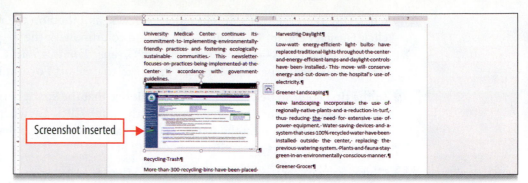

5 With the inserted screenshot selected, on the **FORMAT tab**, in the **Picture Styles group**, click the **Picture Border button arrow**, and then under **Theme Colors**, in the second column, click the first color—**Black, Text 1**.

6 Save 🖫 the document.

Objective 6 | Use Special Character and Paragraph Formatting

Video W3-6

Special text and paragraph formatting is useful to emphasize text, and it makes your newsletter look more professional. For example, you can place a border around one or more paragraphs or add shading to a paragraph. When adding shading, use light colors; dark shading can make the text difficult to read.

Activity 3.24 | Applying the Small Caps Font Effect

For headlines and titles, *small caps* is an attractive font effect. The effect changes lowercase letters to uppercase letters, but with the height of lowercase letters.

1 Under the screenshot, select the paragraph *Recycling Trash* including the paragraph mark.

2 Right-click the selected text, and then on the shortcut menu, click **Font** to display the **Font** dialog box. Click the **Font color arrow**, and then change the color to **Blue, Accent 1, Darker 50%**—in the fifth column, the last color.

3 Under **Font style**, click **Bold**. Under **Effects**, select the **Small caps** check box. Compare your screen with Figure 3.42.

The Font dialog box provides more options than are available on the ribbon and enables you to make several changes at the same time. In the Preview box, the text displays with the selected formatting options applied.

FIGURE 3.42

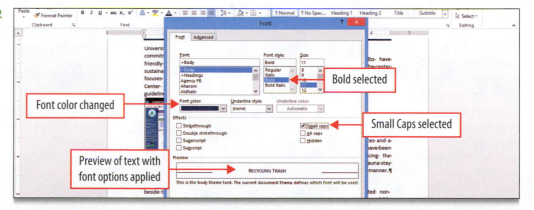

4 Click **OK**. With the text still selected, right-click, and then on the mini toolbar, double-click **Format Painter** 🖌. Then, in the second column, with the 𝐀𝐈 pointer, select each of the heading paragraphs—*Harvesting Daylight*, *Greener Landscaping*, *Greener Grocer*, and *Greener Records*—to apply the same formats. Press Esc to turn off **Format Painter**.

5 In the first column below the screenshot, notice that the space between the *Recycling Trash* subheading and the screenshot is fairly small. Click anywhere in the *Recycling Trash* subheading, and then on the **PAGE LAYOUT tab**, in the **Paragraph group**, click the **Before up spin arrow** two times to set the spacing to **12 pt**.

6 Compare your screen with Figure 3.43, and then **Save** 💾 your document.

FIGURE 3.43

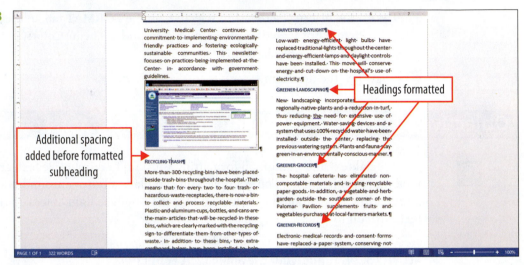

Activity 3.25 | Inserting Symbols and Special Characters

You can insert symbols and special characters in a Word document, including copyright symbols, trademark symbols, and em dashes. An ***em dash*** is a punctuation symbol used to indicate an explanation or emphasis.

1 Press Ctrl + End to move to the end of the document, and then after the name *Emily Lynn* delete the comma and the space that separates her name from her job title—*Facilities Director*.

2 With the insertion point positioned before the *F* in *Facilities*, on the **INSERT tab**, in the **Symbols group**, click **Symbol**. Below the gallery, click **More Symbols** to display the **Symbol** dialog box.

Here you can choose the symbol that you want to insert in your document.

3 In the **Symbol** dialog box, click the **Special Characters tab**. Scroll the list to view the types of special characters that you can insert; notice that some of the characters can be inserted using a Shortcut key.

4 Click **Em Dash**, and then in the lower right portion of the dialog box, click **Insert**. Compare your screen with Figure 3.44.

An em dash displays between the name *Lynn* and the word *Facilities*.

FIGURE 3.44

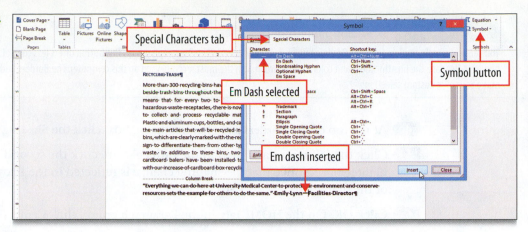

5 > In the **Symbol** dialog box, click **Close**, and then **Save** 🖫 your document.

Activity 3.26 | Adding Borders and Shading to a Paragraph and Inserting a Manual Line Break

Paragraph borders provide strong visual cues to the reader. You can use paragraph shading with or without borders; however, combined with a border, light shading can be very effective in drawing the reader's eye to the text.

1 > At the end of the document, select the two lines of bold text that begin *"Everything we can do."*

The recycle picture may also be selected because it is anchored to the paragraph.

2 > On the **HOME tab**, in the **Paragraph group**, click the **Borders button arrow** ⊞ ▾, and then click **Borders and Shading**.

3 > In the **Borders and Shading** dialog box, be sure the **Borders tab** is selected. Under **Setting**, click **Shadow**. Click the **Color arrow**, and then in the fifth column, click the last color—**Blue, Accent 1, Darker 50%**. Click the **Width arrow**, and then click **1 pt**. Compare your screen with Figure 3.45.

In the lower right portion of the Borders and Shading dialog box, the *Apply to* box indicates *Paragraph*. The *Apply to* box directs where the border will be applied—in this instance, the border will be applied only to the selected paragraph.

FIGURE 3.45

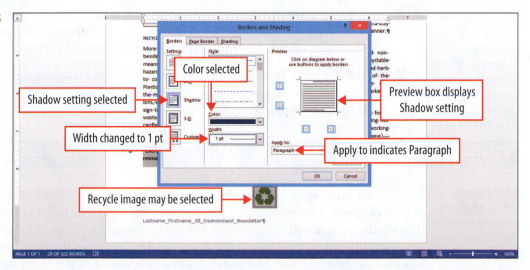

4 At the top of the **Borders and Shading** dialog box, click the **Shading tab**.

5 Click the **Fill arrow**, and then in the fifth column, click the second color—**Blue, Accent 1, Lighter 80%**. Notice that the shading change is reflected in the **Preview area** on the right side of the dialog box.

6 Click **OK**. On the **HOME tab**, in the **Paragraph group**, click **Center** .

7 Click anywhere in the document to deselect, and then compare your screen with Figure 3.46.

FIGURE 3.46

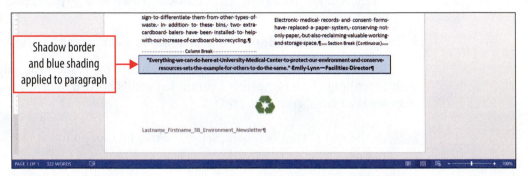

8 In the shaded paragraph, in the second line, click in front of the *E* in the name *Emily*. Hold down Shift and then press Enter.

Holding down Shift while pressing Enter inserts a ***manual line break***, which moves the text to the right of the insertion point to a new line while keeping the text in the same paragraph. A ***line break indicator***, in the shape of a bent arrow, indicates a manual line break.

9 Press Ctrl + Home to move the insertion point to the top of the document. Click the **FILE tab** to display **Backstage** view. On the right, at the bottom of the **Properties** list, click **Show All Properties**.

10 On the list of **Properties**, click to the right of **Tags**, and then type **newsletter, January**

11 Click to the right of **Subject**, and then type your course name and section number. Under **Related People**, be sure that your name displays as the author. If necessary, right-click the author name, click **Edit Property**, type your name, and click **OK**.

12 On the left, click **Print** to display the **Print Preview**, make any necessary corrections, and then **Save** the document. **Close** Word; hold this file until you complete this project. If necessary, close Internet Explorer.

Objective 7   Create Mailing Labels Using Mail Merge

Video W3-7

Word's ***mail merge*** feature joins a ***main document*** and a ***data source*** to create customized letters or labels. The main document contains the text or formatting that remains constant. For labels, the main document contains the formatting for a specific label size. The data source contains information including the names and addresses of the individuals for whom the labels are being created. Names and addresses in a data source might come from a Word table, an Excel worksheet, or an Access database.

The easiest way to perform a mail merge is to use the Mail Merge Wizard, which asks you questions and, based on your answers, walks you step by step through the mail merge process.

Activity 3.27 | Starting the Mail Merge Wizard Template

In this activity, you will open the data source for the mail merge, which is a Word table containing names and addresses.

1 Start Word and display a new blank document. Display formatting marks and rulers. **Save** the document in your **Word Chapter 3** folder as **Lastname_Firstname_3B_Mailing_Labels**

2 With your new document open on the screen, from your student files, **Open** the file **w03B_Addresses**. **Save** the address file in your **Word Chapter 3** folder as **Lastname_Firstname_3B_Addresses** and then add the file name to the footer.

> This document contains a table of addresses. The first row contains the column names. The remaining rows contain the names and addresses.

3 Click to position the insertion point in the last cell in the table, and then press Tab to create a new row. Enter the following information, and then compare your table with Figure 3.47.

FIRST NAME	LAST NAME	ADDRESS 1	UNIT	CITY	STATE	ZIP CODE
Monica	Warren	5626 Summer Road	#234	Lakeland	TN	38002

FIGURE 3.47

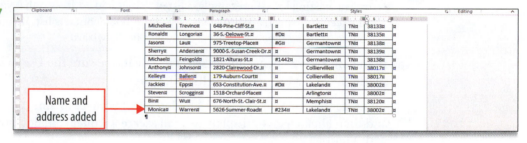

Name and address added

4 Save, and then **Close** the table of addresses. Be sure that your blank **Lastname_Firstname_3B_Mailing_Labels** document displays.

5 Click the **MAILINGS tab**. In the **Start Mail Merge group**, click **Start Mail Merge**, and then click **Step-by-Step Mail Merge Wizard** to display the **Mail Merge** pane on the right.

6 In the **Mail Merge** pane, under **Select document type**, click **Labels**. At the bottom of the **Mail Merge** pane, click **Next: Starting document** to display Step 2 of 6.

7 Under **Select starting document**, be sure **Change document layout** is selected, and then under **Change document layout**, click **Label options**.

8 In the **Label Options** dialog box, under **Printer information**, click the **Tray arrow**, and then if necessary, click **Default tray** (Automatically Select)—the exact wording may vary depending on your printer, but select the *Default* or *Automatic* option so that you can print the labels on regular paper rather than manually inserting labels in the printer.

9 Under **Label information**, click the **Label vendors arrow**, and then click **Avery US Letter**. Under **Product number**, scroll about halfway down the list, and then click **5160 Easy Peel Address Labels**. Compare your screen with Figure 3.48.

> The Avery 5160 address label is a commonly used label. The precut sheets contain three columns of 10 labels each—for a total of 30 labels per sheet.

FIGURE 3.48

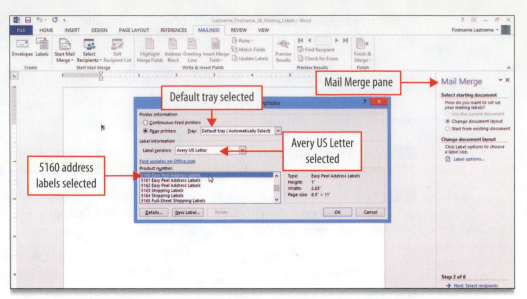

10 ▶ At the bottom of the **Label Options** dialog box, click **OK**. If a message box displays, click **OK** to set up the labels. If the gridlines do not display, on the **Layout tab**, in the **Table** group, click **View Gridlines**. At the bottom of the **Mail Merge** pane, click **Next: Select recipients**.

The label page is set up with three columns and ten rows. Here, in Step 3 of the Mail Merge Wizard, you must identify the recipients—the data source. For your recipient data source, you can choose to use an existing list—for example, a list of names and addresses that you have in an Access database, an Excel worksheet, a Word table, or your Outlook contacts list. If you do not have an existing data source, you can type a new list at this point in the wizard.

11 ▶ In the **Mail Merge** pane, under **Select recipients**, be sure the **Use an existing list** option button is selected. Under **Use an existing list**, click **Browse**.

12 ▶ Navigate to your **Word Chapter 3** folder, select your **Lastname_Firstname_3B_Addresses** file, and then click **Open** to display the **Mail Merge Recipients** dialog box. Compare your screen with Figure 3.49.

In the Mail Merge Recipients dialog box, the column headings are formed from the text in the first row of your Word table of addresses. Each row of information that contains data for one person is referred to as a *record*. The column headings—for example, *Last_Name* and *First_Name*—are referred to as *fields*. An underscore replaces the spaces between words in the field name headings.

FIGURE 3.49

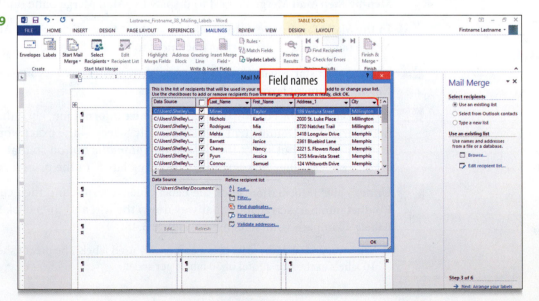

13 In the lower left portion of the **Mail Merge Recipients** dialog box, in the **Data Source** box, click the path that contains your file name. Then, at the bottom of the **Mail Merge Recipients** dialog box, click **Edit**.

14 In the upper right corner of the **Data Form** dialog box, click **Add New**. In the blank record, type the following, pressing Tab to move from field to field, and then compare your **Data Form** dialog box with Figure 3.50.

FIRST_NAME	LAST_NAME	ADDRESS_1	UNIT	CITY	STATE	ZIP CODE
Sharon	Williams	1251 Parker Road	#843	Memphis	TN	38123

FIGURE 3.50

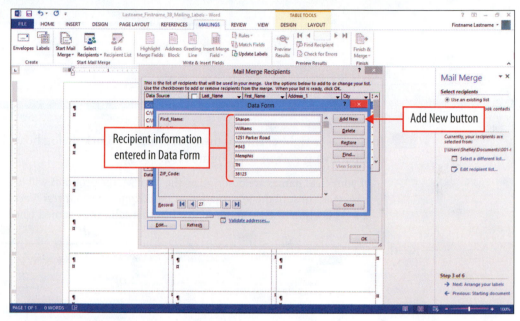

15 In the lower right corner of the **Data Form** dialog box, click **Close**. Scroll to the end of the recipient list to confirm that the record for *Sharon Williams* that you just added is in the list. At the bottom of the **Mail Merge Recipients** dialog box, click **OK**.

Activity 3.28 | Completing the Mail Merge Wizard

You can add or edit names and addresses while completing the Mail Merge. You can also match your column names with preset names used in Mail Merge.

1 At the bottom of the **Mail Merge** pane, click **Next: Arrange your labels**.

2 Under **Arrange your labels**, click **Address block**. In the **Insert Address Block** dialog box, under **Specify address elements**, examine the various formats for names. If necessary, under *Insert recipient's name in this format*, select the *Joshua Randall Jr.* format. Compare your dialog box with Figure 3.51.

FIGURE 3.51

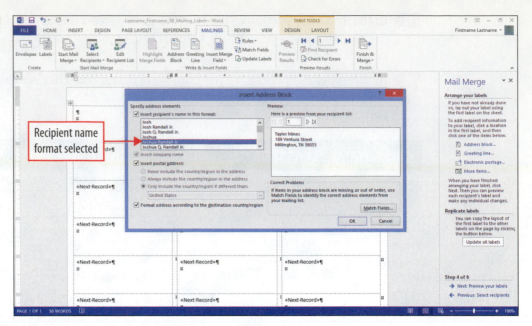

Recipient name format selected

3 ▶ In the lower right corner of the **Insert Address Block** dialog box, click **Match Fields**, and then compare your screen with Figure 3.52.

If your field names are descriptive, the Mail Merge program will identify them correctly, as is the case with most of the information in the *Required for Address Block* section. However, the Address 2 field is unmatched—in the source file, this column is named *Unit*.

FIGURE 3.52

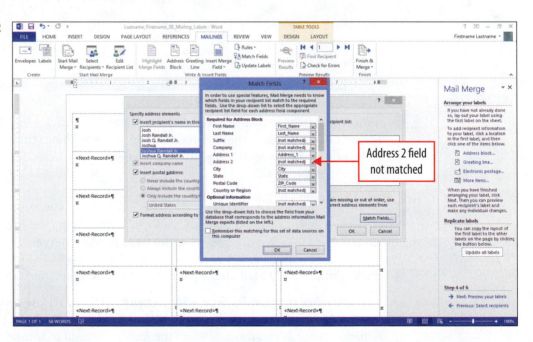

Address 2 field not matched

4 ▶ Click the **Address 2 arrow**, and then from the list of available fields, click **Unit** to match the Mail Merge field with the field in your data source.

5 ▶ At the bottom of the **Match Fields** dialog box, click **OK**. At the bottom of the **Insert Address Block** dialog box, click **OK**.

Word inserts the Address block in the first label space surrounded by double angle brackets. The *AddressBlock* field name displays, which represents the address block you saw in the Preview area of the Insert Address Block dialog box.

6 In the **Mail Merge** pane, under **Replicate labels**, click **Update all labels** to insert an address block in each label space for each subsequent record.

7 At the bottom of the **Mail Merge** pane, click **Next: Preview your labels**. Notice that for addresses with four lines, the last line of the address is cut off.

8 Press Ctrl + A to select all of the label text, click the **PAGE LAYOUT tab**, and then in the **Paragraph group**, click in the **Spacing Before** box. Type **3** and press Enter.

9 Click in any label to deselect, and notice that 4-line addresses are no longer cut off. Compare your screen with Figure 3.53.

FIGURE 3.53

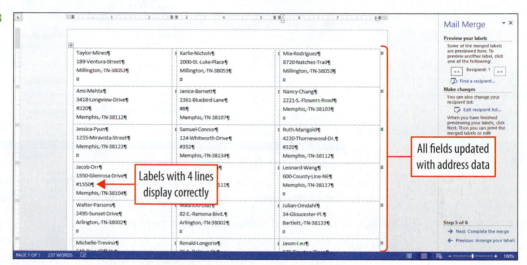

10 At the bottom of the **Mail Merge** pane, click **Next: Complete the merge**.

Step 6 of the Mail Merge displays. At this point you can print or edit your labels, although this is done more easily in the document window.

11 Save 🖫 your labels, and then on the right, **Close** ✖ the **Mail Merge** pane.

Activity 3.29 | Sorting Mail Merge Results

If you discover that you need to make further changes to your labels, you can still make them even though the Mail Merge task pane is closed.

1 Add the file name to the footer, close the footer area, and then move to the top of Page 2. Click anywhere in the empty table row, and then click the **LAYOUT tab**. In the **Rows & Columns group**, click **Delete**, and then click **Delete Rows**.

Adding footer text to a label sheet replaces the last row of labels on a page with the footer text, and moves the last row of labels to the top of the next page. In this instance, a blank second page is created, which you can delete by deleting the blank row.

2 Notice that the labels do not display in alphabetical order. Click the **MAILINGS tab**, and then in the **Start Mail Merge group**, click **Edit Recipient List** to display the list of names and addresses.

3 In the **Mail Merge Recipients** dialog box, click the **Last_Name** field heading, and notice that the names are sorted alphabetically by the recipient's last name.

Mailing labels are often sorted by either last name or by ZIP Code.

4 Click the **Last_Name** field heading again, and notice that the last names are sorted in descending order. Click the **Last_Name** field one more time to return to ascending order, and then click **OK**. Press Ctrl + Home, and then compare your screen with Figure 3.54.

FIGURE 3.54

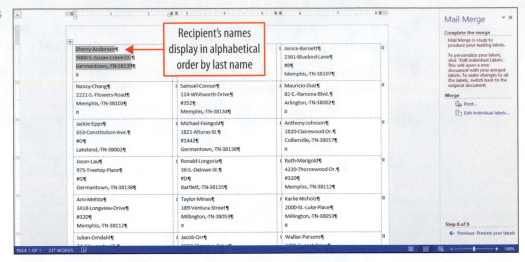

5 Click the **FILE tab**. On the right, at the bottom of the **Properties** list, click **Show All Properties**. On the list of **Properties**, click to the right of **Tags**, and then type **labels**

6 Click to the right of **Subject**, and then type your course name and section number. Be sure that your name displays as the author. If necessary, right-click the author name, click **Edit Property**, type your name, and click **OK**. Save 🖫 the file. **Close** the document, and click **Yes** to save the data source.

7 As directed by your instructor, print or submit electronically.

If you print, the labels will print on whatever paper is in the printer; unless you have preformatted labels available, the labels will print on a sheet of paper. Printing the labels on plain paper enables you to proofread the labels before you print them on more expensive label sheets.

8 In addition to your labels and address document, print or submit your **Lastname_Firstname_3B_Environment_Newsletter** document as directed. **Close** Word.

END | You have completed Project 3B

Objective | Format a Single-Column Newsletter in Word Web App

You can use the Word Web App to insert clip art and to format text. You can change fonts and font color, and modify paragraph spacing.

> **ALERT!**   **Working with Web-Based Applications and Services**
>
> Computer programs and services on the web receive continuous updates and improvements, so the steps to complete this web-based activity may differ from the ones shown. You can often look at the screens and the information presented to determine how to complete the activity.

Activity | Formatting a Single-Column Newsletter

In this activity, you will use the Word Web App to edit a single-column newsletter similar to the one you edited in Project 3B.

1 From the desktop, start Internet Explorer. Navigate to **http://skydrive.com**, and then sign in to your Microsoft account. Open your **GO! Web Projects** folder; or create this folder if necessary.

2 In the SkyDrive menu bar, click **Upload**. Navigate to your student data files, click **w03_3B_Web**, and then click **Open**.

3 Point to the uploaded file **w03_3B_Web**, and then right-click. On the shortcut menu, scroll as necessary, and then click **Rename**. Using your own last name and first name, type **Lastname_Firstname_WD_3B_Web** and then press Enter to rename the file.

4 Double-click the file that you just renamed, and then click **EDIT DOCUMENT**. On the list, click **Edit in Word Web App**.

5 Drag to select the newsletter title—*University Medical Center Goes Green*. On the **HOME tab**, in the

Font group, locate and click the **Grow Font button** two times to change the font size to **18**. With the newsletter title still selected, on the **HOME tab**, in the **Font group**, click **Font Color**, and then in the fifth column, click the last color—**Blue Gray, Accent 1, Darker 50%**. Apply the same **Font Color** to the five subheadings—*Recycling Trash*, *Harvesting Daylight*, *Greener Landscaping*, *Greener Grocer*, and *Greener Records*.

6 Drag to select the first subheading—*Recycling Trash*. On the **PAGE LAYOUT tab**, in the **Paragraph group**, click in the **After box**. Type **12** and then press Enter—or click the arrow as necessary. Apply the same **Spacing After** to the remaining four subheadings—*Harvesting Daylight*, *Greener Landscaping*, *Greener Grocer*, and *Greener Records*. Click anywhere in the document, and then press Ctrl + Home to move to the top of the document. Compare your screen with Figure A.

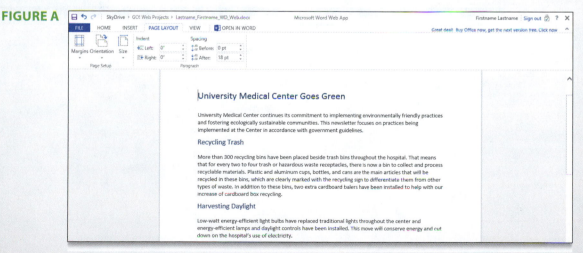

FIGURE A

(GO! with Office Web Apps continues on the next page)

7 Be sure the insertion point is positioned at the top of the document. On the **PAGE LAYOUT tab**, in the **Page Setup group**, click **Margins**, and then click **Custom Margins**. Click in the **Top** box and type **0.5** and then click in the **Bottom** box. Type **0.5** and then click **OK**.

8 On the **INSERT tab**, in the **Pictures group**, click **Clip Art**. In the **Search** box, type **recycling bottles** and then press Enter. Click the image of the recycle bin filled with plastic bottles on a black background. If the image is not available, choose a similar picture. Click **Insert**.

9 On the **FORMAT tab**, in the **Image Size group**, click in the **Scale** box. Type **10** to replace the existing number, and then press Enter. On the **FORMAT tab**, in the **Picture Styles group**, use the ScreenTips to locate and then click **Reflected Rounded Rectangle**.

10 Press Ctrl + End to move to the end of the document, and then press Enter. On the **INSERT tab**, in the **Pictures group**, click **Clip Art**. In the **Search** box, type

green recycle symbol and then press Enter. Click the image of the green recycle symbol that you used in Project 3B. If the image is not available, choose a similar picture. Click **Insert**.

11 On the **FORMAT tab**, in the **Image Size group**, click in the **Scale** box. Type **5** to replace the existing number, and then press Enter. On the **HOME tab**, in the **Paragraph group**, click **Center**.

12 In the last paragraph of the newsletter, click to position the insertion point between the second quotation mark and the letter *E* in *Emily*. Hold down Shift and then press Enter to insert a manual line break. On the **HOME tab**, in the **Paragraph group**, click **Center** to center the three lines of text in the last paragraph. Compare your screen with Figure B.

13 **Save** your file and submit as directed by your instructor. Then, on the ribbon, click the **FILE tab**, and then click **Exit**. Sign out of your SkyDrive.

FIGURE B

GO! with Microsoft Office 365

Andrew Rodriguez / Fotolia; FotolEdhar/ Fotolia; apops/ Fotolia; Yuri Arcurs/ Fotolia

The advantage of using Office 365 is that your organization does not have to purchase and install server hardware and software for sophisticated business applications and does not need a full-time IT person or staff just to manage the technology your teams need.

By using Office 365, you are able to have business-class services for your employees without investing in expensive hardware, software, and personnel. However, at least one person in an organization must be designated as the *Office 365 Administrator*—the person who creates and manages the account, adds new users, sets up the services your organization wants to use, sets permission levels, and manages the SharePoint team sites. You can have more than one Administrator if you want to share these tasks with others.

Microsoft provides easy-to-use instructions and videos to get you started, and you might also have contact with a Microsoft representative. You will probably find, however, that subscribing to and setting up the account, adding users, and activating services is a straightforward process that requires little or no assistance.

After purchasing the required number of licenses, you will add each team member as a user that includes his or her email address.

The Admin Overview page, as shown in the Figure below, assists the Office 365 Administrator. On the left, there are links to manage the users and domains in your Office 365 account. This is where you can add new users, delete users, set permission levels, enter and change passwords, and update the user properties and the licenses.

In the center, you can see the various services available to you in Office 365. In the site shown in Figure A, Outlook, Lync, SharePoint (team sites), and a public-facing website are all part of the services.

Activity | Using a Team Site to Collaborate

This group project relates to the **Bell Orchid Hotels**. If your instructor assigns this project to your class, you can expect to use a SharePoint team site in **Office 365** to collaborate on the following tasks for this chapter:

- If you are in the **Accounting Group**, you and your teammates will finalize the report to shareholders, merge the letter with the labels, and post the final report on the SharePoint team site.

- If you are in the **Engineering Group**, you and your teammates will finalize the report to the three insurance companies, merge the letter with the labels, and post the final report on the SharePoint team site.

- If you are in the **Food and Beverage Group**, you and your teammates will finalize the letter to customers planning a banquet, merge the letter with the labels, and post the final letter on the SharePoint team site.

- If you are in the **Human Resources Group**, you and your teammates will finalize the memo to employees, merge the memo with the labels, and post the final memo on the SharePoint team site.

- If you are in the **Operations Group**, you and your teammates will finalize the letter to job applicants, merge the letter with the labels, and post the final letter on the SharePoint team site.

- If you are in the **Sales and Marketing Group**, you and your teammates will finalize the letter to the 20 professional associations, merge the letter with the labels, and post the final letter on the SharePoint team site.

FIGURE A

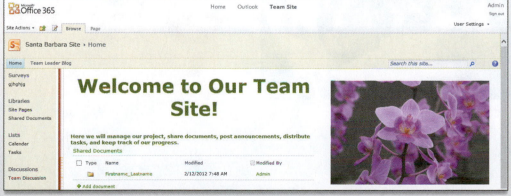

END OF CHAPTER

SUMMARY

Word assists you in formatting a research paper for college or business by providing built-in styles and applies the most commonly used footnote and citation styles for research papers—MLA and APA.

Word helps you create the bibliography for your research paper by recording all of your citations in the Source Manager, and then generating the bibliography—in MLA, called Works Cited—for you.

Newsletters are often used by organizations to communicate information to a specific group. A newsletter can be formatted in two columns with a nameplate at the top that identifies the publication.

The Mail Merge Wizard enables you to easily merge a main document and a data source to create customized letters or labels. The data source can be a Word table, Excel spreadsheet, or Access database.

GO! LEARN IT ONLINE

Review the concepts and key terms in this chapter by completing these online challenges, which you can find at **www.pearsonhighered.com/go**.

Matching and Multiple Choice: Answer matching and multiple choice questions to test what you learned in this chapter. MyITLab®

Crossword Puzzle: Spell out the words that match the numbered clues, and put them in the puzzle squares.

Flipboard: Flip through the definitions of the key terms in this chapter and match them with the correct term.

GO! FOR JOB SUCCESS

Video: Email Etiquette

Your instructor may assign this video to your class, and then ask you to think about, or discuss with your classmates, these questions:

FotolEdhar / Fotolia

Why do you think it is important to follow specific etiquette when composing email?

Why is it important to include a greeting and sign every email that you send?

What are the differences between sending a business email and a personal email, and what are three specific things you should never do in a business email?

END OF CHAPTER

REVIEW AND ASSESSMENT GUIDE FOR WORD CHAPTER 3

Your instructor may assign one or more of these projects to help you review the chapter and assess your mastery and understanding of the chapter.

Review and Assessment Guide for Word Chapter 3			
Project	**Apply Skills from These Chapter Objectives**	**Project Type**	**Project Location**
3C	Objectives 1-4 from Project 3A	**3C Skills Review** A guided review of the skills from Project 3A.	On the following pages
3D	Objectives 5-7 from Project 3B	**3D Skills Review** A guided review of the skills from Project 3B.	On the following pages
3E	Objectives 1-4 from Project 3A	**3E Mastery (Grader Project)** A demonstration of your mastery of the skills in Project 3A with extensive decision making.	In MyITLab and on the following pages
3F	Objectives 5-7 from Project 3B	**3F Mastery (Grader Project)** A demonstration of your mastery of the skills in Project 3B with extensive decision making.	In MyITLab and on the following pages
3G	Objectives 1-7 from Projects 3A and 3B	**3G Mastery (Grader Project)** A demonstration of your mastery of the skills in Projects 3A and 3B with extensive decision making.	In MyITLab and on the following pages
3H	Combination of Objectives from Projects 3A and 3B	**3H GO! Fix It** A demonstration of your mastery of the skills in Projects 3A and 3B by creating a correct result from a document that contains errors you must find.	Online
3I	Combination of Objectives from Projects 3A and 3B	**3I GO! Make It** A demonstration of your mastery of the skills in Projects 3A and 3B by creating a result from a supplied picture.	Online
3J	Combination of Objectives from Projects 3A and 3B	**3J GO! Solve It** A demonstration of your mastery of the skills in Projects 3A and 3B, your decision-making skills, and your critical thinking skills. A task-specific rubric helps you self-assess your result.	Online
3K	Combination of Objectives from Projects 3A and 3B	**3K GO! Solve It** A demonstration of your mastery of the skills in Projects 3A and 3B, your decision-making skills, and your critical thinking skills. A task-specific rubric helps you self-assess your result.	On the following pages
3L	Combination of Objectives from Projects 3A and 3B	**3L GO! Think** A demonstration of your understanding of the chapter concepts applied in a manner that you would outside of college. An analytic rubric helps you and your instructor grade the quality of your work by comparing it to the work an expert in the discipline would create.	On the following pages
3M	Combination of Objectives from Projects 3A and 3B	**3M GO! Think** A demonstration of your understanding of the chapter concepts applied in a manner that you would outside of college. An analytic rubric helps you and your instructor grade the quality of your work by comparing it to the work an expert in the discipline would create.	Online
3N	Combination of Objectives from Projects 3A and 3B	**3N You and GO!** A demonstration of your understanding of the chapter concepts applied in a manner that you would in a personal situation. An analytic rubric helps you and your instructor grade the quality of your work.	Online
3O	Combination of Objectives from Projects 3A and 3B	**3O Cumulative Group Project for Word Chapter 3** A demonstration of your understanding of concepts and your ability to work collaboratively in a group role-playing assessment, requiring both collaboration and self-management.	Online
Capstone Project for Word Chapters 1-3	Combination of Objectives from Projects 1A, 1B, 2A, 2B, 3A, and 3B	A demonstration of your mastery of the skills in Chapters 1-3 with extensive decision making. **(Grader Project)**	In MyITLab and online

GLOSSARY

GLOSSARY OF CHAPTER KEY TERMS

American Psychological Association (APA) One of two commonly used style guides for formatting research papers.

Bibliography A list of cited works in a report or research paper; also referred to as Works Cited, Sources, or References, depending upon the report style.

Brightness The relative lightness of a picture.

Citation A note inserted into the text of a research paper that refers the reader to a source in the bibliography.

Column break indicator A dotted line containing the words *Column Break* that displays at the bottom of the column.

Contrast The difference between the darkest and lightest area of a picture.

Crop A command that removes unwanted or unnecessary areas of a picture.

Crop handles Handles used to define unwanted areas of a picture.

Crop pointer The pointer used to crop areas of a picture.

Data source A document that contains a list of variable information, such as names and addresses, that is merged with a main document to create customized form letters or labels.

Em dash A punctuation symbol used to indicate an explanation or emphasis.

Endnote In a research paper, a note placed at the end of a document or chapter.

Fields In a mail merge, the column headings in the data source.

Flip A command that creates a reverse image of a picture or object.

Footnote In a research paper, a note placed at the bottom of the page.

Hanging indent An indent style in which the first line of a paragraph extends to the left of the remaining lines and that is commonly used for bibliographic entries.

Line break indicator A non-printing character in the shape of a bent arrow that indicates a manual line break.

Mail merge A feature that joins a main document and a data source to create customized letters or labels.

Main document In a mail merge, the document that contains the text or formatting that remains constant.

Manual column break An artificial end to a column to balance columns or to provide space for the insertion of other objects.

Manual line break A break that moves text to the right of the insertion point to a new line while keeping the text in the same paragraph.

Manual page break The action of forcing a page to end and placing subsequent text at the top of the next page.

Modern Language Association (MLA) One of two commonly used style guides for formatting research papers.

Nameplate The banner on the front page of a newsletter that identifies the publication.

Newsletter A periodical that communicates news and information to a specific group.

Note In a research paper, information that expands on the topic, but that does not fit well in the document text.

Office 365 Administrator—the person who creates and manages the account, adds new users, sets up the services your organization wants to use, sets permission levels, and manages the SharePoint team sites.

Page break indicator A dotted line with the text *Page Break* that indicates where a manual page break was inserted.

Parenthetical references References that include the last name of the author or authors, and the page number in the referenced source.

PDF Reflow The ability to import PDF files into Word so that you can transform a PDF back into a fully editable Word document.

Read Mode A view in Word that optimizes the Word screen for the times when you are reading Word documents on the screen and not creating or editing them.

Recolor A feature that enables you to change all colors in the picture to shades of a single color.

Record Each row of information that contains data for one person.

Scale A command that resizes a picture to a percentage of its size.

Screenshot An image of an active window on your computer that you can paste into a document.

Section A portion of a document that can be formatted differently from the rest of the document.

Section break A double dotted line that indicates the end of one section and the beginning of another section.

Small caps A font effect that changes lowercase letters to uppercase letters, but with the height of lowercase letters.

Style A group of formatting commands, such as font, font size, font color, paragraph alignment, and line spacing that can be applied to a paragraph with one command.

Style guide A manual that contains standards for the design and writing of documents.

Suppress A Word feature that hides header and footer information, including the page number, on the first page of a document.

Windows Reader app A Windows Store app with which you can open a PDF or XPS file, zoom, find words or phrases, take notes, save changes, and then print or share the file.

Works Cited In the MLA style, a list of cited works placed at the end of a research paper or report.

CHAPTER REVIEW

Apply 3A skills from these Objectives:

1 Create a Research Paper
2 Insert Footnotes in a Research Paper
3 Create Citations and a Bibliography in a Research Paper
4 Use Read Mode and PDF Reflow

Skills Review Project 3C Diet and Exercise Report

In the following Skills Review, you will edit and format a research paper that contains information about the effects of diet and exercise. This paper was created by Rachel Holder, a medical intern at University Medical Center, for distribution to her classmates studying physiology. Your completed document will look similar to the one shown in Figure 3.55.

PROJECT FILES

For Project 3C, you will need the following file:

w03C_Diet_Exercise

You will save your document as:

Lastname_Firstname_3C_Diet_Exercise

PROJECT RESULTS

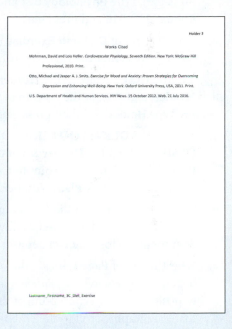

FIGURE 3.55

(Project 3C Diet and Exercise Report continues on the next page)

CHAPTER REVIEW

1 Start Word. From your student files, locate and open the document **w03C_Diet_Exercise**. Display the formatting marks and rulers. **Save** the file in your **Word Chapter 3** folder as **Lastname_Firstname_3C_Diet_Exercise**

a. Press Ctrl + A to select all the text. On the **HOME tab**, in the **Paragraph group**, click **Line and Paragraph Spacing**, and then change the line spacing to **2.0**. On the **PAGE LAYOUT tab**, change the **Spacing After** to **0 pt**.

b. Press Ctrl + Home, press Enter to create a blank line at the top of the document, and then click to position the insertion point in the new blank line. Type **Rachel Holder** and press Enter. Type **Dr. Hillary Kim** and press Enter. Type **Physiology 621** and press Enter. Type **August 31, 2016** and press Enter.

c. Type **Effects of Diet and Exercise** and then press Ctrl + E to center the title you just typed.

2 On the **INSERT tab**, in the **Header & Footer group**, click **Header**, and then at the bottom of the list, click **Edit Header**. Type **Holder** and then press Spacebar.

a. Under **HEADER & FOOTER TOOLS**, on the **DESIGN tab**, in the **Header & Footer group**, click **Page Number**, and then point to **Current Position**. Under **Simple**, click **Plain Number**.

b. On the **HOME tab**, in the **Paragraph group**, click **Align Right**. Double-click anywhere in the document to close the Header area.

c. Near the top of **Page 1**, locate the paragraph beginning *The scientific evidence*, and then click to position the insertion point at the beginning of that paragraph. Scroll to the end of the document, hold down Shift, and then click to the right of the last paragraph mark to select all of the text from the insertion point to the end of the document.

d. On the **HOME tab**, in the **Paragraph group**, click the **Dialog Box Launcher** button. In the **Paragraph** dialog box, on the **Indents and Spacing tab**, under **Indentation**, click the **Special arrow**, and then click **First line**. Click **OK**.

e. On the **INSERT tab**, in the **Header & Footer group**, click **Footer**, and then click **Edit Footer**. In the **Insert group**, click **Document Info**, and then click **File Name**. Click **Close Header and Footer**.

3 Scroll to view the top of **Page 2**, locate the paragraph that begins *Exercise also has*, and then at the end of that paragraph, click to position the insertion point to the right of the period following *Irwin*. On the **REFERENCES tab**, in the **Footnotes group**, click **Insert Footnote**.

a. As the footnote text, type **Physical activity may provide a low-risk method of preventing weight gain. Unlike diet-induced weight loss, exercise-induced weight loss increases cardiorespiratory fitness levels.**

b. In the upper portion of **Page 1**, locate the paragraph that begins *Regular cardiovascular exercise*. Click to position the insertion point at the end of the paragraph and insert a footnote.

c. As the footnote text, type **The objective of the study was to examine the effects of exercise on total and intra-abdominal body fat overall and by level of exercise. Save** your document.

4 At the bottom of **Page 1**, right-click in the footnote you just typed. On the shortcut menu, click **Style**. In the **Style** dialog box, click **Modify**. In the **Modify Style** dialog box, locate the small Formatting toolbar in the center of the dialog box, click the **Font Size button arrow**, and then click **11**.

a. In the lower left corner of the dialog box, click **Format**, and then click **Paragraph**. In the **Paragraph** dialog box, under **Indentation**, click the **Special arrow**, and then click **First line**. Under **Spacing**, click the **Line spacing button arrow**, and then click **Double**.

b. Click **OK** to close the **Paragraph** dialog box, click **OK** to close the **Modify Style** dialog box, and then click **Apply** to apply the new style. **Save** your document.

5 Scroll to view the top of **Page 1**, and then in the paragraph that begins *The scientific evidence*, click to position the insertion point to the left of the period at the end of the paragraph.

a. On the **REFERENCES tab**, in the **Citations & Bibliography group**, click the **Style button arrow**, and then click **MLA** to insert a reference using MLA style. Click **Insert Citation**, and then click **Add New Source**. Click the **Type of Source arrow**, scroll as

(Project 3C Diet and Exercise Report continues on the next page)

CHAPTER REVIEW

necessary to locate and click **Book**, and then add the following information:

Author	Otto, Michael and Jasper A. J. Smits
Title	Exercise for Mood and Anxiety: Proven Strategies for Overcoming Depression and Enhancing Well-Being
Year	2011
City	New York
Publisher	Oxford University Press, USA
Medium	Print

b. Click **OK** to insert the citation. In the paragraph, click to select the citation, click the **Citation Options arrow**, and then click **Edit Citation**. In the **Edit Citation** dialog box, under **Add**, in the **Pages** box, type **3** and then click **OK**.

c. On the upper portion of **Page 2**, in the paragraph that begins *Other positive effects*, in the third line, click to position the insertion point to the left of the period following *substantially*. In the **Citations & Bibliography group**, click **Insert Citation**, and then click **Add New Source**. Click the **Type of Source arrow**, click **Book**, and then add the following information:

Author	Lohrman, David and Lois Heller
Title	Cardiovascular Physiology, Seventh Edition
Year	2010
City	New York
Publisher	McGraw-Hill Professional
Medium	Print

d. Click **OK**. Click to select the citation in the paragraph, click the **Citation Options arrow**, and then click **Edit Citation**. In the **Edit Citation** dialog box, under **Add**, in the **Pages** box, type **195** and then click **OK**.

6 Press Ctrl + End to move to the end of the last paragraph in the document. Click to the left of the period following *loss*. In the **Citations & Bibliography group**,

click **Insert Citation**, and then click **Add New Source**. Click the **Type of Source arrow**, click **Web site**, and then select the **Corporate Author** check box. Add the following information:

Corporate Author	U.S. Department of Health and Human Services
Name of Web Page	NIH News
Year	2012
Month	October
Day	15
Year Accessed	2016
Month Accessed	July
Day Accessed	21
Medium	Web

a. Click **OK**. Press Ctrl + End to move the insertion point to the end of the document. Press Ctrl + Enter to insert a manual page break. On the **HOME tab**, in the **Paragraph group**, click the **Dialog Box Launcher** button. In the **Paragraph** dialog box, on the **Indents and Spacing tab**, under **Indentation**, click the **Special arrow**, and then click **(none)**. Click **OK**.

b. Type **Works Cited** and then press Enter. On the **REFERENCES tab**, in the **Citations & Bibliography group**, be sure **MLA** displays in the **Style** box. In the **Citations & Bibliography group**, click **Bibliography**, and then at the bottom, click **Insert Bibliography**.

c. Click anywhere in the *Works Cited* title, and then press Ctrl + E to center the title. **Save** your document.

7 On the **REFERENCES tab**, in the **Citations & Bibliography group**, click **Manage Sources**. On the left, on the **Master List**, click the entry for *Lohrman, David*, and then click **Edit**. In the **Edit Source** dialog box, in the **Author** box, change the *L* in *Lohrman* to **M** Click **OK**, click **Yes**, and then click **Close**.

a. On **Page 2**, in the paragraph that begins *Other positive effects*, in the third line, on the selected citation, click the **Citation Options arrow**, and then click **Update Citations and Bibliography**.

(Project 3C Diet and Exercise Report continues on the next page)

CHAPTER REVIEW

b. In the bibliography, move the pointer to the left of the first entry—beginning *Mohrman*—to display the pointer. Drag down to select all three references in the field. On the **HOME tab**, in the **Paragraph group**, set the **Line spacing** to **2.0**. On the **PAGE LAYOUT tab**, set the **Spacing After** to **0 pt**.

c. Click the **FILE tab**, and then in the lower right corner, click **Show All Properties**. Add the following information:

Title	**Diet and Exercise**
Tags	**weight loss, exercise, diet**
Comments	**Draft copy of report for class**
Categories	**biomedical research**
Company	**University Medical Center**
Manager	**Dr. Hillary Kim**

END | You have completed Project 3C

d. In the **Subject** box, type your course name and section number. Be sure that your name displays as the Author and edit if necessary. On the left, click **Save** to redisplay your document. On the **VIEW tab**, in the **Views group**, click **Read Mode**. In the upper left, click **TOOLS**, click **Find**, and then in the search box, type **Yale** and notice that the text you searched for is highlighted in the document.

e. In the upper left, click **VIEW**, and then click **Edit Document** to return to **Print Layout** view. **Close** the **navigation pane**. **Save** your document, view the **Print Preview**, and then print or submit electronically as directed by your instructor. **Close** Word.

CHAPTER REVIEW

Apply **3B** skills from these Objectives:

5 Format a Multiple-Column Newsletter

6 Use Special Character and Paragraph Formatting

7 Create Mailing Labels Using Mail Merge

In the following Skills Review, you will format a newsletter regarding professional development opportunities offered by University Medical Center, and you will create mailing labels for staff interested in these opportunities. Your completed document will look similar to Figure 3.56.

PROJECT FILES

For Project 3D, you will need the following files:

New blank Word document

w03D_Career_Newsletter

w03D_Addresses

You will save your documents as:

Lastname_Firstname_3D_Career_Newsletter

Lastname_Firstname_3D_Addresses

Lastname_Firstname_3D_Mailing_Labels

PROJECT RESULTS

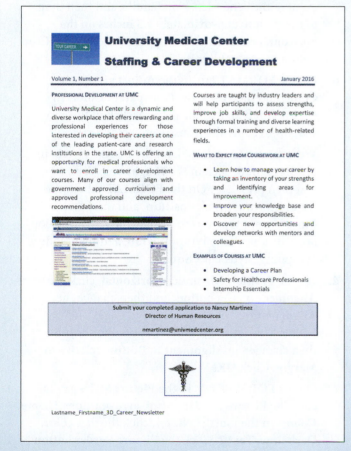

FIGURE 3.56

(Project 3D Career Newsletter continues on the next page)

CHAPTER REVIEW

1 Start Word. On Word's opening screen, in the lower left, click **Open Other Documents**. Navigate to your student files, and then locate and open **w03D_Career_Newsletter**. **Save** the file in your **Word Chapter 3** folder as **Lastname_Firstname_3D_Career_Newsletter** and then add the file name to the footer.

a. Select the first two lines of the document. On the mini toolbar, change the **Font** to **Arial Black** and the **Font Size** to **18**. Select the first three lines of the document. Click the **Font Color button arrow**, and then under **Theme Colors**, in the fifth column, click the last color—**Blue, Accent 1, Darker 50%**.

b. With the text still selected, on the **HOME tab**, in the **Paragraph group**, click the **Borders button arrow**, and then at the bottom, click **Borders and Shading**. In the **Borders and Shading** dialog box, on the **Borders tab**, click the **Color arrow**, and then under **Theme Colors**, in the fifth column, click the last color—**Blue, Accent 1, Darker 50%**.

c. Click the **Width arrow**, and then click **3 pt**. In the **Preview** box, click the bottom border. Click **OK**.

d. Click at the beginning of the paragraph that begins *Professional Development*. Scroll the document, hold down Shift, and then click after the paragraph mark at the end of the *Internship Essentials* line. On the **PAGE LAYOUT tab**, in the **Page Setup group**, click **Columns**, and then click **Two**. With the two columns of text selected, on the **HOME tab**, in the **Paragraph group**, click **Justify**.

e. In the first column, click at the beginning of the paragraph that begins *Courses are taught*. On the **PAGE LAYOUT tab**, in the **Page Setup group**, click **Breaks**. Under **Page Breaks**, click **Column**.

2 Press Ctrl + Home. On the **INSERT tab**, in the **Illustrations group**, click **Online Pictures**. In the **Office.com Clip Art** search box, type **career** and then press Enter. Click the image of the sign with the text *Your Career*. If the image does not display, select a similar picture. Click **Insert**.

a. On the **FORMAT tab**, in the **Size group**, click the **Dialog Box Launcher** button. In the **Layout** dialog box, on the **Size tab**, under **Scale**, be sure the **Lock aspect ratio** and **Relative to original picture size** check boxes are selected. Select the number in the **Height** box, type **10** and then press Tab.

b. In the **Layout** dialog box, click the **Text Wrapping tab**. Under **Wrapping style**, click **Square**.

c. Click the **Position tab**, and then under **Horizontal**, click the **Alignment** option button. Be sure that the **Alignment** indicates **Left** and **relative to Column**. Under **Vertical**, click the **Alignment** option button, and then change the alignment to **Top relative to Margin**. Click **OK**. **Save** your newsletter.

3 Press Ctrl + End to move to the end of the document. On the **INSERT tab**, in the **Illustrations group**, click **Online Pictures**. In the **Office.com Clip Art** search box, search for **caducei healthcare symbol** and then insert the picture of the gray caducei with a gray shadow. If the image does not display, select a similar picture.

a. On the **FORMAT tab**, in the **Size group**, click the upper portion of the **Crop** button. Point to the center right crop handle, and then drag to the left to approximately **5.5 inches on the horizontal ruler**. Point to the center left crop handle, and then drag to the right to approximately **1.5 inches on the horizontal ruler**. Click the upper portion of the **Crop** button to apply the crop.

b. On the **FORMAT tab**, in the **Adjust group**, click **Color**, and then click **Set Transparent Color**. In the lower left area of the picture, click in the gray shadow to apply the transparent color.

c. With the picture selected, on the **FORMAT tab**, in the **Size group**, click in the **Height** box. Type **1** and then press Enter. On the **FORMAT tab**, in the **Arrange group**, click **Position**, and then click **More Layout Options** to display the **Layout** dialog box. Click the **Text Wrapping tab**, and then under **Wrapping Style**, click **Square**.

d. On the **Position tab**, under **Horizontal**, click the **Alignment** option button, and then change the **Alignment** to **Centered relative to Page**. Under **Vertical**, click the **Alignment** option button, and then change the **Alignment** to **Bottom relative to Margin**. Click **OK**.

e. On the **FORMAT tab**, in the **Picture Styles group**, click the **Picture Border button arrow**. Under **Theme Colors**, in the fourth column, click the first color—**Dark Blue, Text 2**. Click the **Picture Border button arrow** again, and then point to **Weight**. Click **1 pt**.

(Project 3D Career Newsletter continues on the next page)

f. On the **FORMAT tab**, in the **Adjust group**, click **Color**. Under **Recolor**, in the first row, click the last option—**Black and White, 75%**. On the **FORMAT tab**, in the **Adjust group**, click **Corrections**. Under **Brightness/Contrast**, in the second row, click the fourth setting—**Brightness: +20% Contrast: −20%**.

4 ▶ In the paragraph that begins *University Medical Center is a dynamic*, click after the period at the end of the paragraph, and then press [Enter]. Start Internet Explorer, maximize the window, and then navigate to **www.ahrq.gov/clinic/**

a. Redisplay your **3D_Career_Newletter** document. With the insertion point positioned in the blank line above the column break, on the **INSERT tab**, in the **Illustrations group**, click **Screenshot**. In the **Screenshot** gallery, click the browser window that contains the website; click **No** in the message that displays.

b. Select the subheading *Professional Development at UMC* including the paragraph mark. Right-click the selected text, and then on the shortcut menu, click **Font**. In the **Font** dialog box, click the **Font color arrow**, and then in the fifth column, click the last color—**Blue, Accent 1, Darker 50%**. Under **Font style**, click **Bold**, and then under **Effects**, select **Small caps**. Click **OK**.

c. With the text still selected, right-click, and then on the mini toolbar, double-click **Format Painter**. In the second column, with the 🖍I pointer, select each of the subheadings—*What to Expect from Coursework at UMC* and *Example of Courses at UMC*. Press [Esc] to turn off **Format Painter**.

5 ▶ Press [Ctrl] + [End] to move to the end of the document, and then select the two lines of bold text—the graphic will also be selected. On the **HOME tab**, in the **Paragraph group**, click the **Borders button arrow**, and then click **Borders and Shading**.

a. In the **Borders and Shading** dialog box, on the **Borders tab**, under **Setting**, click **Shadow**. Click the **Color arrow**, and then in the fifth column, click the last color—**Blue, Accent 1, Darker 50%**. Click the **Width arrow**, and then click **1 pt**.

b. In the **Borders and Shading** dialog box, click the **Shading tab**. Click the **Fill arrow**, and then in the

fifth column, click the second color—**Blue, Accent 1, Lighter 80%**. Click **OK**. On the **HOME tab**, in the **Paragraph group**, click **Center**. In the shaded paragraph, click in front of the *D* in the word *Director*. Hold down [Shift] and then press [Enter].

c. Press [Ctrl] + [Home], and then click the **FILE tab**. At the bottom of the **Properties** list, click **Show All Properties**. Click to the right of **Tags**, and then type **newsletter, careers** Click to the right of **Subject**, and then type your course name and section number. Under **Related People**, if necessary, type your name in the Author box. Display the **Print Preview** and make any necessary corrections. **Save** the document; close Word and close Internet Explorer.

6 ▶ Start Word and display a new blank document. **Save** the document in your **Word Chapter 3** folder as **Lastname_Firstname_3D_Mailing_Labels** With your new document open on the screen, from your student files, **Open** the file **w03D_Addresses**. **Save** the address file in your **Word Chapter 3** folder as **Lastname_Firstname_3D_ Addresses** and then add the file name to the footer. **Save** and then **Close** the file. Be sure that your **Lastname_ Firstname_3D_Mailing_Labels** document displays.

a. Click the **MAILINGS tab**. In the **Start Mail Merge group**, click **Start Mail Merge**, and then click **Step-by-Step Mail Merge Wizard**. In the **Mail Merge** pane, under **Select document type**, click **Labels**. At the bottom of the **Mail Merge** pane, click **Next: Starting document**.

b. Under **Select starting document**, under **Change document layout**, click **Label options**. In the **Label Options** dialog box, under **Printer information**, be sure that the **Default tray** is selected.

c. Under **Label information**, click the **Label vendors arrow**, and then click **Avery US Letter**. Under **Product number**, scroll about halfway down the list, and then click **5160 Easy Peel Address Labels**. At the bottom of the **Label Options** dialog box, click **OK**. At the bottom of the **Mail Merge** pane, click **Next: Select recipients**.

d. In the **Mail Merge** pane, under **Select recipients**, under **Use an existing list**, click **Browse**. Navigate to your **Word Chapter 3** folder, select your **Lastname_ Firstname_3D_Addresses** file, and then click **Open**.

(Project 3D Career Newsletter continues on the next page)

CHAPTER REVIEW

7 In the lower left portion of the **Mail Merge Recipients** dialog box, in the **Data Source** box, click the path that contains your file name. Then, at the bottom of the **Mail Merge Recipients** dialog box, click **Edit**. In the upper right corner of the **Data Form** dialog box, click **Add New**. In the blank record, type the following, pressing `Tab` to move from field to field:

First_Name:	Mia
Last_Name:	Orr
Address_1:	1378 Lima Ave.
Unit:	#82
City:	Memphis
State:	TN
ZIP_Code:	38123

a. In the lower right corner of the **Data Form** dialog box, click **Close**. At the bottom of the **Mail Merge Recipients** dialog box, click **OK**.

b. At the bottom of the **Mail Merge** pane, click **Next: Arrange your labels**. Under **Arrange your labels**, click **Address block**. In the lower right corner of the **Insert Address Block** dialog box, click **Match Fields**.

c. Click the **Address 2 arrow**, and then from the list of available fields, click **Unit**. Click **OK** two times.

d. In the **Mail Merge** pane, under **Replicate labels**, click **Update all labels**. At the bottom of the **Mail**

Merge pane, click **Next: Preview your labels**. Press `Ctrl` + `A` to select all of the label text, click the **PAGE LAYOUT tab**, and then in the **Paragraph group**, click in the **Spacing Before** box. Type **3** and press `Enter`. At the bottom of the **Mail Merge** pane, click **Next: Complete the merge**.

e. Click the **MAILINGS tab**, and then in the **Start Mail Merge group**, click **Edit Recipient List** to display the list of names and addresses. In the **Mail Merge Recipients** dialog box, click the **Last_Name** field heading to sort the names. Click **OK**. **Close** the **Mail Merge** pane.

f. Scroll the document and then click anywhere in the empty table row at the bottom. Click the **LAYOUT tab**. In the **Rows & Columns group**, click **Delete**, and then click **Delete Rows**. Add the file name to the footer, close the footer area, and then click the **FILE tab**. Click **Show All Properties**. As the **Tags**, type **labels** and as the **Subject**, type your course name and section number. Be sure your name displays as the **Author**, and then **Save** your file.

g. As directed by your instructor, print or submit electronically. **Close** the document, click **Yes** to save the data source, and then if necessary, click **Save** to save the labels. In addition to your labels and address document, submit your **3D_Career_Newsletter** document as directed. **Close** Word.

END | You have completed Project 3D

Apply 3A skills from these Objectives:

1 Create a Research Paper
2 Insert Footnotes in a Research Paper
3 Create Citations and a Bibliography in a Research Paper
4 Use Read Mode and PDF Reflow

Mastering Word   Project 3E Skin Protection Report

In the following Mastering Word project, you will edit and format a research paper that contains information about skin protection and the use of sunblocks and sunscreens. This paper was created by Rachel Holder, a medical intern at University Medical Center, for distribution to her classmates studying dermatology. Your completed document will look similar to the one shown in Figure 3.57.

PROJECT FILES

For Project 3E, you will need the following file:

w03E_Skin_Protection

You will save your document as:

Lastname_Firstname_3E_Skin_Protection

PROJECT RESULTS

FIGURE 3.57

(Project 3E Skin Protection Report continues on the next page)

CONTENT-BASED ASSESSMENTS

1 Start Word. From your student files, locate and open the document **w03E_Skin_Protection**. Display formatting marks and rulers. Save the file in your **Word Chapter 3** folder as **Lastname_Firstname_3E_Skin_Protection**

2 Select all the text, change the **Line Spacing** to **2.0**, and then change the **Spacing After** to **0 pt**. At the top of the document, insert a new blank paragraph, and then in the new paragraph, type **Rachel Holder** Press Enter. Type **Dr. Hillary Kim** and press Enter. Type **Dermatology 544** and press Enter. Type **August 31, 2016** and press Enter. Type **Skin Protection** and then press Ctrl + E to center the title you just typed.

3 Insert a header, type **Holder** and then press Spacebar. Display the **Page Number gallery**, and then in the **Current Position**, add the **Plain Number** style. Apply **Align Right** formatting to the header. Insert a footer with the file name. Starting with the paragraph that begins *One way to prevent*, select all the text in the document, and then set a **First line** indent of **0.5"**.

4 On **Page 2**, at the end of the paragraph that begins *In the medical field*, insert a footnote with the following text: **The American Academy of Dermatology recommends using a broad spectrum sunscreen with an SPF of 30 or more.**

5 On **Page 2**, at the end of the paragraph that begins *Individuals should protect*, insert a footnote with the following text: **For babies, the American Academy of Dermatology recommends using a sunscreen that contains only inorganic filters, such as zinc oxide and titanium dioxide, to avoid any skin or eye irritation.**

6 Modify the **Footnote Text** style so that the **Font Size** is **11**, there is a **First line indent** of **0.5"**, and the spacing is **Double**, and then apply the style.

7 On **Page 1**, at the end of the paragraph that begins *According to an article*, click to the left of the period, and then using **MLA** format, insert a citation for a **Journal Article** with the following information:

Author	Frash, D. E., A. S. Jonason, and J. A. Simon
Title	Sunlight and Sunburn in Human Skin Cancer
Journal Name	The Journal of Investigative Dermatology

Year	1996
Pages	136-142
Medium	Print

8 In the report, select the citation you just created, display the **Citation Options**, and then edit the citation to include **Pages 136-142** At the end of the last paragraph of the report, click to the left of the period, and then insert a citation for a **Book** with the following information:

Author	Leffell, David
Title	Total Skin: The Definitive Guide to Whole Skin Care for Life
Year	2000
City	New York
Publisher	Hyperion
Medium	Print

9 In the report, select the citation you just created, display the **Citation Options**, and then edit the citation to include **Page 96** At the top of **Page 2**, at the end of the paragraph that begins *According to Dr.*, click to the left of the period, and then insert a citation for a **Web site** with the following information:

Author	Gibson, Lawrence E.
Name of Web Page	Does Sunscreen Expire?
Year	2011
Month	April
Day	01
Year Accessed	2016
Month Accessed	June
Day Accessed	30
Medium	Web

10 Move to the end of the document, and then insert a manual page break to create a new page. Display the **Paragraph** dialog box, and then change the **Indentation** under **Special** to **(none)**. Add a **Works Cited** title, press Enter, and then click **Insert Bibliography**. **Center** the *Works Cited* title.

(Project 3E Skin Protection Report continues on the next page)

CONTENT-BASED ASSESSMENTS

11 By using the **Manage Sources** command, display the **Source Manager**. On the **Master List**, select the entry for **Frash, D. E.**, and then **Edit** this source—the last name should be **Brash** instead of *Frash*. In the message that displays, update both lists. Locate the citation in the text of the report, display the **Citation Options**, and then **Update Citations and Bibliography**. On the Works Cited page, select the references, apply **Double** line spacing, and then set the **Spacing After** paragraphs to **0 pt**.

12 Update the **Document Properties** with the following information:

Title	**Skin Protection**
Tags	**sunscreen, sun exposure**
Comments	**Draft copy of report for class**
Categories	**Dermatology**
Company	**University Medical Center**
Manager	**Dr. Hillary Kim**

13 In the **Subject** box, type your course name and section number. Be sure that your name displays as the **Author** and edit if necessary. On the left, click **Print** to view the **Print Preview**, and then click **Save** to redisplay your document. Print or submit electronically as directed by your instructor. **Close** Word.

END | You have completed Project 3E

CONTENT-BASED ASSESSMENTS

Apply 3B skills from these Objectives:

5 Format a Multiple-Column Newsletter

6 Use Special Character and Paragraph Formatting

7 Create Mailing Labels Using Mail Merge

In the following Mastering Word project, you will format a newsletter with information about the therapy dogs handled by volunteers at the University Medical Center. You will also create mailing labels so that the newsletter can be sent to the volunteer staff. Your completed documents will look similar to Figure 3.58.

PROJECT FILES

For Project 3F, you will need the following files:

New blank Word document
w03F_Dogs_Newsletter
w03F_Addresses

You will save your documents as:

Lastname_Firstname_3F_Dogs_Newsletter
Lastname_Firstname_3F_Addresses
Lastname_Firstname_3F_Mailing_Labels

PROJECT RESULTS

University Medical Center
Health Improvement Newsletter

Volume 3   Spring 2016

DOGS FOR HEALING

At University Medical Center, therapy dogs have been a welcomed asset to patient care and recovery since 2004. UMC works with several non-profit organizations to bring dedicated volunteers and their canine teams into the hospital to visit children, adults, and seniors. Information regarding service dog regulations, training, and laws is available on the ADA website.

BENEFITS TO PATIENTS

Medical research shows that petting a dog or other domestic animal relaxes patients and helps ease symptoms of stress from illness or from the hospital setting. Studies have shown that such therapies contribute to decreased blood pressure and heart rate, and can help with patient respiratory rate.

CUDDLES

Cuddles, a 4 year-old Labrador, is one of our most popular therapy dogs and is loved by both young and senior patients. You'll see Cuddles in the Children's wing on Mondays with his owner, Jason, who trained him since he was a tiny pup.

BRANDY

Brandy is a 6 year-old Beagle who brings smiles and giggles to everyone she meets. Over the past several years, Brandy has received accolades and awards for her service as a therapy dog. Brandy is owned by Melinda Sparks, a 17-year veteran employee of University Medical Center. Brandy and Melinda can be seen making the rounds on Wednesdays in the Children's wing and on Mondays and Fridays throughout the hospital.

To request a visit from a therapy dog, or to learn how to become involved with therapy dog training, call Carole Yates at extension 2365.

Lastname_Firstname_3F_Dogs_Newsletter

Mary Ackerman
82 E. Roxie Blvd.
Arlington, TN 38002

Jacqueline Epps
653 Vista Ave.
#D
Lakeland, TN 38002

Emily Gold
888 Packard Court
Lakeland, TN 38002

Bin Lee
676 Silver St.
Memphis, TN 38120

Leland Marcus
600 Garfield Ave.
Memphis, TN 38117

Thai Nguyen
179 Sierra Court
Collierville, TN 38017

Erica Scott
124 Susan Drive
#352
Memphis, TN 38134

Simone Thompson
648 Michaela St.
Bartlett, TN 38133

Miranda Yanos
1256 Loma Ave.
#34
Memphis, TN 38123

Anthony Borman
2820 Lincoln Ave.
Collierville, TN 38017

Renee Farnsworth
36 S. Levin St.
#D
Bartlett, TN 38135

Abel Heaphy
55 Amigo Lane
#4
Collierville, TN 38017

Anh Ly
1255 Chestnut Street
Memphis, TN 38122

Walter McKidd
2495 Holly Drive
Arlington, TN 38002

Thomas Norris
492 Mahogany Street
Bartlett, TN 38135

Andrew Sharma
1550 Beverly Drive
#1550
Memphis, TN 38104

David Turnbull
1821 Chelsea St.
#1442
Germantown, TN 38138

Jerry Camden
543 Verde Way
Memphis, TN 38120

Anita Figueroa
9000 S. Masters Dr.
Germantown, TN 38139

Katie Hughes
34 Sadler Pl.
Bartlett, TN 38133

Priya Malik
975 Ricardo Place
#G
Germantown, TN 38138

Sharon Moreno
1330 Golden Ave.
Memphis, TN 38120

Daniel Scofield
1518 Price Place
Arlington, TN 38002

Sara Thompson
4220 Glendora Dr.
#320
Memphis, TN 38112

Jackson Williams
15 Atlantic Rd.
Memphis, TN 38111

Lastname_Firstname_3F_Mailing_Labels

FIGURE 3.58

(Project 3F Dogs Newsletter and Mailing Labels continues on the next page)

CONTENT-BASED ASSESSMENTS

1 Start Word. From your student files, open **w03F_Dogs_Newsletter**. **Save** the file in your **Word Chapter 3** folder as **Lastname_Firstname_3F_Dogs_Newsletter** and then add the file name to the footer. Select the first three lines of the document, and then change the **Font Color** to **Olive Green, Accent 3, Darker 25%**—in the seventh column, the fifth color. With the text selected, display the **Borders and Shading** dialog box. Apply a **3 pt** bottom border in **Black, Text 1**.

2 Click at the beginning of the newsletter title *University Medical Center*. Insert an online picture from **Office.com Clip Art** by searching for **physician symbols** Insert the picture of the physician symbol on top of the green oval with a blue outline. Use the **Set Transparent Color** command to make the green background transparent. Change the **Brightness/Contrast** to **Brightness: 0% (Normal) Contrast: +40%**.

3 **Scale** the picture to **50%** of its **Height**, and then change the **Text Wrapping** to **Square**. Change the **Horizontal Alignment** to **Left relative** to **Margin** and the **Vertical Alignment** to **Top relative** to **Margin**.

4 Starting with the paragraph that begins *Dogs for Healing*, select all of the text from that point to the end of the document. Change the **Spacing After** to **10 pt**, format the text in two columns, and apply **Justify** alignment. Insert a **Column break** before the subheading *Cuddles*.

5 Click at the beginning of the sentence that begins with *Brandy is a 6 year-old Beagle*. Insert an online picture from **Office.com Clip Art** by searching for **beagle** Insert the picture of the beagle sitting on the grass. Rotate the picture using **Flip Horizontal**. Change the picture **Height** to **1.5** and then apply the **Square** layout option. Change the **Horizontal Alignment** to **Right relative** to **Margin** and the **Vertical Alignment** to **Top relative** to **Line**. Apply a **Black, Text 1 Picture Border** and change the **Weight** to **2 1/4 pt**.

6 Start Internet Explorer, navigate to **www.ada.gov/qasrvc.htm** and then maximize your browser window. In your **3F_Dogs_Newsletter** file, click at the end of the paragraph below the *Dogs for Healing* subheading, and then press Enter. In the blank line, insert a **Screenshot** of the website; do not link to the URL. Apply a **Black, Text 1 Picture Border** and change the **Weight** to **1 pt**.

7 Select the subheading *Dogs for Healing* including the paragraph mark. By using the **Font** dialog box, change the **Size** to **16**, apply **Bold**, apply the **Small caps** effect, and change the **Font color** to **Olive Green, Accent 3, Darker 50%**—in the seventh column, the last color. Apply the same formatting to the subheadings *Benefits to Patients*, *Cuddles*, and *Brandy*.

8 Select the last paragraph in the newsletter, and then apply a **1 pt Shadow** border, in **Black, Text 1**. Shade the paragraph with a **Fill** color of **Olive Green, Accent 3, Lighter 80%**—in the seventh column, the second color. Click the **FILE tab**, and then click **Show All Properties**. As the **Tags**, type **dogs, newsletter** As the **Subject**, type your course name and section number. Under **Related People**, if necessary, type your name in the **Author box**. **Print Preview** the document and make any necessary corrections. **Save** the document and **close** Word.

9 Start Word and display a new blank document. **Save** the document in your **Word Chapter 3** folder as **Lastname_Firstname_3F_Mailing_Labels** From your student files, **Open** the file **w03F_Addresses**. **Save** the address file in your **Word Chapter 3** folder as **Lastname_Firstname_3F_Addresses** and then add the file name to the footer. **Save** and **Close** the file. Be sure that your **Lastname_Firstname_3F_Mailing_Labels** document displays.

10 Start the **Step-by-Step Mail Merge Wizard** to create **Labels**. Be sure that the **Default tray** is selected and that the label vendor is **Avery US Letter**. The **Product number** is **5160 Easy Peel Address Labels**. Select the **Use an existing list** option, and then from your **Word Chapter 3** folder, open your **Lastname_Firstname_3F_Addresses** file. Add the following record to your file:

First Name	**Miranda**
Last Name	**Yanos**
Address 1	**1256 Loma Ave.**
Unit	**#34**
City	**Memphis**
State	**TN**
ZIP Code	**38123**

(Project 3F Dogs Newsletter and Mailing Labels continues on the next page)

CONTENT-BASED ASSESSMENTS

11 Insert an **Address block** and match the fields. Match the **Address 2** field to the **Unit** field, and then update the labels. Preview the labels, and then select the entire document. Change the **Spacing Before** to **3** and then **Complete the merge**. Delete the last row from the bottom of the table, and then add the file name to the footer.

12 Display the document properties. As the **Tags** type **labels** and as the **Subject** type your course name and section number. Be sure your name displays in the **Author box**, and then **Save** your file. As directed by your instructor, print or submit electronically. In addition to your labels and address document, submit your **3F_Dogs_Newsletter** document as directed. **Close** Word and Internet Explorer.

END | You have completed Project 3F

CONTENT-BASED ASSESSMENTS

Apply 3A and 3B skills from these Objectives:

1 Create a Research Paper
2 Insert Footnotes in a Research Paper
3 Create Citations and a Bibliography in a Research Paper
4 Use Read Mode and PDF Reflow
5 Format a Multiple-Column Newsletter
6 Use Special Character and Paragraph Formatting
7 Create Mailing Labels Using Mail Merge

In the following Mastering Word project, you will edit and format a research paper and a newsletter, and you will create mailing labels. Your completed documents will look similar to Figure 3.59.

PROJECT FILES

For Project 3G, you will need the following files:

New blank Word document
w03G_Electronic_Records
w03G_Newsletter
w03G_Addresses

You will save your documents as:

Lastname_Firstname_3G_Electronic_Records
Lastname_Firstname_3G_Newsletter
Lastname_Firstname_3G_Mailing_Labels
Lastname_Firstname_3G_Addresses

PROJECT RESULTS

FIGURE 3.59

(Project 3G Research Paper, Newsletter, and Mailing Labels continues on the next page)

CONTENT-BASED ASSESSMENTS

1 Start Word. From your student files, locate and open the document **w03G_Electronic_Records**, and then **Save** it in your **Word Chapter 3** folder as **Lastname_Firstname_3G_Electronic_Records** Display the header area, type **Eisler** and then press Spacebar. From the **Header & Footer group**, add a **Plain Number** page number from the **Current Position** gallery. Apply **Align Right** formatting to the header. Move to the footer area and add the file name to the footer.

Select all the text in the document, change the **Line Spacing** to **2.0**, and then change the **Spacing After** to **0 pt**. **Center** the title *Electronic Health Records*. Beginning with text below the centered title, select the text from that point to the end of the document, and then set a **First line** indent of **0.5"**.

2 At the top of **Page 1**, at the end of the paragraph that begins *There is often*, insert a footnote with the following text: **Electronic Health Records is an evolving concept that shares records in digital format across different health care settings and might include medical history, test results, and x-rays.**

At the top of **Page 2**, in the second line, at the end of the sentence that ends *if they had it*, insert a footnote with the following text: **The EMR (electronic medical record) is the patient record created in hospitals and ambulatory environments; it serves as a data source for other systems.**

3 On **Page 1**, at the end of the paragraph that begins *Those clinical practices*, click to the left of the period, and then using **MLA** format, insert a citation for a **Web site** with the following information:

Author	Sabriel, Barbara A.
Name of Web Page	Do EMRS Make You a Better Doctor?
Year	2008
Month	July
Day	15
Year Accessed	2016
Month Accessed	June
Day Accessed	30
Medium	Web

On **Page 2**, at the end of the paragraph that begins *Further research*, click to the left of the period, and then

using **MLA** format, insert a citation for a **Book** with the following information:

Author	DeVore, Amy
Title	The Electronic Health Record for the Physician's Office, 1e
Year	2010
City	Maryland Heights
Publisher	Saunders
Medium	Print

In the report, select the citation you just created, display the **Citation Options**, and then edit the citation to include **Pages 253**

4 Insert a manual page break at the end of the document. On the new **Page 3**, display the **Paragraph** dialog box, and then change the **Special** indentation to (**none**). Type **Works Cited** and then press Enter. On the **REFERENCES tab**, click **Bibliography**, and then click **Insert Bibliography**. **Center** the *Works Cited* title.

Use the **Source Manager** to change the name of the reference *Sabriel* to **Gabriel** and update both lists. Then in the selected citation in the report, display the **Citation Options** and click **Update Citations and Bibliography**. On the Works Cited page, select the references, apply **Double** line spacing, and then set the **Spacing After** paragraphs to **0 pt**.

Update the **Document Properties** with the following information:

Title	Electronic Records
Tags	EMR, health records
Comments	Draft copy of report for class
Categories	Health Administration
Subject	(insert your course name and section number)
Company	University Medical Center
Manager	Dr. Hillary Kim

On the left, click **Print** to display the **Print Preview**, make any necessary corrections, **save** and **close** the document; leave Word open. Hold this file until you complete this project.

(Project 3G Research Paper, Newsletter, and Mailing Labels continues on the next page)

CONTENT-BASED ASSESSMENTS

5 From your student files, open **w03G_ Newsletter**. **Save** the file in your **Word Chapter 3** folder as **Lastname_Firstname_3G_Newsletter** and then add the file name to the footer. Select the first three lines of the document and apply a **3 pt** bottom border in **Black, Text 1**.

Click at the beginning of the newsletter title *University Medical Center*. Insert an online picture from **Office.com Clip Art** by searching for **microscope** Insert a picture of a black and white microscope. **Recolor** the picture by applying **Blue, Accent color 1 Light**. Apply a **Black, Text 1 Picture Border** and change the **Weight** to **2 1/4 pt**.

Scale the picture to **10%** of its **Height**, and then change the **Text Wrapping** to **Square**. Change the **Horizontal Alignment** to **Left relative to Margin** and the **Vertical Alignment** to **Top relative to Margin**.

6 Starting with the paragraph that begins *Are You Getting a Good Night's Sleep?*, select all of the text from that point to the end of the document. Format the text in two columns, and apply **Justify** alignment. Insert a **Column break** before the subheading *Can Chemistry Help?*

Start and maximize Internet Explorer, and then navigate to **www.nhlbi.nih.gov/health** and then in the middle of the page, click **Sleep Disorders**. In your **3G_Newsletter** file, click at the end of the paragraph below the *Are You Getting a Good Night's Sleep* subheading, and then press Enter. In the blank line, insert a **Screenshot** of the website; do not link to the URL. Apply a **Black, Text 1 Picture Border** and change the **Weight** to **1 pt**.

Select the subheading *Are You Getting a Good Night's Sleep?* including the paragraph mark. From the **Font** dialog box, apply **Bold** and **Small Caps** and change the **Font color** to **Dark Blue, Text 2**—in the fourth column, the first color. Apply the same formatting to the subheadings *Light and Sleep*, *Can Chemistry Help?* and *Sleep Aid Apps*.

7 Select the last paragraph in the newsletter, and then apply a **1 pt Shadow** border using **Black, Text 1**. Shade the paragraph with the **Fill color Dark Blue, Text 2, Lighter 80%**—in the fourth column, the second color. **Center** the text.

Click the **FILE tab**, and then click **Show All Properties**. As the **Tags**, type **sleep, newsletter** As the **Subject**, type your course name and section number. Under **Related People**, if necessary, type your name in the **Author box**. On the left, click **Print** to display the

Print Preview. Make any necessary corrections. **Save** the document and **Exit** Word.

8 Start Word and display a new blank document. **Save** the document in your **Word Chapter 3** folder as **Lastname_Firstname_3G_Mailing_Labels** From your student files, **Open** the file **w03G_Addresses**. **Save** the address file in your **Word Chapter 3** folder as **Lastname_Firstname_3G_Addresses** and then add the file name to the footer. **Save** and **Close** the file. Be sure that your **Lastname_Firstname_3G_Mailing_Labels** document displays.

9 Start the **Step-by-Step Mail Merge Wizard** to create **Labels**. Be sure that the **Default tray** is selected and that the label vendor is **Avery US Letter**. The **Product number** is **5160 Easy Peel Address Labels**. Select the **Use an existing list option**, and then from your **Word Chapter 3** folder, **Open** your **Lastname_Firstname_3G_Addresses** file. Add the following record to your file:

First Name	**Mason**
Last Name	**Zepeda**
Address 1	**134 Atlantic Ave.**
Unit	**#21**
City	**Memphis**
State	**TN**
ZIP Code	**38123**

10 Insert an **Address block** and match the fields. Match the **Address 2** field to the **Unit** field, and then update the labels. Preview the labels, and then select the entire document. Change the **Spacing Before** to **3** and then **Complete the merge**. Delete the last row from the bottom of the table, and then add the file name to the footer.

Display the document properties. As the **Tags** type **labels** and as the **Subject** type your course name and section number. Be sure your name displays in the **Author box**, and then **Save** your file. As directed by your instructor, print or submit your work electronically. In addition to your labels and address document, submit your **3G_Newsletter** and **3G_Electronic_Records** documents as directed. **Close** Word and Internet Explorer.

END | You have completed Project 3G

CONTENT-BASED ASSESSMENTS

Apply a combination of the **3A** and **3B** skills.

GO! Fix It	Project 3H Hospital Materials	Online

GO! Make It	Project 3I Health Newsletter	Online

Build from Scratch

GO! Solve It	Project 3J Colds and Flu	Online

GO! Solve It	Project 3K Cycling Newsletter	

PROJECT FILES

For Project 3K, you will need the following file:

w03K_Cycling_Newsletter

You will save your document as:

Lastname_Firstname_3K_Cycling_Newsletter

The UMC Emergency Department publishes a newsletter focusing on safety and injury prevention. The topic for the current newsletter is bicycle safety. From your student data files, open w03K_Cycling_Newsletter, add the file name to the footer, and then save the file in your Word Chapter 3 folder as **Lastname_Firstname_3K_Cycling_Newsletter**.

Using the techniques that you practiced in this chapter, format the document in two-column, newsletter format. Format the nameplate so that it is clearly separate from the body of the newsletter. Insert column breaks as necessary and apply appropriate formatting to subheadings. Insert and format at least one appropriate online picture and insert a screenshot of a relevant website. Apply a border and shading to the last paragraph.

Add your name, your course name and section number, and the keywords **safety, newsletter** to the Properties area. Submit as directed.

CONTENT-BASED ASSESSMENTS

Performance Level

Performance Criteria	Exemplary: You consistently applied the relevant skills	Proficient: You sometimes, but not always, applied the relevant skills	Developing: You rarely or never applied the relevant skills
Format nameplate	The nameplate is formatted attractively and in a manner that clearly indicates that it is the nameplate.	The nameplate includes some formatting but is not clearly separated from the body of the newsletter.	The newsletter does not include a nameplate.
Insert and format at least one online picture	An sized and positioned online picture image is included.	An online picture is inserted but is either inappropriate, or is formatted or positioned poorly.	No online picture is included.
Border and shading added to a paragraph	The last paragraph displays an attractive border with shading.	An appropriate border or shading is displayed but not both.	No border or shading is applied.
Insert a screenshot	A relevant screenshot is inserted in one of the columns.	A screenshot is inserted in the document but does not relate to the content of the article.	No screenshot is inserted.

END | You have completed Project 3K

OUTCOMES-BASED ASSESSMENTS

RUBRIC

The following outcomes-based assessments are *open-ended assessments*. That is, there is no specific correct result; your result will depend on your approach to the information provided. Make *Professional Quality* your goal. Use the following scoring rubric to guide you in *how* to approach the problem and then to evaluate *how well* your approach solves the problem.

The *criteria*—Software Mastery, Content, Format and Layout, and Process—represent the knowledge and skills you have gained that you can apply to solving the problem. The *levels of performance*—Professional Quality, Approaching Professional Quality, or Needs Quality Improvements—help you and your instructor evaluate your result.

	Your completed project is of Professional Quality if you:	Your completed project is Approaching Professional Quality if you:	Your completed project Needs Quality Improvements if you:
1-Software Mastery	Choose and apply the most appropriate skills, tools, and features and identify efficient methods to solve the problem.	Choose and apply some appropriate skills, tools, and features, but not in the most efficient manner.	Choose inappropriate skills, tools, or features, or are inefficient in solving the problem.
2-Content	Construct a solution that is clear and well organized, contains content that is accurate, appropriate to the audience and purpose, and is complete. Provide a solution that contains no errors in spelling, grammar, or style.	Construct a solution in which some components are unclear, poorly organized, inconsistent, or incomplete. Misjudge the needs of the audience. Have some errors in spelling, grammar, or style, but the errors do not detract from comprehension.	Construct a solution that is unclear, incomplete, or poorly organized; contains some inaccurate or inappropriate content; and contains many errors in spelling, grammar, or style. Do not solve the problem.
3-Format & Layout	Format and arrange all elements to communicate information and ideas, clarify function, illustrate relationships, and indicate relative importance.	Apply appropriate format and layout features to some elements, but not others. Overuse features, causing minor distraction.	Apply format and layout that does not communicate information or ideas clearly. Do not use format and layout features to clarify function, illustrate relationships, or indicate relative importance. Use available features excessively, causing distraction.
4-Process	Use an organized approach that integrates planning, development, self-assessment, revision, and reflection.	Demonstrate an organized approach in some areas, but not others; or, use an insufficient process of organization throughout.	Do not use an organized approach to solve the problem.

OUTCOMES-BASED ASSESSMENTS

Build from
Scratch

GO! Think Project 3L Influenza Report

PROJECT FILES

For Project 3L, you will need the following file:

New blank Word document

You will save your document as:

Lastname_Firstname_3L_Influenza

As part of the ongoing research conducted by University Medical Center in the area of community health and contagious diseases, Dr. Hillary Kim has asked Sarah Stanger to create a report on influenza—how it spreads, and how it can be prevented in the community.

Create a new file and save it as **Lastname_Firstname_3L_Influenza** Create the report in MLA format. The report should include at least two footnotes, at least two citations, and should include a *Works Cited* page.

The report should contain an introduction, and then information about what influenza is, how it spreads, and how it can be prevented. A good place to start is at http://health.nih.gov/topic/influenza.

Add the file name to the footer. Add appropriate information to the Document Properties and submit it as directed.

END | You have completed Project 3L

OUTCOMES-BASED ASSESSMENTS

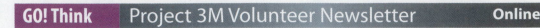

Build from
Scratch

| GO! Think | Project 3M Volunteer Newsletter | Online |

Build from
Scratch

| You and GO! | Project 3N College Newsletter | Online |

| GO! Cumulative Group Project | Project 3O Bell Orchid Hotels |
| | Online |

Glossary

Address bar (Internet Explorer) The area at the top of the Internet Explorer window that displays, and where you can type, a URL—Uniform Resource Locator—which is an address that uniquely identifies a location on the Internet.

Address bar (Windows) The bar at the top of a folder window with which you can navigate to a different folder or library, or go back to a previous one.

Alignment The placement of text or objects relative to the left and right margins.

Alignment guide Green vertical or horizontal lines that display when you are moving or sizing an object to assist you with object placement.

Alignment guides Green lines that display when you move an object to assist in alignment.

American Psychological Association (APA) One of two commonly used style guides for formatting research papers.

App The term that commonly refers to computer programs that run from the device software on a smartphone or a tablet computer—for example, iOS, Android, or Windows Phone—or computer programs that run from the browser software on a desktop PC or laptop PC—for example Internet Explorer, Safari, Firefox, or Chrome.

App for Office A webpage that works within one of the Office applications, such as Excel, and that you download from the Office Store.

Apps for Office 2013 and SharePoint 2013 A collection of downloadable apps that enable you to create and view information within your familiar Office programs.

Artistic effects Formats applied to images that make pictures resemble sketches or paintings.

AutoCorrect A feature that corrects common typing and spelling errors as you type, for example changing *teh* to *the*.

Backstage tabs The area along the left side of Backstage view with tabs to display screens with related groups of commands.

Backstage view A centralized space for file management tasks; for example, opening, saving, printing, publishing, or sharing a file. A navigation pane displays along the left side with tabs that group file-related tasks together.

Bibliography A list of cited works in a report or research paper; also referred to as Works Cited, Sources, or References, depending upon the report style.

Body The text of a letter.

Brightness The relative lightness of a picture.

Bulleted list A list of items with each item introduced by a symbol such as a small circle or check mark, and which is useful when the items in the list can be displayed in any order.

Bullets Text symbols such as small circles or check marks that precede each item in a bulleted list.

Cell The box at the intersection of a row and column in a Word table.

Center alignment The alignment of text or objects that is centered horizontally between the left and right margins.

Citation A note inserted into the text of a research paper that refers the reader to a source in the bibliography.

Click The action of pressing and releasing the left button on a mouse pointing device one time.

Clip art Downloadable predefined graphics available online from Office. com and other sites.

Clipboard A temporary storage area that holds text or graphics that you select and then cut or copy.

Cloud computing Applications and services that are accessed over the Internet with multiple devices.

Cloud storage Online storage of data so that you can access your data from different places and devices.

Collaborate To work with others as a team in an intellectual endeavor to complete a shared task or to achieve a shared goal.

Collaboration The action of working together with others as a team in an intellectual endeavor to complete a shared task or achieve a shared goal.

Column break indicator A dotted line containing the words *Column Break* that displays at the bottom of the column.

Commands An instruction to a computer program that causes an action to be carried out.

Common dialog boxes The set of dialog boxes that includes Open, Save, and Save As, which are provided by the Windows programming interface, and which display and operate in all of the Office programs in the same manner.

Complimentary closing A parting farewell in a business letter.

Compressed file A file that has been reduced in size and thus takes up less storage space and can be transferred to other computers quickly.

Compressed folder A folder that has been reduced in size and thus takes up less storage space and can be transferred to other computers quickly; also called a *zipped* folder.

Content control In a template, an area indicated by placeholder text that can be used to add text, pictures, dates, or lists.

Context menus Menus that display commands and options relevant to the selected text or object; also called *shortcut menus*.

Context-sensitive commands Commands that display on a shortcut menu that relate to the object or text that you right-clicked.

Contextual tabs Tabs that are added to the ribbon automatically when a specific object, such as a picture, is selected, and that contain commands relevant to the selected object.

Contrast The difference between the darkest and lightest area of a picture.

Copy A command that duplicates a selection and places it on the Clipboard.

Cover letter A document that you send with your resume to provide additional information about your skills and experience.

Crop A command that removes unwanted or unnecessary areas of a picture.

Crop handles Handles used to define unwanted areas of a picture.

Crop pointer The pointer used to crop areas of a picture.

Cut A command that removes a selection and places it on the Clipboard.

Data source A document that contains a list of variable information, such as names and addresses, that is merged with a main document to create customized form letters or labels.

Date & Time A command with which you can automatically insert the current date and time into a document in a variety of formats.

Dateline The first line in a business letter that contains the current date and which is positioned just below the letterhead if a letterhead is used.

Decrease Indent A command that moves your paragraph closer to the margin.

Default The term that refers to the current selection or setting that is automatically used by a computer program unless you specify otherwise.

Deselect The action of canceling the selection of an object or block of text by clicking outside of the selection.

Desktop In Windows, the screen that simulates your work area.

Desktop app The term that commonly refers to a computer program that is installed on your computer and requires a computer operating system like Microsoft Windows or Apple OS to run.

Dialog box A small window that contains options for completing a task.

Dialog Box Launcher A small icon that displays to the right of some group names on the ribbon, and which opens a related dialog box or pane providing additional options and commands related to that group.

Document properties Details about a file that describe or identify it, including the title, author name, subject, and keywords that identify the document's topic or contents; also known as *metadata*.

Dot leader A series of dots preceding a tab that guides the eye across the line.

Drag The action of holding down the left mouse button while moving your mouse.

Drag-and-drop A technique by which you can move, by dragging, selected text from one location in a document to another.

Drawing objects Graphic objects, such as shapes, diagrams, lines, or circles.

Edit The process of making changes to text or graphics in an Office file.

Ellipsis A set of three dots indicating incompleteness; an ellipsis following a command name indicates that a dialog box will display if you click the command.

Em dash A punctuation symbol used to indicate an explanation or emphasis.

Embed code A code that creates a link to a video, picture, or other type of rich media content.

Enclosures Additional documents included with a business letter.

Endnote In a research paper, a note placed at the end of a document or chapter.

Enhanced ScreenTip A ScreenTip that displays more descriptive text than a normal ScreenTip.

Extract To decompress, or pull out, files from a compressed form.

Fields In a mail merge, the column headings in the data source.

File A collection of information stored on a computer under a single name, for example a Word document or a PowerPoint presentation.

File Explorer The program that displays the files and folders on your computer, and which is at work anytime you are viewing the contents of files and folders in a window.

Fill The inside color of an object.

Flip A command that creates a reverse image of a picture or object.

Floating object A graphic that can be moved independently of the surrounding text characters.

Folder A container in which you store files.

Folder window In Windows, a window that displays the contents of the current folder, library, or device, and contains helpful parts so that you can navigate the Windows file structure.

Font A set of characters with the same design and shape.

Font styles Formatting emphasis such as bold, italic, and underline.

Footer A reserved area for text or graphics that displays at the bottom of each page in a document.

Footnote In a research paper, a note placed at the bottom of the page.

Formatting The process of establishing the overall appearance of text, graphics, and pages in an Office file—for example, in a Word document.

Formatting marks Characters that display on the screen, but do not print, indicating where the Enter key, the Spacebar, and the Tab key were pressed; also called *nonprinting characters*.

Gallery An Office feature that displays a list of potential results instead of just the command name.

Gradient fill A fill effect in which one color fades into another.

Graphics Pictures, charts, or drawing objects.

Groups On the Office ribbon, the sets of related commands that you might need for a specific type of task.

Hanging indent An indent style in which the first line of a paragraph extends to the left of the remaining lines and that is commonly used for bibliographic entries.

Header A reserved area for text or graphics that displays at the top of each page in a document.

Increase Indent A command moves your paragraph farther away from the margin.

Info tab The tab in Backstage view that displays information about the current file.

Inline Object An object or graphic inserted in a document that acts like a character in a sentence.

Insertion point A blinking vertical line that indicates where text or graphics will be inserted.

Inside address The name and address of the person receiving the letter and positioned below the date line.

Interactive media Computer interaction that responds to your actions; for example by presenting text, graphics, animation, video, audio, or games. Also referred to as rich media.

Justified alignment An arrangement of text in which the text aligns evenly on both the left and right margins.

Keyboard shortcut A combination of two or more keyboard keys, used to perform a task that would otherwise require a mouse.

KeyTip The letter that displays on a command in the ribbon and that indicates the key you can press to activate the command when keyboard control of the ribbon is activated.

Keywords Custom file properties in the form of words that you associate with a document to give an indication of the document's content; used to help find and organize files. Also called *tags*.

Landscape orientation A page orientation in which the paper is wider than it is tall.

Layout Options A button that displays when an object is selected and that has commands to choose how the object interacts with surrounding text.

Leader character Characters that form a solid, dotted, or dashed line that fills the space preceding a tab stop.

Left alignment An arrangement of text in which the text aligns at the left margin, leaving the right margin uneven.

Letterhead The personal or company information that displays at the top of a letter.

Line break indicator A non-printing character in the shape of a bent arrow that indicates a manual line break.

Line spacing The distance between lines of text in a paragraph.

Live Layout A feature that reflows text as you move or size an object so that you can view the placement of surrounding text.

Live Preview A technology that shows the result of applying an editing or formatting change as you point to possible results—*before* you actually apply it.

Location Any disk drive, folder, or other place in which you can store files and folders.

Mail merge A feature that joins a main document and a data source to create customized letters or labels.

Main document In a mail merge, the document that contains the text or formatting that remains constant.

Manual column break An artificial end to a column to balance columns or to provide space for the insertion of other objects.

Manual line break A break that moves text to the right of the insertion point to a new line while keeping the text in the same paragraph.

Manual page break The action of forcing a page to end and placing subsequent text at the top of the next page.

Margins The space between the text and the top, bottom, left, and right edges of the paper.

Metadata Details about a file that describe or identify it, including the title, author name, subject, and keywords that identify the document's topic or contents; also known as *document properties*.

Microsoft Office 365 A set of secure online services that enable people in an organization to communicate and collaborate by using any Internet-connected device—a computer, a tablet, or a mobile phone.

Mini toolbar A small toolbar containing frequently used formatting commands that displays as a result of selecting text or objects.

Modern Language Association (MLA) One of two commonly used style guides for formatting research papers.

MRU Acronym for *most recently used*, which refers to the state of some commands that retain the characteristic most recently applied; for example, the Font Color button retains the most recently used color until a new color is chosen.

Nameplate The banner on the front page of a newsletter that identifies the publication.

Navigate The process of exploring within the organizing structure of Windows.

Navigation Pane In a folder window, the area on the left in which you can navigate to, open, and display favorites, libraries, folders, saved searches, and an expandable list of drives.

Newsletter A periodical that communicates news and information to a specific group.

No Paragraph Style The built-in paragraph style—available from the Paragraph Spacing command—that inserts *no* extra space before or after a paragraph and uses line spacing of 1.

Nonprinting characters Characters that display on the screen, but do not print, indicating where the Enter key, the Spacebar, and the Tab key were pressed; also called *formatting marks*.

Normal template The template that serves as a basis for all Word documents.

Note In a research paper, information that expands on the topic, but that does not fit well in the document text.

Notification bar An area at the bottom of an Internet Explorer window that displays information about pending downloads, security issues, add-ons, and other issues related to the operation of your computer.

Numbered list A list that uses consecutive numbers or letters to introduce each item in a list.

Object A text box, picture, table, or shape that you can select and then move and resize.

Object anchor The symbol that indicates to which paragraph an object is attached.

Office 365 Administrator The person who creates and manages the account, adds new users, sets up the services your organization wants to use, sets permission levels, and manages the SharePoint team sites.

Office Presentation Service A Word feature to present your Word document to others who can watch in a web browser.

Office Web Apps The free online companions to Microsoft Word, Excel, PowerPoint, Access, and OneNote.

One-click Row/Column Insertion A Word table feature with which you can insert a new row or column by pointing to the desired location and then clicking.

Open dialog box A dialog box from which you can navigate to, and then open on your screen, an existing file that was created in that same program.

Option button In a dialog box, a round button that enables you to make one choice among two or more options.

Options dialog box A dialog box within each Office application where you can select program settings and other options and preferences.

Page break indicator A dotted line with the text *Page Break* that indicates where a manual page break was inserted.

Pane A separate area of a window.

Paragraph symbol The symbol ¶ that represents the end of a paragraph.

Parenthetical references References that include the last name of the author or authors, and the page number in the referenced source.

Paste The action of placing text or objects that have been copied or cut from one location to another location.

Paste Options gallery A gallery of buttons that provides a Live Preview of all the Paste options available in the current context.

Path A sequence of folders that leads to a specific file or folder.

PDF The acronym for Portable Document Format, which is a file format that creates an image that preserves the look of your file; this is a popular format for sending documents electronically because the document will display on most computers.

PDF Reflow The ability to import PDF files into Word so that you can transform a PDF back into a fully editable Word document.

Picture Effects Formatting that enhances a picture with effects such as shadow, glow, reflection, or 3-D rotation.

Picture styles Frames, shapes, shadows, borders, and other special effects that can be added to an image to create an overall visual style for the image.

Placeholder text The text in a content control that indicates the type of information to be entered in a specific location.

Point The action of moving your mouse pointer over something on your screen.

Pointer Any symbol that displays on your screen in response to moving your mouse.

Points A measurement of the size of a font; there are 72 points in an inch.

Portable Document Format A file format that creates an image that preserves the look of your file, but that cannot be easily changed; a popular format for sending documents electronically, because the document will display on most computers.

Portrait orientation A page orientation in which the paper is taller than it is wide.

Print Preview A view of a document as it will appear when you print it.

Progress bar In a dialog box or taskbar button, a bar that indicates visually the progress of a task such as a download or file transfer.

Protected View A security feature in Office 2013 that protects your computer from malicious files by opening them in a restricted environment until you enable them; you might encounter this feature if you open a file from an email or download files from the Internet.

pt The abbreviation for *point*; for example, when referring to a font size.

Quick Access Toolbar In an Office program window, the small row of buttons in the upper left corner of the screen from which you can perform frequently used commands.

Read Mode A view in Word that optimizes the Word screen for the times when you are reading Word documents on the screen and not creating or editing them.

Read-Only A property assigned to a file that prevents the file from being modified or deleted; it indicates that you cannot save any changes to the displayed document unless you first save it with a new name.

Recolor A feature that enables you to change all colors in the picture to shades of a single color.

Record Each row of information that contains data for one person.

Ribbon A user interface in both Office 2013 and File Explorer that groups the commands for performing related tasks on tabs across the upper portion of the program window.

Rich media Computer interaction that responds to your actions; for example by presenting text, graphics, animation, video, audio, or games. Also referred to as interactive media.

Right alignment An arrangement of text in which the text aligns at the right margin, leaving the left margin uneven.

Right-click The action of clicking the right mouse button one time.

Rotation handle A symbol with which you can rotate a graphic to any angle; displays above the top center sizing handle.

Salutation The greeting line of a business letter.

Sans serif font A font design with no lines or extensions on the ends of characters.

Scale A command that resizes a picture to a percentage of its size.

Screenshot An image of an active window on your computer that you can paste into a document.

ScreenTip A small box that displays useful information when you perform various mouse actions such as pointing to screen elements or dragging.

Scroll bar A vertical or horizontal bar in a window or a pane to assist in bringing an area into view, and which contains a scroll box and scroll arrows.

Scroll box The box in the vertical and horizontal scroll bars that can be dragged to reposition the contents of a window or pane on the screen.

Section A portion of a document that can be formatted differently from the rest of the document.

Section break A double dotted line that indicates the end of one section and the beginning of another section.

Selecting Highlighting, by dragging with your mouse, areas of text or data or graphics, so that the selection can be edited, formatted, copied, or moved.

Serif font A font design that includes small line extensions on the ends of the letters to guide the eye in reading from left to right.

Shapes Lines, arrows, stars, banners, ovals, rectangles, and other basic shapes with which you can illustrate an idea, a process, or a workflow.

SharePoint Collaboration software with which people in an organization can set up team sites to share information, manage documents, and publish reports for others to see.

Shortcut menu A menu that displays commands and options relevant to the selected text or object; also called a *context menu*.

Single spacing The common name for line spacing in which there is *no* extra space before or after a paragraph and that uses line spacing of 1.

Sizing handles Small squares that indicate a picture or object is selected.

SkyDrive Microsoft's free cloud storage for anyone with a free Microsoft account.

Skype A Microsoft product with which you can make voice calls, make video calls, transfer files, or send messages—including instant message and text messages—over the Internet.

Small caps A font effect that changes lowercase letters to uppercase letters, but with the height of lowercase letters.

SmartArt A designer-quality visual representation of your information that you can create by choosing from among many different layouts to effectively communicate your message or ideas.

Spin box A small box with an upward- and downward-pointing arrow that lets you move rapidly through a set of values by clicking.

Split button A button divided into two parts and in which clicking the main part of the button performs a command and clicking the arrow opens a menu with choices.

Start search The search feature in Windows 8 in which, from the Start screen, you can begin to type and by default, Windows 8 searches for apps; you can adjust the search to search for files or settings.

Status bar The area along the lower edge of an Office program window that displays file information on the left and buttons to control how the window looks on the right.

Style A group of formatting commands, such as font, font size, font color, paragraph alignment, and line spacing that can be applied to a paragraph with one command.

Style guide A manual that contains standards for the design and writing of documents.

Subfolder A folder within a folder.

Subject line The optional line following the inside address in a business letter that states the purpose of the letter.

Suppress A Word feature that hides header and footer information, including the page number, on the first page of a document.

Synchronization The process of updating computer files that are in two or more locations according to specific rules—also called *syncing*.

Syncing The process of updating computer files that are in two or more locations according to specific rules—also called *synchronization*.

Synonyms Words with the same or similar meaning.

Tab stop A specific location on a line of text, marked on the Word ruler, to which you can move the insertion point by pressing the Tab key, and which is used to align and indent text.

Table An arrangement of information organized into rows and columns.

Tabs (ribbon) On the Office ribbon, the name of each activity area.

Tags Custom file properties in the form of words that you associate with a document to give an indication of the document's content; used to help find and organize files. Also called *keywords*.

Taskbar The area along the lower edge of the desktop that displays buttons representing programs.

Team A group of workers tasked with working together to solve a problem, make a decision, or create a work product.

Template An existing document that you use as a starting point for a new document; it opens a copy of itself, unnamed, and then you use the structure—and possibly some content, such as headings—as the starting point for a new document.

Text box A movable resizable container for text or graphics.

Text control A content control that accepts only a text entry.

Text effects Decorative formats, such as shadowed or mirrored text, text glow, 3-D effects, and colors that make text stand out.

Text wrapping The manner in which text displays around an object.

Theme A predesigned combination of colors, fonts, and effects that look good together and is applied to an entire document by a single selection.

Thesaurus A research tool that provides a list of synonyms.

Title bar The bar at the top edge of the program window that indicates the name of the current file and the program name.

Toggle button A button that can be turned on by clicking it once, and then turned off by clicking it again.

Toolbar In a folder window, a row of buttons with which you can perform common tasks, such as changing the view of your files and folders or burning files to a CD.

Triple-click The action of clicking the left mouse button three times in rapid succession.

Trusted Documents A security feature in Office that remembers which files you have already enabled; you might encounter this feature if you open a file from an email or download files from the Internet.

Uniform Resource Locator An address that uniquely identifies a location on the Internet.

URL The acronym for Uniform Resource Locator, which is an address that uniquely identifies a location on the Internet.

USB flash drive A small data storage device that plugs into a computer USB port.

Window A rectangular area on a computer screen in which programs and content appear, and which can be moved, resized, minimized, or closed.

Windows Reader app A Windows Store app with which you can open a PDF or XPS file, zoom, find words or phrases, take notes, save changes, and then print or share the file.

Wordwrap The feature that moves text from the right edge of a paragraph to the beginning of the next line as necessary to fit within the margins.

Works Cited In the MLA style, a list of cited works placed at the end of a research paper or report.

Writer's identification The name and title of the author of a letter, placed near the bottom of the letter under the complimentary closing—also referred to as the *writer's signature block*.

Writer's signature block The name and title of the author of a letter, placed near the bottom of the letter, under the complimentary closing—also referred to as the *writer's identification*.

XML Paper Specification A Microsoft file format that creates an image of your document and that opens in the XPS viewer.

XPS The acronym for XML Paper Specification—a Microsoft file format that creates an image of your document and that opens in the XPS viewer.

Zipped folder A folder that has been reduced in size and thus takes up less storage space and can be transferred to other computers quickly; also called a *compressed* folder.

Zoom The action of increasing or decreasing the size of the viewing area on the screen.

Index